A Stone in Spain's Shoe

A Stone in Spain's Shoe

THE SEARCH FOR A SOLUTION
TO THE PROBLEM OF GIBRALTAR

PETER GOLD

LIVERPOOL UNIVERSITY PRESS

First published 1994 by
LIVERPOOL UNIVERSITY PRESS
PO BOX 147
LIVERPOOL
L69 3BX

**British Library Cataloguing-in-
Publication Data**
A British Library CIP Record is available
ISBN 0–85323–209–1 cased
ISBN 0–85323–219–9 paper

Set in Linotron 202 Meridien by
Wilmaset Limited, Birkenhead, Wirral
Printed and bound in the European Union by
Bell and Bain Limited, Glasgow

To my Mother, who has always supported me, to the memory of my Father, and to Anne and all our children for their love and forbearance.

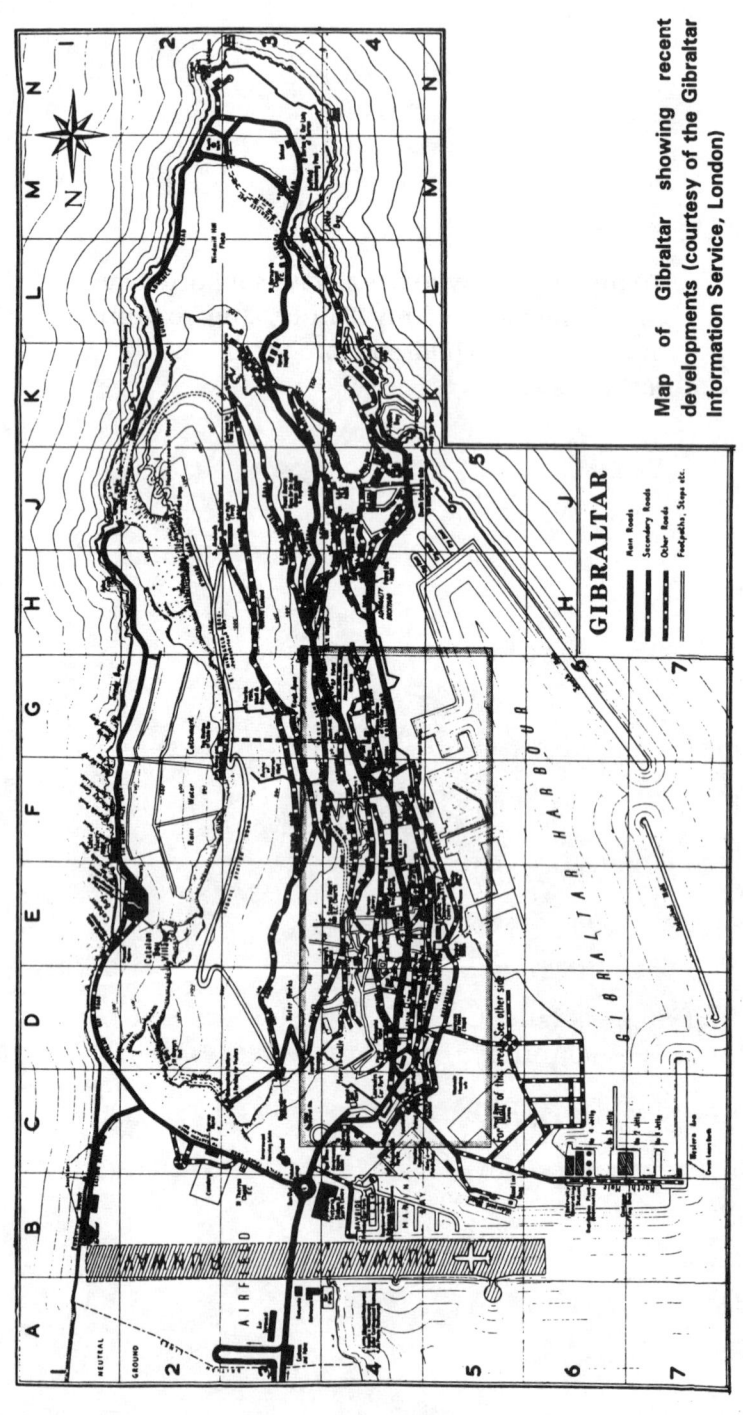

Map of Gibraltar showing recent developments (courtesy of the Gibraltar Information Service, London)

CONTENTS

ACKNOWLEDGEMENTS

I am grateful to the British Council and to the Spanish Ministerio de Educación y Ciencia in Madrid for providing 'Acciones integradas' funding for this project. I thank Sr D. Agustín Gervas Sánchez of the Ministerio de Asuntos Exteriores and Mr Geoffrey Gilham of the British Embassy in Madrid for their helpful comments and useful material. My thanks also to John Kingdom of Sheffield Hallam University for reading the manuscript and giving me helpful advice.

ONE

INTRODUCTION

For the British, Gibraltar is a visit to the dentist once a year when we meet to talk about it. For us, it is a stone in the shoe all day long. (Felipe González, Spanish Prime Minister, in an interview for *The Financial Times*, 9 May 1991)

The British colony of Gibraltar, a rocky promontory which rises to a height of about 420 metres, is a little over six kilometres in length, about 1,200 metres wide and covers an area of some seven square kilometres. It is connected to the southern tip of Spain by a low-lying isthmus about 800 metres wide at the border crossing. Eight kilometres away across the bay to the west of Gibraltar lies the Spanish port of Algeciras, while on the other side of the Strait of Gibraltar lies Morocco, thirty-two kilometres distant.

The British have occupied the Rock since 1704, following its capture during the War of the Spanish Succession by an Anglo-Dutch force led by Admiral Sir George Rooke. Under the Treaty of Utrecht, signed in 1713, the territory was ceded to Britain in perpetuity.[1] Less than a hundred Spaniards remained on the Rock, but they have since been joined by Britons, Genoese, Maltese, Moroccans, Portuguese, Minorcans, Sephardic Jews from North Africa and, more recently, migrants from the Indian sub-continent. The population currently numbers about 30,000, of whom some 20,000 are Gibraltarians, 5,000 are other British subjects including military personnel and their families, and 5,000 are aliens (mostly Moroccans). Despite their mixed origins, the way of life of the majority is essentially British. Pubs, British schools and police officers in British 'bobby' uniforms are typical manifestations of the essential Britishness of the colony, although most Gibraltarians can speak Spanish as well as English.

Several attempts have been made to retake Gibraltar by force, the most recent and most notable between 1779 and 1783, when General Eliot held out against a combined French and Spanish force. But Spain has never renounced its claims to sovereignty over the territory and since the 1960s, in an international climate supportive of decolonisation, has had the backing of numerous UN resolutions to resolve the issue. In 1969 the Spanish dictator General Franco tried to force Britain's negotiating hand by removing Spanish workers from Gibraltar, closing the border between the Rock and mainland Spain and cutting off all other direct communications in the hope of irreparably damaging the Gibraltarian economy and bringing Britain to the negotiating table. Not only did the move not have the desired effect, but it stiffened the Gibraltarians' resolve to remain tied to Britain and by isolating them Franco alienated them from Spaniards, with whom thereafter they could have little direct contact.

The fact is that, even without the Spanish blockade, the British Government would never have contemplated a transfer of sovereignty to Spain while the Franco regime was still in power. But with the restoration of democracy in Spain following Franco's death in 1975 and Spain's gradual reincorporation into international affairs, the way has been open for Britain and Spain to seek a settlement for the future of what is the only remaining colony in Europe. In the late 1970s, with Spain eager to join the European Community* and to become a member of NATO (although not to integrate into its military structure), a solution to what was generally seen to be an anachronism and an impediment to good bilateral relations became not only desirable but necessary. The signing of the Lisbon Agreement in 1980, which this work takes as its main starting point, was the first important step in that process. Subsequently Britain and Spain agreed, through the signing of the Brussels Declaration in 1984, to solve all of their differences over Gibraltar, including the issue of sovereignty.

Progress has been extraordinarily slow and tortuous, and fourteen years on from Lisbon the negotiations are far from nearing their end. The problem is that Gibraltar's decolonisation process is complicated both by its history and its geography.

As far as history is concerned, there are three factors at work. First, even if an independent, decolonised Gibraltar were a viable

---

*The term European Community (EC) is used with reference to the period prior to the signing of the Maastrict Treaty in December 1991. Thereafter, the term European Union (EU) is used.

entity, the Treaty of Utrecht, if properly observed, does not allow Gibraltarians to seek independence, but rather says that if Britain should wish to 'grant, sell or by any means to alienate' ownership of Gibraltar, Spain should be given first preference to it.[2] Hence Gibraltar is not a straightforward case of a colony seeking independent status from a colonial power (although there are many in Gibraltar who would like it to pursue that course). It is a third party, Spain, which has been calling for Gibraltar to be decolonised, not in order to secure Gibraltarian independence but to reabsorb the territory into Spain. The problem is that although Britain might be willing to decolonise Gibraltar (the territory), the Gibraltarians are not willing to become Spanish citizens, and Britain feels bound, morally and constitutionally, to respect their wishes.

Second, Franco's policy of isolation, which was in place for 16 years and is now seen even within Spain to have been a grave mistake, has had the effect of making the Gibraltarians' attitude towards Spaniards at best mistrustful, at worst hostile. Although Spain has made it quite clear that it is interested in re-establishing its territorial integrity and not in turning Gibraltarians into Spaniards, the process of undoing the damage caused by the blockade, a process which the Spaniards have called 'osmosis', is by definition one which requires time and patience—and not a little effort, too. But after a wait of nearly three centuries patience does not come easily.

The third historical factor is the Falklands/Malvinas conflict of 1982 and its effect on negotiations over Gibraltar. The claim by Argentina (a former Spanish colony and therefore a member of the Hispanic family of nations) against Britain over another of its colonies struck a chord in Spain; the use of force was condemned, but the spirit which inspired it was applauded. The events in the South Atlantic, which are explored in some detail in Chapter 5, had two main consequences. First, the parallels which Spain inevitably drew between the two situations alienated the British Foreign Office and made negotiations over Gibraltar more difficult, and second, in practical terms, progress in implementing the Lisbon Agreement was put back years by the Falklands/Malvinas War. If the Lisbon Agreement had not already been signed almost exactly two years before the war, it is certain that the process of negotiation over Gibraltar would have taken much longer even to get as far as it has done.

The role of Gibraltar's geography in the decolonisation process is in some respects self-evident. Gibraltar controls the seaway between the Mediterranean and the Atlantic Ocean, as well as being at the crossroads between southern Europe and North Africa. Every vessel which enters or leaves the Mediterranean has to pass through the Strait of Gibraltar, including oil-tankers and merchant fleets as well as warships, making the Rock a key strategic location between East and West. As a supply base and ship-repair facility it has proved invaluable, especially in time of war, and it may well be that nuclear warheads are stored in the bowels of the Rock. It is not surprising that Gibraltar has been so important to Britain (and subsequently to NATO) for so long, and why Britain is reluctant to relinquish sovereignty, especially as Spain's involvement in NATO is both recent and incomplete.

The second geographical factor in Gibraltar's case is its size. It is smaller in terms of both territory and population than most independent states and it would be difficult for it to achieve self-sufficiency in economic or defence matters. If it were larger, it would be possible for Britain to argue through the UN (and probably with its support) that the Treaty of Utrecht was no longer applicable, that it made no more sense for Gibraltar to be part of Spain than it did for it to continue as a British colony, and that it should therefore be granted independence. In the absence of that option, Spain can use the Treaty to insist on being given first preference if there is to be any change of sovereignty.

The third aspect of Gibraltar's geography which impinges upon any change in sovereignty is the fact that it is located in Europe. Its proximity to Britain makes it a much more sensitive and immediate issue as far as domestic British politics are concerned than would be the case if it were an African or Asian colony, and therefore it is more difficult for a British government to ride roughshod over the wishes of the affected population. Lord Carrington is quoted as having said that 'the problem for Spain is that Gibraltar is in Europe . . . the issue would be settled, just like Rhodesia and Hong Kong, if the Spaniards were black or Chinese'.[3]

The fourth geographical aspect concerns the fact that there are really two separate areas which are under negotiation: the Rock itself, and also the isthmus which connects the Rock to the Spanish mainland. The isthmus is territory which has been occupied by Britain since 1815 (when it sought and was granted—albeit on a provisional basis—permission from Spain to build huts to house those escaping yellow fever epidemics in the town) and on which it built the fence in 1908 and the airport during the Second World War. But it is not part of the Treaty of Utrecht, so that whereas Britain can use *de jure* arguments in relation to the promontory, it has to rely on the more contentious *de facto* arguments of possession by prescription in relation to the isthmus and the airport (now used by both civil and military aircraft), which have come to be seen by Spain as more fruitful territory for negotiation.

There is one further factor which has some bearing on the issue, and that is the question of the Spanish enclaves of Ceuta and Melilla in North Africa. Melilla, which is less than 13 square kilometres and has a population of 56,000, has belonged to Spain since 1497, when Spain pursued some of the last Muslims to be expelled from the Peninsula across the Strait of Gibraltar. In 1912 it was declared a Spanish protectorate, which enabled it to become more than just a fortress around the castle. Ceuta, 160 kilometres to the west, is under 20 square kilometres and has 68,000 inhabitants. The fort was established by the Portuguese in 1415 and ceded to Spain in 1668. Both Ceuta and Melilla were retained by Spain as fortified enclaves when Morocco became independent in 1956. Many of the inhabitants of the enclaves are Muslims, and the introduction by Madrid of a new aliens law in July 1985 led to disturbances there. Following negotiations, those who had been resident in the enclaves for 10 years became eligible for Spanish nationality. These territories are claimed by Morocco, and Spain knows that when progress is made on Gibraltar, Morocco will be demanding parallel progress regarding its claims. The North African enclaves help to explain why at times it has appeared that Spain has not applied pressure on reaching a solution on Gibraltar quite as forcefully as it otherwise might have done.

These historical and geographical factors have weighed heavily on the negotiating process, which this book explores in some detail. In essence, that process has consisted of pressure from Spain for Britain to return the colony and so allow Spain to restore its territorial integrity. In return Britain has shown an apparent willingness to respond positively to such pressure, but at the same time a reluctance to force the Gibraltarians to do anything against their democratically expressed wishes.

In one sense all three protagonists—Britain, Spain and Gibraltar—have been playing for time. As the relationships between them have evolved, each has in turn hoped that the new circumstances would provide an opportunity for an advantageous solution. Most of the leading figures in the dispute now agree that if and when a change in Gibraltar's status occurs it will be Britain's and Spain's membership of the European Union which will have provided the framework. The nature and timing of that change will depend largely upon the ways in which the Union develops new political structures and how long these take to evolve. Given the state of progress on these matters, all the signs are that a solution to the question of Gibraltar is still some way off.

Notes

1 For the text of Article X of the Treaty of Utrecht, see Appendix 1.

2 Observance of the details of the Treaty has depended upon which party has been doing the observing. Britain (in order not to offend Spain) and Spain (because it seeks the reintegration of Gibraltar) both argue that the Treaty rules out Gibraltarian independence. Gibraltar claims that as the agreement was between Crown and Crown, the Treaty became invalid when Spain became a republic (first in 1873, and again in the 1930s). Moreover, since all sides choose to ignore the fact that the Treaty prohibits communication between Gibraltar and Spain by land, and that it also prohibits residence on the Rock by Jews and Moors, Gibraltarians—with some justification—question the consistency of adherence to certain commitments in the Treaty but not to others.

3 Quoted in *El País*, 4 August 1987, p. 7. Spain has inevitably drawn parallels between Gibraltar and Hong Kong, as later chapters will illustrate.

TWO
GIBRALTAR INCOMMUNICADO 1963–1979

On 8 June 1969 Spain ordered the closure of the customs post and border gates between Spain and Gibraltar at La Línea. On 25 June the ferry service from Algeciras to Gibraltar was suspended with effect from 27 June, leaving the weekly BEA flight from London via Madrid as the only communication between Spain and the Rock. So began the fifteenth and longest siege of Gibraltar.

The British Foreign Secretary Michael Stewart commented in the House of Commons on 26 June that the interruption of the ferry service not only flouted 'standards of international behaviour accepted by modern governments', but also that it was in breach of the Treaty of Utrecht, which implies that there should be sea communication between Spain and Gibraltar. He accused Spain of subjecting the Gibraltarians to a policy of economic and psychological pressure.[1] In an *aide-mémoire* handed to the Spanish Ambassador in London when he was summoned to the Foreign Office on 27 June, the Foreign Secretary said, prophetically: '. . . a policy of deliberate hostility against the inhabitants of Gibraltar can only be self-defeating . . . Her Majesty's Government find it impossible to understand what interests can be well served by severing all means of surface communications between two closely-linked communities . . .'.

If General Franco and, more particularly, his hard-line Foreign Minister Sr Castiella thought that a policy of isolating Gibraltar would both bring Gibraltar to its knees economically and result in the inevitable transfer of Gibraltar to Spain as the only path to its survival, they were clearly very much mistaken on both counts. Not only did Gibraltar survive economically, largely through the support of successive British Governments, but its isolation from 1969 to 1985 had the predictable effect of making a closer relationship with Spain—even a democratic and modern Spain which is now a fellow-member of NATO and the EU—significantly less attractive than would have been the case if communications had been maintained throughout those years. So what prompted Spain to take such a drastic step?

The answer can only be that it was taken out of a sense of frustration which had built up over a six-year period. During that time Spain applied fruitless diplomatic pressure to get Britain to negotiate the transfer of sovereignty, while suffering immense irritation at the measures which Britain took, either to confirm its determination to defend the wishes of the Gibraltarians or to enhance the colony's self-sufficiency. The problem was that Britain made it quite clear for most of that period that the one issue which it would refuse to discuss was the question of a transfer of sovereignty to Spain, while this appeared to be the only aspect of the problem in which the Spanish Government was interested. The harder Spain tried to exert pressure on Britain to negotiate, the more determined Britain became to resist. It was an extraordinarily short-sighted policy pursued by General Franco and his Foreign Minister, but it was fuelled by the constant encouragement which the climate of decolonisation at the United Nations offered throughout this period, from 1960 onwards.

At Spain's request the United Nations Committee of 24[2] discussed the question of Gibraltar for the first time in September 1963, but no conclusions were reached. Discussions did not resume until the next session in September and October 1964, and it was during that session that Jaime de Pinies, on behalf of the Spanish Government, threatened for the first time to cut communications with Gibraltar if Britain did not withdraw. He called upon Britain to negotiate with Spain to implement UN Resolution 1514 of December 1960 on the ending of colonialism. At the end of the session on 16 October 1964, the Committee noted that there was 'a disagreement, even a dispute, between the UK and Spain over the status and the situation of the territory of Gibraltar', and called upon the two sides to negotiate. However, Britain's representative, Cecil King, did not accept that there was a dispute over the status of Gibraltar. He said that the British Government would not feel bound by the terms of any recommendations the Committee might make on questions of sovereignty, and that they were not prepared to discuss sovereignty over Gibraltar with Spain.

Meanwhile, in August 1964 the British Government had introduced constitutional changes in Gibraltar which gave the colony a greater degree of internal self-government, and elections to the new Legislative Council were held in September. Spanish Government reaction to this and to British intransigence at the UN in October was to restrict the passage of people, traffic and goods across the border. The economic effects on the Rock were significant, and they prompted steps to be taken during the Spring of 1965 to increase the colony's self-sufficiency[3] in case Spain carried out its threat—as it was to do four years later—to close the border completely.

Exchanges of diplomatic notes took place between November 1964 and March 1965, with Spain trying to get Britain to agree to talk without pre-conditions (although it then promptly proposed one itself), to which Britain's reply was that it would not do so under duress. The British Government published a White Paper in April 1965 which set out its view of events since the Autumn of 1963.[4]

In reply Spain published a 550-page Red Book in December the same year setting out the Spanish case.[5] Four sessions of fractious bilateral talks were held in London between May and October 1966, but without achieving any rapprochement of the views held by the two sides. On the eve of the fourth session in October, the communications issue grew worse when Spain closed the customs post at La Línea to all vehicles entering and leaving Gibraltar, and later that month closed the border except for pedestrians. As a consequence Britain proposed that the legal issues in dispute between the two governments should be taken to the International Court of Justice at The Hague.[6]

From 12 November Gibraltarian passports were no longer recognised at La Línea, which effectively banned Gibraltarians from entering Spain. Following a ban on British military aircraft flying over Spanish territory from 4 August 1966, a further exchange of diplomatic notes occurred in relation to alleged violations of the ban and to the question of sovereignty over the isthmus.

At the UN in December 1966 a resolution called upon Britain and Spain to continue their negotiations 'taking into account the interests of the people of the territory', and called upon Britain to expedite the decolonisation of Gibraltar. Gibraltar's Chief Minister, Sir Joshua Hassan, told the Assembly's Trusteeship Committee that Gibraltarians already enjoyed a considerable degree of self-government, and that they had no wish to become part of Spain or to come in any way under Spanish sovereignty.

In March 1967, in compliance with the UN resolution, Britain proposed that talks should start on 18 April. These were called off by Britain, however, when on 12 April Spain, claiming persistent violations of its airspace, introduced a ban on all flights by foreign aircraft in an area contiguous to Gibraltar. When Britain called for negotiations on the ban, Spain responded by calling for talks on the decolonisation question. Although talks did resume on 5 June, they broke down three days later when Britain, having failed to persuade Spain to discuss the particular technical issue of aerial restrictions, took the dispute to the International Civil Aviation Authority, but they were unable to resolve a problem which was essentially a political one. This was quickly followed by an announcement on 14 June in the House of Commons that a referendum would be held in September inviting Gibraltarians to choose between continued association with Britain or Spanish sovereignty.

Not surprisingly this drew strong objections from Spain, who argued that the referendum violated UN General Assembly Resolutions by being held without consultation with Spain, and also that it contravened the Treaty of Utrecht. The UN Committee of 24 passed a Resolution on 1 September in support of Spain's objections (although it is difficult to see on what legal grounds) and called upon Britain and Spain to negotiate directly. Britain and Gibraltar denounced the UN Committee's Resolution as a wholly partisan document, and went ahead with the referendum on 10 September. The result was about as decisive as it could be without being unanimous, 12,138 Gibraltarians voting in favour of continuing association with Britain and 44 voting for Spanish sovereignty out of 12,762 registered voters.

Before the result was announced, Spain had already requested the resumption of talks on 6 September. However, when Britain agreed and proposed that they be held towards the end of November, Spain replied that Britain would first have to invalidate the referendum, which it refused to do. A dispute over the violation of Spanish territorial waters in the Bay of Algeciras blew up in early December.

A second Red Book was published by the Spanish Government on 11 December 1967, in which the negotiations since May 1966 were analysed.[7] On 16 December the UN General Assembly's Trusteeship Committee passed a resolution, endorsed on 19 December by the General Assembly, which regretted the interruption of talks on Gibraltar, described the referendum as a contravention of the 1966 Assembly Resolution and of the one passed by the Committee of 24 on 1 September 1967, and called upon Spain and Britain to resume talks with a view to ending the colonial situation in Gibraltar. The British permanent representative, Lord Caradon, described the resolution as 'unworthy of the UN and a disgrace to the [Trusteeship] Committee', while Gibraltar's Chief Minister, Sir Joshua Hassan, complained that 'abuse of fact, distortion, and deliberate lies have won the day.'

In January and February 1968 Spain again called for talks on the return of Gibraltar to Spanish sovereignty. On 15 March a group of six Gibraltarian lawyers and businessmen calling themselves the 'Doves' published a letter calling for a negotiated settlement with Spain. Following a further letter on 4 April, rioting and violent attacks on their property took place.

Talks were resumed in Madrid on 18 March 1968 but two days later broke down because Spain insisted that they be based exclusively on the UN Resolution. On 5 May, as a result of what Spain described as 'Britain's refusal to comply with the UN Resolution', Spain closed the land frontier to all traffic, including pedestrians, except for permanent residents and those Spaniards with permits to work on the Rock. On 7 May an emergency debate was held in the House of Commons, during which the UN Resolution was described as 'contemptible' and 'disgraceful'. The Commonwealth Secretary, George Thomson, spoke of the possibility that Spain might in future prevent its nationals from continuing to work in Gibraltar.[8]

British reaction to Spain's attitude hardened. Mr Thomson visited Gibraltar later that month and agreed that constitutional talks between Britain and the colony would take place in Gibraltar in July. These were agreed on 24 July in a joint communiqué which covered Gibraltar's links with Britain and its internal constitution. As part of the former, it was agreed that the Preamble to the Order in

Council promulgating the new Constitution would include a declaration to the effect that 'Gibraltar is a part of Her Majesty's Dominions and will remain so unless and until an Act of Parliament otherwise provides'. More significantly, the Preamble also included the commitment from the British Government that it will 'never enter into arrangements under which the people of Gibraltar would pass under the sovereignty of another State against their freely and democratically expressed wishes'. Ever since then, this commitment has given the Gibraltarians a virtual power of veto as far as the transfer of sovereignty is concerned and has given the British Government a let-out clause over the aspect of the issue in which Spain is interested above all others. Because of the opportunity it provides for the status quo to be maintained, it has proved to be the single most significant statement made on the sovereignty of Gibraltar since the signing of the Treaty of Utrecht itself.

Spain condemned the talks in a statement issued on 24 July 1968 which was sent to the UN Secretary General. It argued that the measures constituted a gratuitously unfriendly act towards Spain, a defiance of the United Nations, and a further obstacle to the solution to Gibraltar's future. Britain's delegation to the UN responded by pointing out that UN resolutions were recommendations, not binding decisions, and that when a resolution conflicted with the UN Charter[9] the obligation under the Charter had to take precedence. Britain's response went on that it looked forward to a time when Spain realised that its crude pressure was misguided and when it understood the need for patient endeavour to eradicate the distrust and hostility which its policy had created. Such a time was, at this juncture, a long way off.

Gibraltar was back on the UN agenda in December 1968, when the most strongly-worded Resolution thus far proposed was adopted. It declared the colonial situation in Gibraltar to be incompatible with the UN Charter and with previous Assembly Resolutions, called upon Britain to terminate the colonial situation in Gibraltar by 1 October 1969 and called upon the British and Spanish Governments to begin negotiations without delay. Lord Caradon, for the British Government, told the Assembly that the resolution would not and could not be put into effect.

Gibraltar's new constitution was published on 30 May 1969 as an Order in Council and came into immediate effect, with elections scheduled for 30 July.[10] The Spanish Government described it as open disregard by Britain of UN Resolutions and as a violation of Article 10 of the Treaty of Utrecht. It was at a meeting of the Spanish Cabinet on 6 June that the decision was taken to carry out the threat made over four years earlier to cut Gibraltar off from the mainland. Two days later Gibraltar's 16-year period of physical and psychological isolation from Spain began.

The deadline of 1 October, contained in the UN resolution of December 1968, had no sooner passed than Spain increased Gibraltar's isolation by severing telephone links. Britain described the act as 'malicious', 'inhumane' and 'small-minded'. But surprisingly, a change in the tone of Spanish policy soon occurred with the replacement of Fernando María Castiella as Foreign Minister by Gregorio López Bravo on 30 October. Spanish propaganda broadcasting to Gibraltar was stopped, and Spain decided in November not to raise the question of Gibraltar at the current session of the UN General Assembly. Telephone links were restored over Christmas for 36 hours.

The most immediate effect in Gibraltar of the frontier closure was the need to find replacements for the 4,800 Spanish workers—about one-third of the labour force—who hitherto had crossed daily to work on the Rock. Replacements were largely achieved through a combination of troops, Government employees taking on extra part-time jobs, and the hiring of housewives and Moroccans. Britain's commitment to assist Gibraltar's economy following the severance of communications was now turned into hard currency, when a visit to London in early December 1969 by the new Chief Minister, Robert Peliza, produced a commitment of £4 million over three years for development aid.

During the first half of 1970 there were rumours that behind-the-scenes negotiations were taking place, but until restrictions were lifted by Spain Britain made it clear that serious talks could not get under way. There was a change of British Government in June, and the new Conservative Foreign Secretary, Sir Alec Douglas-Home, had a brief meeting with his Spanish counterpart Sr López Bravo in Luxemburg on 30 June. Little happened for nearly a year. Informal talks took place in Madrid on 3 June 1971 at the level of Permanent Under-Secretary of State on the British side, with the Spanish Foreign Minister and senior officials on the other, but it was reported that the attitudes of the two sides remained unchanged. Sir Alec Douglas-Home went to Gibraltar for talks on 24 September, and in October Sr López Bravo spoke of his feeling that a climate for dialogue now existed.

Talks did in fact take place at Foreign Minister level in Madrid in February 1972, but no progress was made. Further discussions on Gibraltar were held during an official visit by the Spanish Foreign Minister to London in July, and contact was renewed in November between Sir Alec Douglas-Home and his Spanish counterpart. Their views were sufficiently far apart for the joint communiqué to state that they had not yet reached the stage at which formal negotiations might begin.

Britain formally entered the European Community on 1 January 1973. Gibraltar was accorded special status under Article 227(4) of the Treaty of Rome, through which it became a member but did not contribute VAT, nor participate in the Common Agricultural Policy or the Common External Tariff. By the same token, the colony had no official representation in any of the Union's institutions in its own right, including the European Parliament. Britain's Accession Treaty with the EU made it clear that this status could be safeguarded because Britain would have the right of veto over any proposal to change it.

The next round of talks between the two Foreign Ministers took place in May 1973, when Spain tabled some new proposals,[11] predicated upon the transfer of sovereignty, which Britain was unable to accept.

The situation looked bleak at this point, with no communiqué issued and no date set for a further meeting. Sr López Bravo's replacement as Foreign Minister, Laureano López Rodó, informed the UN Secretary General, Dr Kurt Waldheim, on 18 July that discussions had definitely been broken off because of British intransigence. On 6 August communications by small craft from Gibraltar to Algeciras, which had been permitted since November 1970, were halted. On 26 November Spain renewed its call to the UN Trusteeship Committee for a British withdrawal from Gibraltar, and the consensus recommended by this Committee was adopted by the General Assembly. It appeared that after four years of a softer line from Sr López Bravo, which had been unproductive from a Spanish point of view, a harder line was once more being taken under his successor.

Britain, under the new Labour Government, responded to the UN consensus by proposing exploratory and non-committal talks in Madrid, which took place at the end of May 1974. One issue which Britain raised was safe access to Gibraltar airport, but Spain refused to discuss it separately from the decolonisation question. No decisions were taken and no date was set for a subsequent meeting. At the UN General Assembly on 3 October Spain's Foreign Minister, Pedro Cortina Mauri, accused Britain of having been unwilling to discuss matters of substance during the May talks.[12] In November, Roy Hattersley, Minister of State at the Foreign and Commonwealth Office, stated that the Government had no plans for further talks with Spain, and none were forthcoming for some time.

Financial commitments by the British Government to Gibraltar were by this stage taking on an air of permanence. In November 1974 capital aid of over £7.6 million was agreed for the period 1975–78, following talks in London with Gibraltar's Chief Minister, who called for a shift of emphasis in Gibraltar's aid programme from short-term temporary measures towards investment designed to increase Gibraltar's self-sufficiency.

In September 1975 Roy Hattersley paid an official visit to Gibraltar. He confirmed the British Government's position, but also made it clear that he ruled out any prospect of future integration with Britain.

The possibility of progress being made on the Gibraltar question was improved by the death of General Franco on 20 November 1975 and the replacement of his dictatorship by a constitutional monarchy, the introduction of democratic reforms and the potential integration of Spain into the European Community. It was clear that there would be no sudden and dramatic progress, however, when King Juan Carlos emphasised in his accession speech that Spain would continue to attempt to reclaim sovereignty over Gibraltar. But the first sign of the end of Gibraltar's isolation occurred in December, when telephone links between Spain and the Rock were restored between Christmas and the New Year, and again over Easter in April 1976.

Early in 1976 an inter-party Constitution Committee in Gibraltar proposed constitutional changes involving greater integration with Britain, and in June a delegation visited London to discuss them. In a Memorandum the British Government declared that 'it is impossible to consider decolonisation in the form of integration with Britain or independence'. They rejected the proposed reforms because they wanted to avoid taking measures which might hamper 'the development of a more favourable Spanish attitude'. They also rejected the idea of a permanent economic link with Britain because it would 'decrease the options which might eventually be open to the Gibraltarians'.[13] On 19 September Sir Joshua Hassan (who was shortly to be re-elected as Chief Minister)[14] wrote a perceptive letter to *The Sunday Times*, in which he envisaged a time when a solution to the Gibraltar question might be achieved: 'Should a more humane and modern European policy be adopted in the future [by Spain], one can see possibilities of an honourable long-term solution, in a European context, which would safeguard our political freedoms, the continuation of our links with Britain and our way of life as a minute but identifiable community'.

Following the first post-Franco general elections in Spain on 15 June 1977, the Spanish Government's main preoccupation was the introduction of a new constitution.[15] But it did not waste any time in reiterating at the first cabinet meeting on 12 July its claim to Gibraltar as part of Spanish territory, and in the first foreign affairs debate of the new Parliament held on 20 September all parties agreed on 'the decolonisation of Gibraltar'.

On 5 September Dr David Owen became the first British Foreign Secretary to visit Spain since Sir Alec Douglas-Home went there in 1961. He called for the lifting of the restrictions on communications before negotiations could begin, although he expressed Britain's support for Spain's application to the EC (which had been formally submitted in July) and also to NATO (which it was considering).

The Spanish Prime Minister, Adolfo Suárez, visited London on 19 October and discussed the Gibraltar issue with his British counterpart, James Callaghan, and with Dr Owen. Sr Suárez was confident that the autonomy statutes in the Spanish constitution held the key to the resolution of the problem, leading to the 'reintegration of Gibraltar into Spanish territory in conformity with UN resolutions'. But he refused to lift the restrictions, as this would have represented a partial solution to the problem rather than a global one.

In November 1977, following discussions in London with Gibraltarian representatives, it was agreed that exploratory talks to break the deadlock should be held between the British and Spanish

Governments, including—for the first time—Gibraltarian representation. Accordingly Dr Owen, Sir Joshua Hassan and Maurice
Xiberras (an independent deputy and former leader of the Integration with Britain Party) met Marcelino Oreja, the Spanish Foreign
Minister, in Strasbourg on 24 November on the occasion of Spain's
entry into the Council of Europe. The meeting was reconvened in
Paris on 15 March 1978, when it was agreed to set up Anglo-Spanish
working groups on telephone and maritime communications, and
also on pensions for former Spanish workers in Gibraltar. The
groups met in London in July and in Madrid in December 1978.

When the general election brought the Conservatives back into
government in May 1979, Lord Carrington, the new Foreign Secretary, quickly confirmed that there would be no change in British
policy towards Gibraltar. What was needed, he said, was a shift in
the attitude of the Spanish Government towards the re-opening of
the border. The shift was eventually to come in March 1980,
brought about by a number of factors, including a general strike in
La Línea in October 1979, and ongoing negotiations on Spain's
membership of both NATO and the EC.

But despite the transition to democracy, there had been a remarkably consistent (even persistent) attitude by Spain towards Gibraltar
throughout this period. All Spanish Governments had clung with
tenacity to a position in which the nation's desire to reclaim the
sovereignty of Gibraltar was unquestioned and unquestionable: the
remarks of King Juan Carlos and Adolfo Suárez on Gibraltar could
have been made by General Franco or any of his Ministers. For Spain,
democracy had changed nothing as far as the issue of Gibraltar was
concerned. But for Britain it was clearly going to be easier to discuss
the Gibraltar issue with a democratic Spain, especially one with
which Britain would be tied through joint membership of a supranational organisation. Not only would it be easier, but also essential:
Spain would have to put an end to the blockade, as there would have
to be free movement of people and goods across borders, and Britain
would have to seek a way of satisfying the territorial claims of
another Community state. The problem would be to convince the
Gibraltarians themselves that change was either desirable or necessary. After over a decade of isolation, and several more years of it to
come, that would be an uphill task.

Notes

1 See *Hansard*, 5th Series, Vol. 785, cols. 1709–15.

2 Its full title was the UN Special Committee on the Situation with regard to the Implementation of the Declaration on the Granting of Independence to Colonial Countries and Peoples.

3 From November 1966 the British Government provided economic assistance for a development programme designed to make Gibraltar's economy independent of that of Spain.

4 *Gibraltar—Recent Differences with Spain*, HMSO, Misc. No. 12 (1965).

5 *Documentos sobre Gibraltar*. Documentos presentados a las Cortes Españolas por el Ministro de Asuntos Exteriores, Madrid, 1965.

6 In a statement in the Commons on 31 October 1966, the Foreign Secretary, George Brown, referring to the British proposal, said that 'it will be for the Court to decide on all questions referred to it, including the question of sovereignty. The Spanish Government and Her Majesty's Government would be bound by the Court's decision'. (*Hansard*, 5th Series, Vol. 735, cols. 34–35.) This was the first time that Britain had been prepared to allow for any discussion on the sovereignty issue.

7 *Negociaciones sobre Gibraltar*, Documentos presentados a las Cortes Españolas por el Ministro de Asuntos Exteriores, Madrid, 1967.

8 See *Hansard*, 5th Series, Vol. 764, 7 May 1968, Cols. 245, 267, 271, 276–77.

9 They referred to Article 73 and the need for the British Government to safeguard the interests of the inhabitants of non-self-governing territories for which it was responsible.

10 The elections resulted in the formation of a coalition, led by Major Robert Peliza as Chief Minister, between five members of the Integration with Britain Party and three Independents. This marked a brief interruption in the premiership of Sir Joshua Hassan.

11 These had originally been conveyed to Gibraltar's Chief Minister, Sir Joshua Hassan (who had been re-elected in the elections held in 1972), while on a visit to Brussels in February 1973, but had not been made public. They remained confidential until 7 November 1974, when a series of letters were exchanged through the columns of *The Times* between 14 October and 12 November.

12 In January 1975 the Moroccan Government called on the UN Committee of 24 to declare that Spain's claim to Gibraltar was not consistent with its continued presence on Moroccan territory in Ceuta and Melilla.

13 *Memorandum by Her Majesty's Government on the Report of the Constitution Committee*, 26 June 1976, known as the Hattersley Memorandum.

14 In the elections held on 26 September, the Integration with Britain Party, whose demise had begun a year or so earlier, was replaced as the main opposition party by the Gibraltar Democratic Movement. This was led by Joe Bossano, a founder member of the Integration with Britain Party, but when three of the four GDM representatives crossed the floor of the Assembly in 1977, Bossano formed

the Gibraltar Socialist Labour Party. As leader of the GSLP, Bossano became Chief Minister in 1988.

15 The autonomy statutes for various regions of Spain which the constitution eventually contained, aroused interest as a possible solution to the problem of Gibraltar. In September 1977 the Party for the Autonomy of Gibraltar was formed with this in mind, and unsuccessfully put up three candidates in the elections in February 1980.

THREE
THE LISBON AGREEMENT
July 1979–April 1980

Sir Ian Gilmour, Minister of State at the Foreign Office, visited Gibraltar on 17 and 18 July 1979 in order to convey the new Conservative Government's views directly to the Gibraltarians. He said that the Government considered the Spanish restrictions to be unjustifiable, that it was inconceivable that the frontier should remain closed in an enlarged European Community, and described the restrictions as an act of hostility.

Thus far the British Government had maintained that Britain would fully support Spain's application for membership of the European Community, and that the Gibraltar dispute was irrelevant to Britain's attitude. But when a member of the British Government linked the two as Sir Ian did, suspicions arose in the minds of Spaniards as to whether there might not be some connection being made between the two issues, especially as the EC negotiations frequently ran into opposition from Britain on the question of fishing.

Nevertheless, Spain's negotiations to join the EC continued, while those on Gibraltar did not. Lord Carrington, the Foreign Secretary, met his Spanish counterpart Sr Oreja in New York on 24 September during the General Assembly of the UN, but nothing of substance emerged.

Pressure on the Spanish Government to shift the logjam on negotiations came from a new quarter in October 1979. A 24-hour general strike was called in La Línea for 9 October to protest against the Government's failure to compensate the Campo region for the economic hardship it had suffered over the past ten years through the closure of the frontier. Unemployment in La Línea currently affected some 4,000 workers, representing between 20% and 25% of the active workforce. The PSOE, the main opposition party, called upon the Government to respond. Pressure from the British and the

Gibraltarians to reopen the border was one thing; calls from disgruntled Spanish workers—and voters—was quite another.

However, little had changed by the time that the Foreign Minister, Marcelino Oreja, appeared before the Senate Foreign Relations Committee on 6 December and took the opportunity to set out Spain's current position on the Gibraltar issue. Spain was prepared to concede a considerable degree of autonomy, dual nationality and customs privileges in exchange for joint control (rather than NATO control) of the military base and a definite timescale for the transfer of sovereignty. He defended the current restrictions by referring to Article 10 of the Treaty of Utrecht, which prohibits communication by land between Gibraltar and Spain, arguing that Gibraltarians were free to enter Spain by any other route. Technically he was correct; in practical terms his statement was not at all helpful, least of all in improving the diplomatic climate.

The heart of the matter was clearly whether Britain would be willing to agree to negotiate explicitly on sovereignty; this appeared to be the only concession Britain could make which would achieve the end of the blockade of Gibraltar by Spain. One ray of hope on the Spanish side that this might be possible was the fact that Lord Carrington was now Foreign Minister. Having demonstrated his ability to persuade the British Government to make important concessions in the case of Rhodesia, it was felt in Spain that he might be able at least to persuade his Government to discuss the Gibraltar sovereignty issue. But no immediate moves were forthcoming.

The general election held in Gibraltar on 6 February 1980 saw Sir Joshua Hassan's AACR party returned to power, with eight of the fifteen seats. The Integration with Britain Party (now reformed as the Democratic Party of British Gibraltar) won six seats, with Joe Bossano as the sole GSLP representative. On 8 February the Spanish daily *El País* reported the results and noted that negotiations on Gibraltar were unlikely in the near future, since the British Foreign Office would argue that the international situation prevented Gibraltar from being one of its priorities, commenting that 'there is always an Afghanistan somewhere in the world'.[1] The fact was, the paper said, that the situation in Afghanistan had once again underlined the strategic importance of Gibraltar whenever there was a confrontation between East and West; when Britain decided to send three frigates and an amphibious assault ship to the Eastern Mediterranean in January to reinforce the US Sixth Fleet, the ships came from Gibraltar.[2]

Lord Carrington and the Spanish Foreign Minister, Marcelino Oreja, were due to meet in Lisbon on 10 April 1980 at a Council of Europe meeting. It was hoped that they might take the opportunity to have informal talks about Gibraltar with a view to establishing a framework for negotiations. The Spanish Parliament tried to give its representative a strong hand at the meeting by unanimously supporting a PSOE resolution on Gibraltar on 27 March. The resolution reaffirmed the will of the Spanish people to reintegrate Gibraltar into Spain; urged the Spanish Government to invite the British Government once more to start negotiations, in accordance with UN Resolutions; invited the Government to re-establish land communications step-by-step as negotiations permit; and called for cultural, economic, scientific and other exchanges between Gibraltar and the Campo region and the implementation of a plan to revive the Campo economy. The PSOE deputy, Luis Yañez, who presented the resolution, concluded his long speech with the words of the President of the Second Spanish Republic in Exile, Claudio Sánchez Albornoz, who said: 'There cannot be a Spaniard worthy of the name, who can write, without blushing, that Gibraltar is not part of Spain. And if there is anyone who can write that without blushing, I take the liberty of blushing for him, as a liberal Spaniard in exile'.[3]

Here at last was an opening—a proposal from the entire, democratically-elected representative body of the Spanish people—which the Spanish Government could use in order to justify the re-establishment of communications with Gibraltar, a measure which would allow the British Government—leaving on one side the predictable call for the reintegration of Gibraltar into Spain—to agree to start negotiations. But as the leader writer in *El País* on 28 March pointed out, while Spain would have to be prepared for Britain to use the protection of the Gibraltarians' interests as their main negotiating weapon, Spain could argue that 'since the restoration of democratic freedoms in Spain there are no civil rights that the Gibraltarians can lose through reintegration into Spain'. Their rights, he argued, would be as well—if not better—protected under Spain's autonomy statutes than they are by holding 'mythical, obsolete and novelesque British passports'.

The declaration from the Spanish Parliament was sent privately to the Foreign Office in London as the basis for the 'talks about talks' in Lisbon in April. There was a great deal of secrecy about the Carrington-Oreja encounter, largely (it was suggested) at Sr Oreja's request, because reports to the press by the Gibraltarians following the meeting he had in Strasbourg with Dr Owen in 1977 had led to friction in later talks.

The two Foreign Ministers met for three-quarters of an hour on 9 April. Although no official statement was issued, it appeared that the main achievement of this encounter was to enable both sides to make their position clear: on the British side that they were determined to seek a solution but that the views of the Gibraltarian people would be decisive, and on the Spanish side that Spain was prepared to re-establish communication by land to coincide with the start of negotiations, and that the new Spanish Constitution offered a suitable solution to the people of Gibraltar.

Lord Carrington and Sr Oreja met again the following day, and it was at the end of their discussions that the declaration which came to be known as the Lisbon Agreement was made. The six points of the Agreement were that the British and Spanish Governments agreed to resolve the problem of Gibraltar, to start negotiations 'in order to resolve all their differences' and to re-establish direct communications in the region. They also agreed— in a phrase which was to create immediate difficulties—that future co-operation should be 'on the basis of reciprocity and full equality of rights'. In addition the Spanish Government, while reaffirming its position regarding the re-establishment of Spain's territorial integrity, agreed to ensure that the interests of the Gibraltarians would be safeguarded, while the British Government would maintain its commitment (as indicated in the Preamble to the 1969 Gibraltarian Constitution) to respect the freely and democratically expressed wishes of the Gibraltarians. It was agreed that by 1 June officials of both sides would prepare the way for the objectives of the agreement to be met, including an agenda and timetable.[4]

At the press conference at which the joint declaration was announced, both sides were clearly satisfied with the outcome of their two days of talks. The practical result was that what *The Times* leader of 12 April called the 'major irritant' of the eleven-year

Spanish blockade of Gibraltar could now be finally lifted. But agreeing to discuss the Gibraltar problem—which was in itself a major step forward—was one thing; perceiving how to resolve it would be quite another. In reality the Agreement represented a statement of the positions held on each side: Spain would pursue discussion of the issue of sovereignty (resolving 'all their differences' clearly implied this), while Britain would respect the wishes of the Gibraltarians. Since it was unlikely in the foreseeable future that the wishes of the Gibraltarians and of the Spanish Government would coincide, these two conflicting positions would inevitably ensure that the negotiations would be neither easy nor brief.

Nevertheless, the achievement of the Lisbon Agreement should not be minimised. The editorial writer of *El País* on 12 April was clearly in no mood to do so, although he gave a generally realistic assessment of the situation. Describing the agreement as 'historic' (despite his recognition that the word was much abused), he saw it as offering 'a coherent strategy for the recovery of the sovereignty over the Rock with the consent of the Gibraltarians'. Democratic Spain was no different, the writer argued, from democratic Britain; whether the human rights of the Gibraltarians could be properly defended was no longer an issue.[5] But the fact that their freedoms and political rights *can* be maintained within the framework of Spanish sovereignty should not be confused, he wrote, with whether they *wish* to accept such a change in their status as citizens. The negotiations were going to have to find a way of reconciling Spain's determination to restore its territorial integrity with Britain's equal determination to defend the wishes of the Gibraltarians. He said that a period of 'osmosis' was about to begin (the first occasion on which the term appeared) between the populations of Gibraltar and Spain. The writer warned that Morocco would be watching to see how Spain handled the Gibraltar issue. While states can make claims for their territorial integrity, he argued, in both cases respect for the rights of people comes before rights over the land.[6]

Reaction in Gibraltar itself was generally—though by no means universally—favourable. Sir Joshua Hassan suggested that the British Government had done Spain a favour by finding a way forward on the Gibraltar problem so that it no longer threatened to get in the way of Spain's negotiations to join the EC. He also underlined the mistrust of Spaniards which had grown over the past eleven years, and urged that that be taken into account when the border was opened.

The importance of Sir Joshua's exhortation was underlined by the fact that on 13 April 2,000 Gibraltarians demonstrated in protest at the opening of negotiations. The man heading the protest was Joe Bossano, leader of the GSLP, whose views were later to lead him to be elected as Chief Minister. He argued at a rally that if there were to be any negotiations about the future of the Rock, they should be held between Britain and the inhabitants of Gibraltar, without any participation by the Spanish Government. There was also concern about the effect that the opening of the border might have on Gibraltar's economy, given the lack of development of its infrastructure during its period of isolation.[7]

No doubt these matters were discussed when Sir Joshua Hassan and Peter Isola of the Integration with Britain Party met Lord Carrington in London on 14 April, the same day that the Foreign Secretary reported to the House of Lords on his meeting with Sr Oreja in Lisbon. In his statement to the House, Lord Carrington pointed out that the process of negotiation was likely to be a very long one, although Lord Gladwyn wondered what the negotiations would be about, given the Government's commitment to do nothing against the wishes of the Gibraltarians. Lord Carrington's reply was that the negotiations would consist of anything anyone wanted to talk about, subject to the proviso regarding the Gibraltarians' wishes. In the Commons Sir Ian Gilmour made a statement and, in answer to a question, agreed that there was nothing to prevent the discussion of sovereignty in the negotiations.

When Marcelino Oreja made a statement on the Lisbon Agreement to the Spanish Foreign Affairs Committee on 16 April, he argued that while Spain was prepared to safeguard and recognise the interests of the Gibraltarians, it would never recognise their right to dispose of 'something which does not belong to them and has never belonged to them: the sovereignty of Gibraltar'. He too conceded that the negotiations would be long and difficult.

Clearly, the starting points of the two sides in the negotiations were going to be some way apart. On the question of sovereignty, the British approach was that, under the terms of the agreement, it was a legitimate subject for discussion, but that the known position of the Gibraltarians made it extremely unlikely that any movement on the issue would be possible. For their part, the Spaniards saw discussions on sovereignty within the context of the UN Resolutions as a move towards decolonisation. As for the Gibraltarians, it was their 'wishes' which would be paramount for Britain, whereas Spain was prepared only to respect their 'interests'.

But at least the negotiating process could now get under way. In addition, Spain was in the process of conducting two other series of negotiations which had a bearing on the Gibraltar question: entry into the European Community and membership of NATO. It was the latter which took centre stage in the months following April 1980.

Notes

1 A reference to the invasion of Afghanistan by Soviet forces in September 1979, followed by the overthrow and execution of President Amin. Because the situation involved one of the superpowers, initially it constituted a major international crisis. The withdrawal of Soviet troops was not completed until almost ten years later.

2 *El País* was not always consistent in its attitude towards the strategic importance of Gibraltar. On 28 March, the leader writer wrote: 'Whatever this country's position might be . . . on our entry into the Atlantic Alliance, it is clear to everyone that Gibraltar is no longer the "key to the Mediterranean" and that modern military strategy is not in fact based on fortified towns'. The fact is that Gibraltar has played an important role in practically every international incident in the European theatre (and in many cases beyond it, as the South Atlantic crisis was graphically to illustrate) since the Second World War.

3 *El País*, 28 March 1980, p. 14.

4 For the full text of the Lisbon Agreement, see Appendix 2.

5 An attempted coup within the year was nearly to prove him wrong (see below, Chapter 4, p. 28).

6 This was a reiteration of the British position of July 1968 (see above, p. 12).

7 Groups who would be likely to suffer the effects of the opening of the border were owners of Moroccan ferries who operated on the five- to six-hour crossing from Tangiers to Algeciras, the inhabitants of Ceuta (where Spaniards went shopping for tax-free goods which in future they would be able to get in Gibraltar), and above all Moroccan workers in Gibraltar, who feared they might be replaced by Spaniards. On the latter point, on 15 April Joe Bossano, leader of the GSLP, issued a statement calling upon the Gibraltarian authorities to guarantee jobs, first to Gibraltarians and Moroccans currently working in Gibraltar, second to workers from EC countries, and third to Spaniards.

FOUR
SPAIN'S APPROACHES TO NATO
June 1980–March 1982

In a wide-ranging interview on the foreign policy of the UCD Government published in *El País* on 15 June 1980, Spain's Foreign Minister, Marcelino Oreja, announced that it was the intention of the Government to apply to join NATO some time in 1981. He made an explicit link with Gibraltar by indicating that the only conditions of Spain's application were guarantees that negotiations on Spain's membership of the EC would continue and that those on the transfer of the sovereignty of Gibraltar would be under way.

In fact negotiations on Gibraltar were not yet under way, although technical talks on practical matters such as setting up customs posts had started. But the start of negotiations on the text of the Lisbon Agreement had been delayed because Spain wanted reciprocal treatment of Spaniards in Gibraltar and Gibraltarians in Spain (referred to in Paragraph 3 of the Agreement) to begin at the same time as communications were restored, whereas as far as reciprocity was concerned Britain (and Gibraltar) put that in the context of the words 'future cooperation' in the text. The timetable, starting with the deadline of 1 June for negotiations to get under way, had fallen at the first hurdle.

The negotiations had still not started by the time that Sir Ian Gilmour, Commons Spokesman on Foreign Affairs, went to Madrid on 7 January 1981 for two days of talks with the new Spanish Foreign Minister, José Pedro Pérez-Llorca, on bilateral and international matters, including Gibraltar. Neither side had budged on the question of reciprocal treatment, and the problem had not been helped in December by a resolution passed in the Gibraltarian House of Assembly (and assumed in Spain to have the backing of Britain) which stated that Spanish nationals should not enjoy the same rights as nationals of other EC countries until Spain was a full member of the Community.

The result of the meeting as far as the Gibraltar issue was concerned was disappointing. Spanish demands were now for equality for Spaniards going to Gibraltar in anticipation of Spain's entry into the European Community (currently expected to be in January 1984), but Sir Ian was not prepared to make any concessions. This was seen in Spain as a clear hardening of the British position, although Sir Ian maintained that through reciprocal rights Spaniards could acquire almost the same advantages in Gibraltar as nationals of other EC countries. It was clear on the British side that Spain was held responsible for the delay in starting talks.

Later in January 1981 Leopoldo Calvo Sotelo took over as Prime Minister from Adolfo Suárez. Before he had had the chance fully to take over the reins of office, there was an attempted coup led by Colonel Tejero on 23 February. Although it failed, it did not enhance Spain's cause in winning the hearts and minds of Gibraltarians, although in other respects (perhaps surprisingly) it does not appear to have affected progress on negotiations on Gibraltar: it has never been suggested that the Gibraltar question would be harder to resolve as a consequence of the vulnerability of Spanish democracy to military intervention. In that respect it may have been an advantage that, at the time, talks on Gibraltar had ground to a halt; if they had been in full swing in February 1981, it is likely that the attempted coup would have represented a severe setback to their progress. As far as the Spanish Government was concerned, they will have wanted to use the attempted coup to put pressure on Britain to move negotiations forward, and thereby bolster the international standing of the democratic regime.

The first contact at Foreign Minister level since the signing of the Lisbon Agreement was arranged for 13 July 1981 in Brussels. The reason for the meeting concerned Spain's application to join the European Community, but Lord Carrington and Sr Pérez-Llorca also briefly discussed Gibraltar. There was speculation before the meeting that Spain would indicate its readiness to open the border gates without insisting on simultaneous reciprocity of rights, but this proved to be unfounded. Instead, there was a more pessimistic fear that unless one side or the other changed its position, the border would not open until 1984 at the earliest.

Anglo-Spanish relations took a turn for the worse when the Foreign Office announced that the Prince and Princess of Wales would fly to Gibraltar to start their honeymoon on the royal yacht *Britannia* on 1 August, following their wedding on 29 July. As a result of the announcement the Spanish King and Queen felt obliged not to attend the wedding ceremony. As the event more or less coincided with the 277th anniversary of the seizure of the Rock on 4 August, several Spanish newspapers took the opportunity to attack Britain over the Gibraltar issue.

Lord Carrington tried to mend the bridges on 16 August, at the end of his holiday in Spain, by asking for a meeting in Madrid with his Spanish counterpart and other officials. The media were not informed of the meeting until after it had taken place, and the comment issued from the Spanish Foreign Ministry was that there had been 'some progress'.

Further speculation about a new proposal from the Spanish side appeared in *The Sunday Times* on 23 August and was repeated in *El País* two days later, to the effect that Spain would propose that Gibraltar should be converted into a full-scale military base under NATO command. The Spanish Government would hope that an agreement with London would take the wind out of the sails of left-wing opposition to Spain's membership of the Atlantic Alliance, which the Government now planned to initiate in the autumn.

Spain had several reasons to want to join NATO: to play a part in mainstream Western international activity; to reinforce its application to join the EC; to modernise the armed forces and give them a non-political focus; to change the nature of its relationship with the US as far as defence is concerned;[1] and last but not least, to provide a context in which an acceptable solution to the Gibraltar issue might be found. It is no doubt for this last reason that the speculation arose as to what Spain might propose in relation to the Gibraltar negotiations.

The PSOE had chosen 3 September as the day to launch their anti-NATO campaign, and they used the Gibraltar issue to stir up Spanish emotions by arguing that once in NATO, Spain would be obliged to defend a British colony if Gibraltar were attacked. The PSOE leader, Felipe González, called for recognition by the other members of the

Atlantic Alliance of Spanish sovereignty over Gibraltar, an action which he knew full well was out of the question. The PSOE spokesman on the Senate Foreign Relations Committee, Fernando Morán, argued that if Gibraltar became a NATO base with a Spanish command, that would make the transfer of sovereignty even more difficult, not easier as the Government was suggesting. The PSOE clearly saw Gibraltar as something of an Achilles' heel for the Government's stance on NATO; its desire to push through membership of NATO could not wait upon a solution to the Gibraltar issue, and would therefore leave Spain with this hypothetical dilemma of having to defend a British colony.

Meanwhile, the Spanish position on Gibraltar had been given a boost on 28 August when the House of Commons Select Committee on Foreign Affairs published a report on Gibraltar. This followed fact-finding visits by a five-member delegation of the Committee, led by Sir Anthony Kershaw, to both Gibraltar and Madrid in April. The Committee's report recommended 'on the lifting of restrictions, to give to Spaniards in Gibraltar the rights they would have as citizens of an EEC country', because it would anticipate their change in status by only a short time. There was recognition that the present Spanish constitutional structure providing for regional autonomy within Spain could be an important element in resolving the dispute. The report also questioned British jurisdiction over the isthmus in the light of the Treaty of Utrecht. And there was the suggestion that the Gibraltarians should be reminded that, whilst accepting Britain's obligations to them, the British Government's primary responsibility is to the British Parliament.[2] Not surprisingly, the report was well received in Spain (it was the main front page news story in *El País* on 28 August), where it was viewed as supporting many of Spain's own positions, particularly regarding the Lisbon Agreement.

The Foreign Minister, José Pedro Pérez-Llorca, met Lord Carrington in New York on 23 September at the UN, where they discussed what by now were the standard three issues: the EC, NATO and Gibraltar. Sr Pérez-Llorca made it clear that he saw Spain's membership of NATO as a means of making progress on the Gibraltar question. There was a clear division of opinion between the UCD Government and the PSOE opposition on whether membership of NATO would help or hinder Spain's aspirations regarding the sovereignty of Gibraltar.

The Spanish Prime Minister, Leopoldo Calvo Sotelo, was scheduled to visit Britain in December, and took the opportunity on 3 October to prepare the ground publicly by announcing that he would be looking for a number of concessions in return for agreeing to open the border gates. They included the hope that the British Government would (a) reject the amendment to the British Nationality Bill which would grant Gibraltarian passport holders the right to apply for British citizenship;[3] (b) support the House of Commons Foreign Affairs Committee report on Gibraltar published in August; and (c) as the current holders of the Presidency of the Council of Ministers, propose at the heads of government summit in November that the date for Spain to join the EC should be 1 January 1984. In addition, Sr Calvo Sotelo hoped to accelerate Spain's membership of NATO by receiving an invitation for Spain to join when the Foreign Ministers of NATO members met in early December. This would enable the Spanish Government to demonstrate to the Spanish people the connection between progress in the four areas of current external negotiations (Gibraltar, EC, NATO and the treaty with the USA), and to win support for Spain's entry into NATO.

An article commenting on the Gibraltar question—of the kind that was to proliferate during the Falklands/Malvinas conflict—appeared under the title of 'The dénouement' in *El País* on 6 October. Its author, José María de Areilza, a former Foreign Minister, noted that in Spain there was political unanimity about Spain's claim to sovereignty. In Britain there is cross-party opinion that a solution needs to be found, but this is not universal; as well as being an important strategic base, Gibraltar is also 'a national myth with deep sentimental roots'. In Gibraltar, the past 12 years have induced a climate of growing hostility towards any solution which proposes the restoration of Spanish sovereignty.

As far as solutions are concerned, Sr de Areilza advocates the opening of the border gates, which is easy to achieve and will bring a 'positive dynamism' to other aspects of the negotiating process, without insisting upon the simultaneous reciprocity of rights, which involves 'putting an end to a degrading discrimination.' He also fails to see why Spain should be concerned that entry into the Atlantic Alliance would make a transfer of sovereignty more difficult, since the Lisbon Agreement referred to the resolution of all differences over Gibraltar and that included re-establishing the territorial integrity of Spain. He is not concerned about the internationalisation of the Gibraltar base, because the base at Cartagena can be given superior status to Gibraltar once Spain is a NATO member. As far as the Gibraltarians themselves are concerned, it should be possible, he argues, for them to live in Spain with their own statute, given that about 4 million British people come to Spain every year.

The article reflects a view of the problem which, as events have since borne out, places too little emphasis on the attitude of the British Government towards the wishes of the Gibraltarians and the extent to which these are made paramount. Whilst it acknowledges the existence of the myth and the sentimental roots, it does not accord them sufficient importance. The fact is that, although many of the inhabitants of the Rock could not claim British ancestry, their way of life had, over the decades, become quintessentially British. Institutions and systems were based on British models, and the visible presence of a British colonial Governor, the British military, British-style police uniforms and the other trappings of 'the old country' created a psychological barrier which made the idea of being part of Spain anathema to the vast majority.

For three days between 6 and 8 October the Spanish Foreign Affairs Committee discussed Spain's entry into NATO. During the final day the Foreign Minister, Sr Pérez-Llorca, argued that his Government was intending to go ahead with its application, despite the fact that the question of the sovereignty of Gibraltar had not been resolved. But he threatened that if there was no progress on the Gibraltar issue Spain would leave NATO. The opposition parties opposed NATO membership prior to the recognition of Spanish sovereignty over Gibraltar, on the grounds that, first, one of Spain's fellow-members had a military base on 'its' territory, and second, in the event of an attack, Spain would have to go to Gibraltar's defence with the Rock still under British control.[4] The draft resolution approved by the Foreign Affairs Committee included the desire to see progress towards a solution to the Gibraltar problem.

The plenary debate on NATO membership in the Spanish Parliament was held three weeks later on 27 and 28 October. The arguments divided largely on left-right lines, with the UCD, Acción Democrática, and the Basque and Catalan Nationalist parties lining up in favour of Spanish entry. The main issue was whether Spain was prepared to commit itself to membership of the Western-Atlantic block, but the restoration of Gibraltar to Spanish sovereignty figured amongst the three subsidiary issues, together with the North African enclaves, and the maintenance of Spain's non-nuclear policy. On all three of these issues, the PSOE and other left-wing opposition parties demanded guarantees before entry, but the Government and its supporters rejected such a position.

The Prime Minister Calvo Sotelo argued that a better solution to the Gibraltar issue could be achieved with Spain inside NATO, and that the decolonisation process had been assisted by the British Parliament's decision on 27 October to grant Gibraltarians the right to British citizenship, following the approval of an amendment in the House of Lords in July. The text authorising the Spanish Parliament to proceed with negotiations included a recommendation to the Government that they pay special attention to the fact that 'the restoration of Spanish sovereignty over Gibraltar is a top priority'.[5]

Such a statement only added to British suspicions as to the Spanish Government's motives for pushing ahead with NATO membership. As has been indicated, there were several reasons why Spain wanted to join NATO, but if it hoped that its membership would enable it somehow to circumvent Britain's adherence to the principle of respecting the wishes of the Gibraltarians as far as sovereignty was concerned, that would only serve to stiffen the resolve of the British Government to adhere to that principle. Whilst Britain wanted Spain to join NATO as a means of strengthening the Alliance's southern flank, it was determined that that would have no effect on its attitude towards Gibraltarian sovereignty.

The Gibraltarians were no doubt glad of that, but they must have wondered what kind of message the British Government was really trying to send to Spain, when on 23 November it announced its intention to close the Royal Navy dockyard at Gibraltar in 1983, with the predicted direct loss of 950 jobs, a total of two thousand jobs threatened (20% of the labour force) and inevitable damage to the economy. In addition, the RAF airfield would operate for fewer hours. In Spain the dockyard closure was taken as a further sign that Britain was trying to reconcile its interests and the defence of Gibraltar with the arguments about Gibraltar put by Spain.

With the parliamentary hurdle concerning NATO out of the way,

Spanish entry into the Atlantic Alliance could now go ahead during 1982. Thus, around the turn of the year, the Gibraltar issue ceased to be linked with NATO, but reverted back to the bilateral talks and the implementation of the Lisbon Agreement. Since the autumn of 1981, work had proceeded between the two Foreign Offices to pave the way for a visit by the Spanish Prime Minister and Foreign Minister to Downing Street on 8 January 1982. The visit was not exclusively concerned with Gibraltar, but it was high on the agenda.

It was expected prior to the meeting that the start of negotiations would be announced, and these expectations were not disappointed, despite an inauspicious snow-storm which coincided with the Spaniards' arrival in London. A joint communiqué was issued to the effect that the date of 20 April 1982 had been set for the start of negotiations on the basis of the 1980 Lisbon Agreement, with the simultaneous opening of the border between Gibraltar and Spain. Although it was not stated in the communiqué, an official at the press conference added that formal written assurances had been given to Sr Calvo Sotelo by means of an exchange of notes that Spanish workers would be able to stay overnight in Gibraltar and would also be given equality of labour rights. The Spanish side had clearly been satisfied that the simultaneity of opening the border and reciprocity of rights would now occur, and it was this which had shifted the logjam. However, Gibraltarians insisted that there had been no discrimination against Spaniards for some time, and also pointed out that in the unlikely event of more jobs in Gibraltar becoming available, workers from other EC-member countries would still have preference over Spaniards.

Reaction in Spain to the announcement was generally favourable. The leading article in *El País* on 9 January welcomed the outcome of the talks and took the opportunity to condemn the policy of Franco and his Foreign Minister Castiella. Amongst the political parties, the only cynical view came from Simón Sánchez Montero of the PCE, who saw the agreed date as part of the Government's attempt to persuade Spaniards that the Gibraltar issue was tied in with Spain's entry into NATO. In Andalusia the head of the Autonomous Government, Rafael Escuredo, looked forward to the time when Gibraltar itself became autonomous and was incorporated into the Autonomous Community of Andalusia. He pointed out that the Autonomy Statute for Andalusia had been drafted to allow for such a step. Other leaders in the region welcomed the announcement, although they were concerned about the impression which the state of the infrastructure in the Campo de Gibraltar would give to people coming from the Rock. Juan Carmona, mayor of La Línea, feared that Gibraltarians would scarcely want to become Spanish when they saw what La Línea was like.

The British press generally welcomed the agreement. *The Times* leader-writer on 9 January argued that it would remove the 'irritant' of the blockade from Anglo-Spanish relations. The paper insisted that 'the interests of the Gibraltarians must be safeguarded', but also warned that as far as the economy is concerned 'the Gibraltarians cannot expect to remain indefinitely in a British cocoon', and that 'it is not excluded for all time that Gibraltar might become part of Spain'.

Such views will not have been well received in Gibraltar itself. Sir Joshua Hassan gave an interview to Spanish National Radio, in which he said that the trouble with the Lisbon Agreement was that it tried to reconcile the irreconcilable, because as far as 'this generation' was concerned no more than half a dozen Gibraltarians were willing to accept Spanish sovereignty. Nevertheless, there were fears amongst the Gibraltarians that the opening of the border and the start of negotiations, together with the announcement about the shipyards, marked the start of a shift in the economy of the Rock and an eventual sell-out by the British Government. By an unfortunate coincidence the first reductions in the shipyard workforce were due to occur on 20 April, the day that the negotiations were set to begin.

On the positive side, Gibraltarians welcomed the fact that land communications would shortly be restored, leading to an increase in tourism and related trade, and that there was the possibility of a marina development. However, an influx of tourists' cars would put pressure on Gibraltar's roads and in anticipation of the opening of the border, over one thousand old cars had been pushed over the cliff into the sea at Europa Point during 1981. There were also fears about the possible entry of troublemakers and an increase in crime.[6]

Whether such fears had any foundation would have to wait until after the opening of the border. The last official contact before the planned opening occurred on 23 March, when the British Foreign Minister Lord Carrington briefly met his Spanish counterpart Sr

Pérez-Llorca in Brussels to discuss 'questions of procedure'. What neither of them could know was that 10 days later, thousands of miles from Gibraltar, General Galtieri of Argentina would set back progress on the Gibraltar issue for many a long month.

Notes

1 Spain had already started negotiations with the USA on renewal of the treaty concerning US bases, which was due to expire in October 1981. In view of its NATO application, these were suspended and the existing treaty extended.

2 House of Commons, Seventh Report from the Foreign Affairs Committee (Session 1980–81), *Gibraltar: The Situation of Gibraltar and United Kingdom Relations with Spain* (HMSO, 1981).

3 Such was the strength of feeling in the debate in the House of Commons on 2 June 1981 that the British Government accepted the amendment later that month (see below, p. 33).

4 There was also concern expressed in the Foreign Affairs Committee debate as to whether there should be some reference in the protocol about Ceuta and Melilla, since the North Atlantic Treaty excludes territory in Africa. It was argued that specific mention of the enclaves could upset Morocco. It was decided in the end not to mention them by name.

5 See *El País*, 30 October 1981, p. 13.

6 One further interested party in what was happening between London and Madrid over Gibraltar was the government in Morocco. In the days following the Calvo Sotelo-Thatcher meeting in London, several statements were issued in Morocco calling for Madrid to adopt the same attitude towards Ceuta and Melilla as they wished London to adopt towards Gibraltar.

FIVE

'DIFFERENT AND DISTANT'? THE FALKLANDS/MALVINAS DISPUTE
April–June 1982

'On 2 April 1982 in an act of unprovoked aggression against British sovereign territory and British people Argentine forces invaded the Falkland Islands.'[1]

The Spanish press showed an immediate fascination for and obsession with the Falklands/Malvinas crisis, reporting it in such detail that an observer from another planet might have been forgiven for thinking that the islands were a Spanish colony rather than a British one. In *El País*, the news was on the front page for several days, it was the main international news story (on page 2 and following) every day for two months from 4 April to 5 June (when Israel invaded Lebanon), and it reappeared on the front page from 14 to 17 June at the time of the Argentine surrender and its aftermath.

However, what was to distinguish Spanish coverage of the South Atlantic crisis from the way in which it was reported in the British press was the fact that in Spain, throughout the months of April and May 1982, the connection was repeatedly made between Argentina's dispute with Britain over the Falklands/Malvinas and Spain's dispute with Britain over Gibraltar. In Britain, for the most part, Gibraltar could not have been further from the minds either of politicians or newspaper editors.

The references in Spain sometimes involved the drawing of

parallels or distinctions between the two issues; at others the question was raised of the effect that the Falklands/Malvinas crisis would have on the progress of negotiations on the Gibraltar question. But whatever the context might be, these references served to reinforce the identification by Spain with the Argentine cause on an emotional level, even though (apart from the extreme right wing) it rejected the manner in which Argentina had attempted to restore its territorial integrity. If the Foreign Office ever had time during the crisis to turn their attention from across the Atlantic to study reaction to it in Spain, they would not have been very pleased at this constant linkage of the two issues, except to note that even the right-wing press such as *El Alcázar* was not advocating a Galtieri-style invasion of the Rock.

On 4 April, the day following the extraordinary Saturday debate in the House of Commons, *El País* linked the two issues on two occasions. The first was in an editorial, entitled 'Las Malvinas, entre la razón y la fuerza' ('The Falklands, between reason and force'), which seized the opportunity to draw distinctions and parallels between the two British colonies. Both the British Government and the Gibraltarians would have been relieved to read that 'the use of force is to be deplored wherever there are diplomatic means to resolve conflicts', although perhaps not so happy with the conclud-ing remark that 'what has happened [in the Falklands/Malvinas] may help the British . . . to appreciate that with colonial questions patience is not infinite'.[2]

Elsewhere in the same edition there was a substantial report on the Commons debate, and alongside it a report of an impromptu press conference given by the Spanish Prime Minister, Leopoldo Calvo Sotelo, who on the Saturday happened fortuitously to be campaigning for the Andalusian elections in Algeciras across the bay from Gibraltar, and was therefore able to have himself photo-graphed giving the press conference with the Rock in the back-ground.

He, like the editorial, made the point that the two problems of the Malvinas and Gibraltar were 'distintos y distantes' ('different and distant'). But what they had in common, of course, was a centuries-old dispute over sovereignty. It is not surprising to find, therefore, that the headline of the article on the Commons debate ('Thatcher reaffirms British sovereignty over the Islands') is echoed by Sr Calvo

Sotelo, who is reported as having said that the opening of the gates between La Línea and the Rock, scheduled for 20 April, would start Spain upon the path towards the rapid recovery of the sovereignty of Gibraltar. Throughout the next two months, the connection between the two issues was never going to be far from the minds of Spanish newspaper editors, and probably not entirely absent from those of Spanish politicians.

Concern about the effect of the Falklands/Malvinas crisis upon the Gibraltar issue quickly centred upon whether it would interfere with the timetable for the opening of the frontier gates and the initiation of negotiations in the Portuguese town of Sintra over the future of the Rock. With the proposed date only two weeks away, a leading article in *El País* on 6 April wondered whether it would be wise for them to take place as planned, given that the Foreign Office team in Britain had just resigned over the Falklands/Malvinas invasion and was now headed, not by Lord Carrington (whose skills in the decolonisation of Zimbabwe and Belize were recalled in an article elsewhere in the same edition), but by Francis Pym, whom they viewed as a hard-liner.[3] Moreover, the article questioned whether it would be advisable at this juncture to attempt to discuss the question of the sovereignty of one of Britain's colonies when it had just sent a task force to 'liberate' another.[4] The judgement was that they ought at least to wait and see what the British navy would do once it reached its destination, and that under present circumstances the negotiations would probably lead to a failure which would benefit neither side.

There were several other reasons why negotiations would be difficult at this time. First, the Portuguese Foreign Affairs Minister had indicated that Portugal would respond favourably to a request from Britain to use the Azores as a supply base for the British fleet. Clearly, Spain would find it diplomatically uncomfortable to be negotiating on Portuguese soil under those circumstances. Second, Spain had abstained in the UN Security Council vote on Resolution 502 condemning the act of Argentine agression,[5] a position which would almost certainly cloud Anglo-Spanish negotiations. Third, Spain found itself between the devil and the deep blue sea on the question of the Falklands/Malvinas issue; as it explained to the Council of Europe on 7 April, while it opposed the use of force as a means of resolving international disputes, it supported the

UN principle of decolonisation and yet it found itself in conflict with the UK, a member of NATO (which it was about to join) and of the European Community (membership of which it was in the process of pursuing).[6] Finally, the British Navy would be using as a supply base for its Falklands/Malvinas venture the very territory in dispute between Spain and Britain.

Speculation regarding a possible postponement did not have to go on for very long. Indeed it was only delayed at all by the British insistence upon agreeing a definite new date and place for the talks. On 8 April, a joint communiqué was issued simultaneously in Madrid and London to the effect that the talks and the opening of the frontier would be postponed until 25 June.[7] No reason was given, but clearly none was necessary.

Not only was the climate not right, but (as an editorial in *El País* put it on 9 April) Francis Pym's mind would inevitably be on other things. The two Governments were anxious for it to be known that they had both agreed to the postponement,[8] that it was being accepted in a spirit of understanding, and that they were both standing by their commitment in the Lisbon Agreement to 'solve all their differences over Gibraltar.'

There was disappointment on both sides of the border at the postponement, and not a little embarrassment in La Línea where the Council would have to change their plans to call the road running to Gibraltar 'Avenida del 20 de Abril'. The mayor of La Línea, Juan Carmona, accepted the logic of the decision but lamented the fact that many businesses in the town, which had suffered at the time Franco closed the border and had received little government assistance by way of compensation, had been borrowing money in anticipation of improved trade when the border reopened and were now going to be financially overstretched. The Chairman of the local branch of the Association for Small and Medium Businesses, Jaime Martínez, estimated that the figure was between 1,000 million and 1,500 million pesetas (£5 million to £7.5 million). By contrast, the Gibraltarians had not made significant investments in advance of the opening of the border, since they had learned their lesson in 1980 when there had been similar expectations which had come to nothing.

Members of divided families, who had to travel via Tangiers to see each other, had also been looking forward to 20 April. More generally, the inhabitants of the Campo de Gibraltar would have to wait two more months before they could enjoy the benefits agreed by Sr Calvo Sotelo and Mrs Thatcher in London in January, namely the right to stay on the Rock overnight, and the same labour, union and welfare rights as Gibraltarians themselves.

Gibraltar's Chief Minister, Sir Joshua Hassan, was piqued, perhaps as much by the fact that he was not consulted about the postponement as about the postponement itself. He did not feel that a delay of two months was justified. But the general consensus amongst Spanish politicians was that a combination of the occupation of the Falklands/Malvinas, the resignation of Lord Carrington and the sensitivity of British public opinion regarding colonial issues meant that it was wise to delay the talks. The postponement also served to remind the foreign affairs spokesman of the right-wing Alianza Popular Party that the two problems of the Falklands/Malvinas and Gibraltar were not as 'different or distant' as the Spanish Prime Minister had tried to suggest. 'Both', he said, 'are problems of decolonisation'.[9]

The House of Commons held a second debate on the Falklands/Malvinas crisis on 7 April and an emergency debate (for which members had to be recalled during the Easter recess) on 14 April. It was during the latter that reference was made on several occasions to the Gibraltar issue, notably by John Stokes, who reminded the House that their response to Argentina would be noted in Gibraltar, and by Alexander Lyon who, while recognising that his was a minority view, suggested that the inhabitants of Britain's remaining colonies could not assume that they could remain British indefinitely just because they said they wanted to.[10] *El País* picked up the point on 15 April made by Judith Hart that, by postponing the opening of the frontier, the British Government had accepted for the first time that communications with the Rock had been cut off. The paper's reporter pinpointed the British Government's position in relation to both colonies: a change of sovereignty cannot occur without the consent of the inhabitants.

The status of the inhabitants of the two colonies was explored by the London correspondent of *El País*, Andrés Ortega, in a collection of articles about colonialism published in the 18 April edition. Britain had recently passed the new Nationality Act, due to come into force the following year. Under the Act, British passport holders in Gibraltar were made exceptions to the patriality rule (whereby one of the grandparents had to be of British origin in order that the colonial citizen might be eligible for the right of abode in Britain). Even the Falkland Islanders, at that time, did not enjoy the same privilege (although the events of 1982 caused the Act later to be amended).

The Washington correspondent, in another of the 18 April articles about the UN and decolonisation, cites Gibraltar as 'another clear case of the ineffectiveness of UN Assembly decisions and their recommendations in favour of decolonisation'. The articles were prompted by the situation in the South Atlantic, but the significance of the problem was undoubtedly seen to be much closer to home.

It was not just *El País'* foreign correspondents who saw the connection between the two colonial problems. In the Letters to the Editor column the same day, one self-confessed member of the right-wing Falange Española Independiente reminded readers that Latin American countries had always supported Spain in its claims to Gibraltar and called upon Spain to support Argentina, 'who is giving us a lesson in dignity'. Indeed, the right-wing parties took to the streets in Madrid on 19 April to demonstrate in favour of Argentina's action in the Falklands/Malvinas, to call for the return of Gibraltar to Spain and (for good measure) to denounce Spanish democracy and the monarchy. Some 5,000 demonstrators (or 15,000 according to the organisers) shouted slogans such as 'Por un Borbón perdimos el Peñón' ('Thanks to a Bourbon we lost the Rock'),[11] 'Gobierno gallina, aprende de Argentina' ('The Government is chicken, they should learn from Argentina'), 'Tejero aguanta, España se levanta' ('With people like Tejero, Spain stands tall') and 'Tejero sal y toma Gibraltar' ('Tejero, come and take Gibraltar').[12] A Spanish flag, signed by 'Soldiers' Wives', was used as a banner and inscribed with slogans saying 'Long live the Argentine Army', 'The Malvinas belong to Argentina' and 'Gibraltar belongs to Spain'. Former Prime Minister Adolfo Suárez came under verbal fire, as the demonstration congregated outside his office to sing the Falange hymn 'Face to the Sun'. While the Spanish flag and those of Fuerza Nueva and the Falange were fluttering in the breeze, two Union Jacks were ceremoniously set alight.

By contrast to all this bellicosity from the Right, a psychiatrist, Carlos Castilla del Pino, wrote an article for *El País* on 18 April in which he observed that it was just as ridiculous for Galtieri to expect Britain to hand over the Falklands/Malvinas as it was for Spain under Franco to expect Britain to hand over Gibraltar—although, he added, it was now quite reasonable for Spain to expect Britain to settle the Gibraltar question once and for all.

Similarly, in an article in the same paper on 22 April, the Socialist Senator for the Canary Islands in the Spanish Parliament and member of the Foreign Affairs Committee, Alberto de Armas, recalled that Franco had tried to distract the population of Spain from domestic difficulties by raising the Gibraltar question, in exactly the same way as Galtieri was currently doing in Argentina. However, he was critical of the Spanish Government for abstaining in the UN Security Council vote because, he argued, democratic Spain ought to be seen to be condemning armed aggression as a way of conducting international relations.

The Canaries Senator brought in the further dimension that, although Spain's claim to Gibraltar is sound and will be relentlessly pursued, both it and Argentina ought to avoid using the argument that geographical proximity gives justice to their claims, since the Canaries are far closer to Africa than they are to Spain (or than the Falklands/Malvinas are to Argentina), and Spain would do well to be seen to be supporting peaceful claims to territorial disputes in case the Canaries ever become of interest to other nations, whether for possible oil deposits or for strategic reasons in the context of East-West confrontation.

Spain was not the only nation with a conflict of interests, of course. The United States had from the outset tried to adopt an even-handed approach to the South Atlantic conflict, since it involved a fellow-member of NATO on the one hand and a fellow-member of the Organisation of American States on the other. When Secretary of State Haig's attempts at shuttle diplomacy finally failed, the USA had to decide which side of the wall to come down on. America's decision to offer logistical support to Britain and to declare general sanctions against Argentina not unnaturally led Spain to consider once more its own conflict of interests.

On 1 May *El País* reported that at the meeting of the Council of Europe, the Spanish representative, Gabriel Mañueco (deputising for the Foreign Minister Pérez-Llorca so that the latter would not have to have any awkward contact with British representatives), had been the only one to abstain on the Council's resolution supporting Britain's position.

The editorial in the same issue explained, in remarkably aggressive terms, why it was that Spain found itself between the devil and the deep blue sea. On the one hand, Britain's position in the South Atlantic was 'a blatant abuse of imperialism . . . without the slightest justification in international law'; on the other hand, the Argentine regime can be challenged not only because of its recourse to force in this dispute but also because of the way in which the military oligarchy treats its own citizens in order to remain in power. 'If democrats anywhere in the world cannot accept a strengthening of the Junta's position, they must also condemn the naked and blatant imperialism of the United Kingdom [. . .] As the war approaches—unless someone's last-minute good sense prevails—it is almost impossible to distinguish between the Goodies and the Baddies.'

Clearly—if this view was representative of public and Government opinion—Spaniards virtually equated (in terms of evil) an act of international aggression by a ruthless military regime with anachronistic colonialism. Their thinking on such matters could only have been coloured in this way because of the issue of Gibraltar.

As for Spain's own position regarding the South Atlantic conflict, the editorial writer took issue with the Spanish Prime Minister's clever word-play of the Falklands/Malvinas and Gibraltar being 'distinto y distante'. They are not so 'different', because they are both British colonial issues which need to be resolved. And they are not 'distant' considering the dilemma which faces Spain regarding how it should respond. On the one hand, Spain is a European country with its own colonial tradition, a country about to enter NATO, hoping to join the EC and 'almost blindly allied to the US'. On the other hand, Argentina is a sister nation with whom Spain has strong historical links. Although democratic Spain despises the Argentine regime, nevertheless socialist regimes including the Soviet Union and Cuba have been lining up with both Latin American democracies and Latin American ultra-right dictatorships in support of Argentina.

Whereas Spain could have offered to mediate, according to the writer it appears instead to have done nothing. As far as Argentina is concerned, this is tantamount to playing Britain's colonial game and is an attitude which is not appropriate for Spain given that it has a foreign colony (Gibraltar) on its territory.

However, the writer concludes that although Spain's attitude has not so far been particularly brilliant, it has at least been intelligent. After all, if a quick diplomatic solution was feasible, why rush to take sides? But now that the dispute has been internationalised, Spain's neutral position cannot continue. And that means answering some difficult questions. Given that a large part of the British fleet set sail from Gibraltar, could Spain declare an air and naval blockade around the Rock in the event of fighting breaking out so that it could not be used further to support Britain's war effort? Is Spain prepared to support the European trade boycott against Argentina, or will it lend its material and moral support? Will Spain continue to abstain in the UN Security Council, as though all this had nothing to do with it? If Spain continues to show ambiguity, Argentina will interpret that as alignment with its enemy's interests; but if Spain shows sympathy for Buenos Aires, that will undermine its relations with Washington. The Spanish Prime Minister's task (the writer concludes) is to act in accordance with the hearts and minds of the Spanish people.

Such ambivalence can scarcely have impressed the British Government. Historical ties and colonial parallels are all very well, but (they would have argued) unprovoked aggression by a ruthless military dictatorship should be condemned outright and any other sentiments should be put to one side. Even if the Falklands/Malvinas dispute was settled quickly—whether through diplomacy or by armed conflict—Spain's attitude could not have enhanced its negotiating position when talks on Gibraltar resumed.

The Spanish press was clearly interested in the reaction in Britain to Spain's position. The London correspondent of *El País* reported on 4 May that Spain's attitude of opposition to the use of force but support for Argentina on the 'colonial question' had provoked little debate, although unofficially there had been regret at Spain's abstention both at European and at UN forums. *The Times* was quoted as having referred to 'the diplomatic isolation of Madrid within Western Europe', and as having suggested that this will make future negotiations over Gibraltar more difficult, although Sr Ortega hastened to point out that this was just the view of a journalist and no official comment about Spain's abstentions had been made.

Meanwhile, there were signs that Spain was after all going to try to use its good offices to mediate in the dispute. It was reported on 4 May that the Spanish Foreign Minister, José Pedro Pérez-Llorca, had gone to New York one day earlier than had been expected in order to express to the UN Secretary General, Javier Pérez de Cuellar, Spain's concern at the escalation of the conflict and possibly to offer Spain's services. However, the reporter, Carlos Mendo, doubted whether London would consider Spain to be an appropriate mediator, especially as the Spanish Government had on 1 May offically expressed 'grave concern' at the bombing of Port Stanley by Britain and had warned Britain of the 'serious historical error' that it might be committing—comments which had been well received in Buenos Aires.

In the same issue, *El País* linked Spain's position with regard to the Falklands/Malvinas crisis and its relations with the EC and NATO. The paper's correspondent in Brussels (where the presidency of the European Community resided at that time) reported that the Belgian Foreign Minister, Leo Tindemans, had stated that as Spain was not yet a member of either the EC or NATO, its support for Buenos Aires had not caused any difficulty for those two organisations (although one conservative Belgian newspaper suggested that Spain had alienated British support for its application to the EC, and that Spain's Latin American interests were incompatible with its European vocation). Spain was, however, clearly concerned to make sure that its prospective colleagues would understand its position, as it had been keeping the EC, NATO and Britain directly informed.

There was a further delicate problem in relation to Spain and NATO, namely the question of the nationality of the commander of the NATO base in Gibraltar. Fortunately, it seemed unlikely that the subject would come up for discussion within NATO for several months, time enough for London to have 'forgotten' about Spain's position during the Falklands/Malvinas crisis. However, if the issue of the Falklands/Malvinas had not been fully settled by the time that the subject was raised, it was suggested that Britain would be unlikely to accept a Spanish commander in Gibraltar, since Gibraltar was clearly needed for British naval protection of the South Atlantic.

The connection between Spain's membership of NATO and negotiations over Gibraltar was made once more by one of Spain's smaller parties, Acción Democrática, who proposed to the Spanish Parliament on 4 May that Spain's entry into NATO should not proceed until negotiations with Britain over the future of Gibraltar had been restarted. The party's leader, Francisco Fernández Ordóñez (later to become Foreign Minister when the PSOE came to power), criticised the Government both for not offering to mediate sooner and for their timid support for Latin America. The double criticism was a reflection of Spain's dilemma: an offer to mediate implied a neutrality which would not go down well in Buenos Aires, whereas strong support for Argentina would offend Britain and rule Spain out as a mediator. Hence the Government's delay in doing either. Acción Democrática also considered that Britain's use of Gibraltar in its South Atlantic campaign was an affront to Spain's dignity, and called on the Spanish Government to protest.

Spain's offer to mediate in the Falklands/Malvinas dispute was taken a stage further on 5 May when King Juan Carlos proposed his good offices. Whereas the Spanish Government's offer was fraught with difficulties, the King's personal intervention could be seen as far less contentious. Not only was the King recognised as being the key figure in Spain's transition to democracy, but he also had the advantage of family ties with the British royal family and a constitutional role which enabled him to rise above political issues. However, on 7 May *El País* reported that little attention had been paid to the King's offer.

By this time, Galtieri's forces had been occupying the Falklands/Malvinas for over a month. The longer Argentinian troops remained, the more the Spanish right was encouraged to think that Spain could attempt a similar show of force and occupy Gibraltar. In an article in *El País* on 7 May entitled '¿Cómo se dice Malvinas en marroquí?' ('How do you say Malvinas in Moroccan?'), a socialist member of the Spanish Parliament, Luis Solana, reminded those who were advocating such a move that aside from the fact that Britain would respond, the use of force by Spain could well prompt Morocco to attempt an invasion of Ceuta and Melilla. He pointed out that since thousands of Spanish troops were stationed in these North African enclaves, such an invasion would undoubtedly be bloody. Since Spain's North African possessions are often linked with Gibraltar, it is surprising that it took so long after the invasion of the Falklands/Malvinas for the link to be made in the Spanish press.

Criticism of the Government by Spanish opposition parties for the opportunities it had missed and the foreign policy it was pursuing began to grow. On 8 May, the leader of the PSOE, Felipe González, wondered why Pérez-Llorca had gone to the United States, arguing that Spain should have made use of its dual position as a Western European country and also one with links with Latin America, whilst making it clear that it adhered to the international principle of a rejection of the use of force.

Fernando Morán (at the time a Socialist Senator and, like Fernández Ordóñez, later to become Foreign Minister) saw that the Falklands/Malvinas crisis impinged upon four aspects of Spanish foreign policy: Gibraltar, NATO, the EC and the harmonisation of its relationship with Europe and with Latin America. On the Gibraltar issue, Morán claimed that the use of the Rock as a supply base for a military operation 'underscored the unacceptability of a part of our territory remaining in foreign hands'. But his criticism was that in its haste to make Spain acceptable to Europe and to its NATO allies the Spanish Government 'had been shedding its clothes like an impatient bride on the staircase' and so shaping the country's foreign policy exclusively in accordance with these present and future alliances.[13]

For the Communists, Enrique Curiel was similarly critical of the foreign policy of Calvo Sotelo's Government: having chosen 'the Atlantic option', Spain could either forget about Gibraltar or else risk alienating its Alliance partners by adopting an anti-colonial position. For the PCE, which wanted Spain to be independent, non-aligned and actively neutral, the Government's posture was an unhappy one. Since Curiel doubted whether Calvo Sotelo knew what to do next, he was not surprised that the Spanish Prime Minister refused to allow the Spanish Parliament to debate the matter.

Guillermo Kirkpatrick, the Assistant General Secretary of the right-wing Alianza Popular, was also critical of the ambiguity and incomprehensibility of the Government's position. His sympathy for the Argentinian position was clear: the conflict could only be solved through the recovery by 'our great brother nation' of its territorial integrity, although this should be achieved through negotiation. 'The age of colonialism is over', he said, recalling that the UN had often said this in connection with Gibraltar.

It was not just the views of Spanish opposition parties that were sought, however, but opportunities to establish the views of leading British politicians (especially regarding British reaction to Spain's position) were eagerly seized upon. When Shirley Williams, President of the one-year-old SDP, visited Madrid on 9 May for a meeting of the International Press Institute, she was asked not only whether she thought that Spain's alignment with Argentina would affect its entry into the EC (to which Mrs Williams replied that she did not think it would), but also whether the Falklands/Malvinas question was different from that of Gibraltar. She replied that it was, because the two sides had agreed to negotiate over Gibraltar, but added that the way in which the problem of the Falklands/Malvinas' sovereignty is solved would help to solve the problem of Gibraltar. Perhaps fortunately for her, the questioner did not then ask her what way she thought this might be, for it is doubtful whether she had an answer. Certainly at this stage no-one else seemed to have one.

The Spanish Government's view was put by Javier Rupérez, at that time a UCD spokesman for foreign relations. He argued that 'democratic Spain had clearly given a priority to Europe and to the West' in its approach to foreign affairs, but that 'this does not exclude—on the contrary—an imaginative and pragmatic relationship with Latin America'. Spain was now a participant in the system which defended Western values, he said, and it is through that system that Gibraltar will finally be recovered.[14]

A connection between the conflict over the Falklands/Malvinas and Spain's own conflict over Gibraltar was clearly unavoidable when Spain's reaction to the situation in the South Atlantic was under discussion by politicians of every persuasion. But it was underlined by the fact that Gibraltar itself was implicated in the Falklands/Malvinas War through the use of the Rock as a base for British supply lines. This became a central issue in the Foreign Affairs Committee debate which took place on 11 and 12 May.

On the first day of the debate, Foreign Minister Pérez-Llorca defended the Government's position on the Falklands/Malvinas as coherent and uncompromising, insisting that the problem was, like Gibraltar, basically a colonial one. For that reason, Spain had been unable to support UN Resolution 502, which simply called for the withdrawal of Argentine troops, or the EC's economic boycott of Argentina, or the Council of Europe's condemnation.

Amongst the opposition speakers, Ramón Tamames (formerly of the PCE and now sitting in the Grupo Mixto) recalled that Calvo Sotelo's distinction between the Falklands/Malvinas and Gibraltar as 'different and distant' was invalid, while Francisco Fernández Ordóñez, leader of Acción Democrática, pointed out that there were connections between the two issues, such as the postponement of negotiations over Gibraltar as a result of the Falklands/Malvinas crisis and the use of Gibraltar as a base. The PNV member Antoni Monforte was the only one to call the Argentines 'aggressors', but got no reply when he asked the Foreign Minister what Spain's attitude would be if a similar aggression were committed against Ceuta and Melilla. The Coalición Democrática representative and former Minister of Culture, Ricardo de la Cierva, asked whether any protest had been lodged against the use of Gibraltar by the United Kingdom. Pérez-Llorca's reply was that there had been some Spanish reaction, which had not yet received an official reply, but that since that reaction British use of Gibraltar had been reduced and was more careful.

When the debate was renewed on the second day, the Communist leader Santiago Carrillo criticised the Government for adopting the 'Atlantic option' because it went against the nation's interests in Latin America and the Third World, and had resulted in the King's offer to mediate failing to gain support. Carrillo was concerned that if Morocco were to attempt to take Ceuta and Melilla by force, NATO would not support Spain, and he therefore supported Fernández Ordóñez's call (as did Manuel Marín for the PSOE) for the suspension of the NATO negotiations until Spain received guarantees concerning Gibraltar and the North African enclaves.

In his response Pérez-Llorca rejected the criticism, and with regard to Ceuta and Melilla he strongly rejected the comparison between the colonial situation of the Falklands/Malvinas 'and the situation in these Spanish towns'. He added that 'the mention of these towns at the present time is against Spanish interests'.[15]

There is a touch of irony in the fact that the Communist Carrillo is at least being consistent in seeing parallels not only between territories claimed by Spain and Argentina, but also between those territories and others claimed *against* Spain, whereas the UCD Foreign Minister is keen to raise the issue of Gibraltar in the context of the Falklands/Malvinas, but rejects even the mention of territories claimed by Morocco, even though the reference was made in the context of Spain's desire to defend them. Indeed, there was a timely reminder from Joaquín Muñoz Peirats, Head of the Spanish Delegation to the Council of Europe and a UCD representative in Congress, that 'specifically Spanish matters should not be brought into the Falklands/Malvinas conflict. Those politicians who want to take advantage of these circumstances to discuss the conditions of our entry into NATO or who look for parallels with our dispute over Gibraltar do not understand international reality or else have other intentions which I would prefer not to go into here'.[16]

Spain was clearly in a dilemma over its stance on the Falklands/ Malvinas crisis, a dilemma which was explored in an editorial in *El País* on 18 May entitled 'The tribulations of foreign affairs' and inspired by the Spanish Foreign Minister's absence from a meeting in Luxembourg of the North Atlantic Council to which he had been invited as an observer. 'Throughout the crisis', wrote the leader writer, 'our diplomacy has chosen to stay in the shade. For Spaniards, the conflict in the South Atlantic, in addition to its intrinsic complexity, has the added difficulty of our links with Latin America, our claim over Gibraltar and' (*pace* Pérez-Llorca) 'the permanent threat of Moroccan irredentism over Ceuta and Melilla . . . our Atlantic commitment squares uncomfortably with our Latin American vocation, but is made much worse with the Gibraltar situation— which after the Falklands/Malvinas the British will doubtless not let go so easily—and with our doubts about what support we would really get from NATO if Morocco were to do in Ceuta and Melilla what Galtieri's regime decided to do in the Falklands/Malvinas'.[17]

The South Atlantic crisis was reaching its climax. On 22 May, British troops began their assault on the Falkland Islands which was to result in their recapture. That day *El País* wrote a leader entitled 'That war of fools', while paradoxically *The Times* chose to make Gibraltar the subject of a leading article for the first time since January that year.[18] The Spanish daily maintained, as it had throughout the conflict, its condemnation of the use of force to solve international disputes, whilst at the same time justifying Argentina's claim to sovereignty on historical grounds as well as those of international law. Then came the inevitable parallel with Spain's dispute with London, in which the writer recalled that it was during General Franco's time that the phrase was coined 'Gibraltar is not worth the life of a single Spanish soldier'. The article went on to condemn the British Government's response to the invasion; 'they have launched their citizens on a race in which national pride and prestige are at stake. In the process they have not hesitated to apply pressure on the serious Press and the media, nor to challenge European unity, nor to arouse the people with the most ugly kind of propaganda'.

Had *The Times'* writer seen the article in *El País* he might not have been so generous to the Spaniards in his own. *The Times*, under the heading 'Gibraltar should not suffer', expressed understanding for the difficulties experienced by the Spanish Government in maintaining its 'moderate position' of support for Argentina's claim while deploring its use of force. Spain's dismay at Mrs Thatcher's action on the Falklands/Malvinas was seen as salutary 'in so far as it has dissipated any Spanish illusions that Britain may be willing to force the Gibraltarians into joining Spain against their will'. But the article urged Spain not to abandon the path of re-establishing contact and rebuilding confidence with Gibraltar, as this was seen as essential to the whole process of change. Moreover, it was seen to be in Britain's interests for the Gibraltar problem to be solved so that its relationship with a new NATO and European Community member could be regularised, and it was pointed out both that Spain's entry into the Community could not happen without the frontier being open and also that, once Spain was a member, its nationals would have access to Gibraltar in the same way as those from any other member state. Finally, the process of regional devolution in Spain (the Andalusians were to elect their first autonomous parliament the following day) was seen to offer the possibility of Gibraltar one day taking its 'natural' place as a self-governing unit within a decentralised Spain. 'But that can happen only when the Gibraltarians themselves are convinced of it,' the writer said, suggesting that they would be well advised to follow the example of Dr Garrett Fitzgerald (the Fine Gael Prime Minister of Ireland who adopted a more moderate approach to the future of Northern Ireland) rather than that of his Fianna Fail counterpart Charles Haughey.

The Spanish press thereafter continued to report the final stages of the Falklands/Malvinas War, but it is noteworthy that the references to Gibraltar in such reporting virtually disappeared. That is not to say, however, that Gibraltar itself was relegated to a back seat amongst the concerns of the press. On the contrary, it figured just as prominently in the early days of June. The difference was that it now came to be closely linked with Spain's membership of NATO, which was formalised on 30 May, prior to the June NATO summit.

At the same time, as the War drew to a close, the issues of Gibraltar, the Falklands/Malvinas and NATO became closely inter-twined. The connection was, of course, evident during the conflict when Britain used Gibraltar as a supply base for its Falklands/Malvinas campaign. But that connection was to be made explicit in an extraordinary juxtaposition of events over a period of three days in June, which saw Britain accept the surrender of the Falklands/Malvinas by one of Spain's former colonies, whilst welcoming Spain as a military ally, despite the latter's continuing support for its vanquished cultural offspring and despite the unresolved colonial problem of Gibraltar which stood between the two NATO partners.

Notes

1 *The Falklands Campaign: The Lessons*, HMSO, Cmnd 8758, December 1982, p. 5.

2 *El País*, 4 April 1982, p.10. The editorial writer also learned how careful he would have to be when writing about the Falklands/Malvinas issue. In explaining the difference between Gibraltar and the Falklands/Malvinas, he said that 'the Falklands/Malvinas had never belonged to Argentina', and a correction had to be published following the editorial on 6 April (p. 10) to the effect that Argentina had formally held sovereignty between 1820 and 1833.

3 This view of Pym was softened a few days later, when he was described as a man of great experience and flexibility, and even mentioned as a possible Prime Minister in the event of a political crisis. See *El País*, 9 April 1982, p. 9.

4 The Spanish press always put the word 'liberar' in inverted commas, as it did not wish to be seen to be supporting the British view of the issue.

5 It was unofficially recognised, however, that the fact that Spain abstained rather than voting with Argentina, as it would normally have done, was a gesture towards the British Government. However, the Socialist opposition felt that Spain ought to have supported Britain's proposal. In addition, abstention by a potential member of the European Community was not well received in Brussels.

6 Spain was the only country to abstain in a vote by the Council of Europe in support of Britain's position at the meeting held in Strasbourg on 30 April.

7 Either both sides expected that the Falklands/Malvinas conflict would be settled within that time span and that the air would have cleared sufficiently for the talks to get under way successfully, or else Britain felt that a longer delay could

arouse feelings of bad faith on its part, and if necessary a further postponement could be proposed. The second possibility seems the more realistic one.

8 The same editorial suggested that the original intention on the British side had been to keep to the original schedule. But when London indicated uncertainty as to who would head the British delegation, the Spaniards made it clear that they would insist upon foreign affairs ministers or nothing, and so London responded accordingly.

9 *El País*, 9 April 1982, p. 10.

10 *The Falklands Campaign: A Digest of Debates in the House of Commons 2 April to 15 June 1982*, HMSO, 1982, pp. 90–91.

11 A reference to Louis XIV's grandson, Phillipe d'Anjou, who as Felipe V and one of King Juan Carlos' ancestors became the first of the Bourbon kings of Spain in 1700 and signed the Treaty of Utrecht which handed Gibraltar to Britain.

12 Colonel Francisco Tejero was the leader of the attempted coup on 23 February 1981.

13 *El País*, 9 May 1982, p. 13.

14 Idem, 12 May 1982, p. 4.

15 Idem, 13 May 1982, p. 23.

16 Ibid, p. 4.

17 Idem, 18 May 1982, p. 12. The Ceuta and Melilla question was also raised in the context of Spain's membership of NATO since the Secretary General Joseph Luns had declared that the Spanish enclaves would not come under the umbrella of NATO. In contrast, the article pointed out, Britain's NATO allies had expressed solidarity over the Falklands/Malvinas islands which were close to the Antarctic and therefore well outside the theatre of NATO operations.

18 It was the first article of any kind in *The Times* about Gibraltar since 5 April, apart from a short piece on 18 May quoting an interview with the Spanish Defence Minister published in a Madrid daily, in which he expressed the view that the Falklands/Malvinas conflict would not have any bearing on the Gibraltar problem. The Madrid article may well have prompted *The Times* to produce a leading article on the issue.

SIX

SPAIN JOINS NATO
May–June 1982

As we have observed, Spain's membership of NATO was seen to be closely linked to the resolution of the Gibraltar question. An article in *El País* on 23 May 1982 dealing with the defence changes which would follow Spain's entry referred briefly to Gibraltar as the most important issue (but not the only one) requiring clarification before entry could take place.

Alongside it appeared an article specifically about the relationship between Gibraltar and Spain's membership of the Atlantic Alliance. Three possibilites were considered regarding the military control of the Gibraltar base: first, things would stay as they were, which would be intolerable for Spain as well as illogical from an operational point of view; second, the separate command GIBMED would disappear and become part of the Western Mediterranean subcommand under a Spanish admiral based elsewhere (a possibility opposed by Britain); third, there would be joint British-Spanish command of the Gibraltar base, with the command alternating every couple of years. The article further hypothesised that if the bilateral talks over the future of Gibraltar were to fail, there could be considerable difficulties if a Spaniard were in command, especially if there were to be another episode like the Falklands/Malvinas when the British (or the USA) wanted to use Gibraltar. For this reason, the writer suggested, before Spain becomes part of the military structure of NATO, the position of Gibraltar should be clarified, at least with regard to the role of the Spanish navy on the Rock and responsibility for the costs involved in maintaining or modernising the base.

When Spain became the sixteenth member of NATO on 30 May 1982, it was still unclear exactly how she would fit into the command structure: whether she would form part of SACEUR (with its HQ in Belgium), or whether (as Spain itself preferred) a new Spanish command would be created, covering the whole of the Iberian peninsula (an arrangement which Portugal, currently part of the SACLANT command based in Norfolk, Virginia, would view with mixed feelings) together with the Balearic Islands and the Canaries.

That was one problem. The other was the question of Gibraltar itself. Leaving aside the whole sovereignty issue, the British in particular were concerned about the Spanish government's opposition (in the event that command of the base were shared) to the presence of nuclear-armed warships using Gibraltar's naval docks.

A third problem was that of Ceuta and Melilla. The North Atlantic Treaty, as General Secretary Joseph Luns had made clear on more than one occasion, specifically excluded the African territories, but Spain considered them to be part of its national territory (and not colonies like Gibraltar or the Falklands/Malvinas) and was determined to include them under NATO protection.

Although Spain's membership of NATO marked one further step towards its international rehabilitation after the Franco years, it was not the most auspicious time, either on the national or international scene, for it to take such an important as well as such a controversial decision. The international backdrop was that the event took place while the Falklands/Malvinas conflict remained unresolved, a conflict which saw all of Spain's future NATO partners in support of the British position while Spain supported Argentina. On the national stage, the sentences on those responsible for the attempted military coup of 23 February the previous year were handed down a few days after entry. The fact that both Spain and the other NATO members persevered with the process despite these factors is testimony as much to the powers of persuasion of the Spanish Government and military leaders (including the Commander-in-Chief, King Juan Carlos) as it is to the determination of the other NATO members not to allow Spanish democracy to slip backwards, nor to lose the opportunity to embrace this strategically vital part of Western Europe.

There was another national factor to consider, namely that there was by no means a consensus amongst the Spanish people that membership of NATO was the right step for the country to take. To bring the point home, the PSOE, which had made plain its opposition to that step, had just won a resounding victory in the Andalusian elections. This lent weight to the motion which the PSOE had put before the Spanish Parliament to postpone Spain's entry into the Alliance at least until the negotiations on Gibraltar had been restarted. For the Spanish Government would now have to accept that after the bloody conflict in the South Atlantic over one of its colonies, Britain would not lightly relinquish its hold over another closer to home. Moreover, Spain's position as a member of NATO not only left it little room for manoeuvre as a mediator over the Falklands/Malvinas, but also restricted its negotiating position over Gibraltar. From now on, negotiations would have to take into account Spain's obligations to the North Atlantic Treaty.

The official ceremony to mark Spain's membership was held in Brussels on 5 June. In his speech to the extraordinary session on the North Atlantic Council, Spain's Foreign Minister José Pedro Pérez-Llorca made no specific reference to Gibraltar, although he did explain the historical ties which led his country to adopt a different attitude towards the Falklands/Malvinas conflict from that of other NATO members. In the press conference, however, he recognised that the question of the command of Gibraltar would not be solved in the short term, and that the solution to the sovereignty issue was more important. In the same conference, the Defence Minister Alberto Oliart denied that Spain would consider sharing the command with Britain and argued that the Spanish position was that Gibraltar should be controlled directly from Brussels and have a Spanish commander.

In the final ceremony connected with Spain's entry into NATO—the summit on 10 June in Bonn—Prime Minister Calvo Sotelo did refer to Gibraltar when he called for the Alliance's cooperation in matters such as its incorporation into the EC, the fight against terrorism, and 'a rapid, negotiated settlement to the Gibraltar problem'. As the leading article in *El País* on 11 June pointed out, until that happens Gibraltar remains a British base which is at NATO's disposal and not subject to the Spanish Government's denuclearisation policy.

So Spain and Britain became military allies for the first time since Britain helped to expel Napoleon's troops from Spanish soil 170 years earlier (although relations between Britain and Spain were bad even at that time, in part due to the Gibraltar issue). It was hoped that this new alliance would be a good omen for the talks on Gibraltar which were scheduled to start two weeks later, following the postponement from 20 April.

SEVEN

THE BORDER REMAINS CLOSED
June–October 1982

25 June 1982 had been fixed as the date for the renewal of talks between Britain and Spain and the opening of the border between Spain and Gibraltar.

In anticipation of the talks, Spain realised that the Falklands/Malvinas War had rather changed the atmosphere. In particular, although Britain remained committed to the Lisbon Agreement to resolve all the differences between it and Spain over the Rock, Britain's attitude had changed ever since Spain aligned itself with Panama in the UN Security Council resolution, which called for a cease-fire in the Falklands/Malvinas without it being linked to an Argentine withdrawal. It was also reported in Spain that Britain was concerned about the fact that during the South Atlantic crisis the Spanish media (particularly television) had given greater credence to reports from Buenos Aires than to those emanating from London.

In the climate of euphoria in London following the Falklands/Malvinas victory, it was not surprising, therefore, that there were those in Spain who suspected that the British representatives might go to Sintra 'simply to have their photo taken' and who, in the absence prior to the talks of any firm indication of Britain's stance, preferred the talks to be cancelled.[1] There were others who felt that Britain might be more sympathetic to negotiations over Gibraltar, given the contrast between Madrid's civilised approach and the Argentinians' use of force in the South Atlantic.

Anticipation was greatest in the frontier town of La Línea. It had suffered most when the frontier was closed in 1969, both in trade and in jobs. In 1982, 38% of the active population was unemployed and millions of pesetas' worth of trade, especially in foodstuffs, had been lost. Once the frontier was opened, it was hoped that some 500 jobs would become available in Gibraltar to residents in La Línea, that some Gibraltarians would come and live in the growing town given the housing waiting list of 1,600 in Gibraltar itself, and that the tourist trade would bring new life to bars, restaurants and hotels. But having made investments totalling 3,000 million pesetas (£15 million), including 1,500 million pesetas (£7.5 million) in increased stocks, in anticipation of the opening both now and two months earlier, many businesses were at the limit of their credit. The mayor, Juan Carmona, was all in favour of opening the frontier, and argued that Spain did not need to use its opening as a condition for the start of talks. Gibraltarians, too, wanted the frontier to be opened without further delay.

Foreign Ministers Pym and Pérez-Llorca met in Luxembourg on 21 June as part of the negotiations relating to Spain's membership of the EC. It had become clearer by then that Spain had been pressing London to agree that the communiqué after the Sintra talks should be able to include an indication that the question of sovereignty had been discussed and that a timetable had been set for negotiations. A Spanish note sent to the Foreign Office about the Sintra talks had suggested a new treaty to replace that of Utrecht, which would guarantee and safeguard all the legitimate interests and the well-being of the inhabitants of Gibraltar, but re-establish Spain's territorial integrity. Not surprisingly given the climate of the day, Britain was unwilling to agree to this, and the Spanish Government decided to postpone the talks without setting a new date and to keep the frontier closed.

In their statements in Luxembourg announcing the decision, Francis Pym blamed Spanish domestic politics, while his Spanish counterpart put the postponement down to the emotionally-charged atmosphere in Britain which would prevent the talks getting off to a positive start. Pérez-Llorca may have been persuaded (probably rightly) that since the Falklands/Malvinas War, Britain was quite likely to insist that the views of the Gibraltarians would be paramount, and he hoped that the passage of time might lessen the chances of a statement to this effect being made.

Reaction in La Línea was one of bitter disappointment. Representatives of the town's political, economic and social interests agreed to send a commission to Madrid to ask for the region to be declared a disaster area, and considered other measures such as blocking the road from Algeciras to Cádiz, calling for a massive demonstration, sending thousands of telegrams to the Foreign Affairs Minister or even hunger strikes.

It was in this climate that two days later, on 23 June, *El País* ran a front-page story based upon an interview given by Mrs Thatcher for Danish, Swedish and Norwegian television, in which she stated that Britain was not prepared to talk about the sovereignty of Gibraltar with Spain. She did, however, consider independence for Gibraltar a possibility, despite the stipulations of the Treaty of Utrecht, provided that Spain agreed to it and the Gibraltarians wanted it.[2] The Spanish Foreign Office was furious at these remarks, and the British Ambassador Richard Parsons could hardly have been surprised to find himself summoned to the Palacio de Santa Cruz to try to explain what Mrs Thatcher meant. He reaffirmed Britain's commitment to the Lisbon Agreement and suggested that Mrs Thatcher must have meant by her remarks that Britain could not enter talks with preconditions having been set. A spokesman at the British Embassy in Madrid suggested that the interview was supposed to be about the Falklands/Malvinas, and that Mrs Thatcher was not prepared for a question about Gibraltar. In order that it could hear and see exactly what Mrs Thatcher did say, the Foreign Affairs Ministry in Madrid asked for a video of the broadcast.

In the House of Commons, Francis Pym expressed regret that the opening of the frontier had been postponed, and warned Spain that it could not enter the EC without a change in that situation. But he must have been acutely embarrassed by Mrs Thatcher's remarks (not least because they made it quite clear that he was not in control of British foreign policy) and he had to reassert that Britain would honour the Lisbon accord. In Gibraltar the GSLP, which had always been opposed to the Lisbon Agreement, seized the opportunity to organise a rally to demonstrate that sovereignty was not negotiable. British diplomatic sources were quoted in the Spanish press as having conceded in private that Mrs Thatcher had 'put her foot in it'.

Coming as they did so soon after the Falklands/Malvinas conflict, Mrs Thatcher's remarks were scarcely surprising. But they were nonetheless damaging and seemed to justify Spain's fears that the Falklands/Malvinas War represented a considerable setback to the negotiation process over Gibraltar, not just because the start of talks had been indefinitely postponed, but because the sentiments contained in the Lisbon Agreement were now clearly threatened. It would have to await the Brussels Declaration nearly two years later for those sentiments to be reaffirmed to Spain's satisfaction.

Notes

1 *El País*, 20 June 1982, p. 14.

2 In New York on 23 June she declined to confirm that she had made this statement (see *El País*, 24 June 1982, p. 14)

EIGHT
FELIPE OPENS THE GATES
October–December 1982

Spain's first post-Franco Socialist Government came to power on 28 October 1982 with a comfortable overall majority. The new Prime Minister, Felipe González, addressed the nation on television at 2.35 am from his party's HQ in the Hotel Palace. His message was brief, but such is the prominence given to the Gibraltar issue in Spanish foreign affairs that even on this occasion he made reference to it by saying that 'we also reaffirm our unflagging aspiration to reintegrate Gibraltar into our national sovereignty', words which were highlighted in the reaction the next day by the British press to the PSOE's victory.[1]

On 7 December Felipe González held his first Cabinet meeting and afterwards gave a press conference. The Cabinet agreed that on 15 December the frontier with Gibraltar would be opened to visitors on foot on humanitarian grounds. At the press conference the Prime Minister explained that, although the frontier would be open 24 hours a day, people would only be allowed to make one crossing per day in each direction.

The following day the British Government reacted favourably to the proposal as far as it went, although the Foreign Office took the opportunity to point out that Britain had always kept its side of the border gates open (at least from 6.00 am to 1.00 am the next morning). A British observer was quoted as saying that the Spanish proposal was a master stroke, since by restricting access to pedestrians it would provide economic benefits to the Campo region but not to Gibraltar.

Before the border was actually opened, however, Francis Pym and Fernando Morán agreed during an encounter at a NATO meeting in Brussels on 10 December that negotiations over Gibraltar would be reopened some time during the spring of the following year, and would coincide with the full opening of the border. Sr Morán took the opportunity to reiterate the fact that the Lisbon Agreement referred to discussion by both sides of all points of disagreement and, whilst recognising the need to change the climate amongst the people of Gibraltar, he asserted that Spain's objective continued to be that 'in the near future, Gibraltar once again becomes part of Spanish sovereignty'.[2] This agreement to negotiate under the terms set in Lisbon was the first official indication that the new Spanish Government would pursue the diplomatic procedures established by its predecessor.

The historic day when the border would be officially opened approached. As it did so, a certain amount of diplomatic sparring took place. On the same day as the Foreign Ministers met in Brussels, the Spanish Government decided that only Spanish passport holders and British citizens resident in Gibraltar would be allowed to cross the frontier. Both the British and Gibraltarian authorities declared this to be discriminatory, and in retaliation Gibraltar's Council of Ministers reversed its decision of 9 December and decided in an emergency meeting two days later not to open the border gates for 24 hours a day, but to continue to close them between 1.00 am and 6.00 am, although Spaniards would still be allowed to spend the night on the Rock. The Spaniards in the Campo were annoyed, but put the change of heart about 24-hour opening down to reaction by Gibraltarian businesses against the Spanish decision to restrict passage to pedestrians, thus denying the businessmen any commercial advantages.

However, that decision was once more reversed under pressure from the Foreign Office in London on the night of 14 December, and with just over an hour to go before the opening was due, Sir Joshua Hassan appeared on Gibraltar television to announce that the gates would remain open permanently after all.

When midnight struck, some 500 people were at the border gates to see them opened on the Spanish side for the first time in 13 years. There was some disagreement between the Civil Guard and the National Police as to who should perform the ceremony, and the problem was resolved by the Head of Customs, who did it himself. A 52-year-old man from La Línea but resident in Gibraltar succeeded in becoming the first person to cross (from the

Gibraltar side, because those crossing from the Spanish side had to cover about 100 yards of no-man's-land). The atmosphere was festive, with singing, champagne and emotional reunions. Inevitably there were some disappointments, as the initial arrangements did not allow some 200 Gibraltarians resident in La Línea to cross into Gibraltar (this ban was lifted on 10 January); nor did they allow the non-Spanish or non-Gibraltarian spouses of those entitled to cross to do so. But for most there was a sense of relief and a feeling that at last tangible progress was being made towards the normalisation of communications between Gibraltar and Spain.[3]

Not surprisingly, there was some political fall-out for Gibraltar's Chief Minister at having been overruled by the Foreign Office. Joe Bossano, leader of the GSLP, could not resist the jibe: 'I suspect that this is the first occasion that Hassan has done something off his own bat, and look what happens'. The Chief Minister gave a press conference the day after the opening, and said he had not considered resignation. He said that Francis Pym had given him 'exceptional reasons to make him take the decision to keep the gates open, but now is not the time to go into them'. [4] Clearly, Mr Pym did not want to give Spain the diplomatic initiative by being seen to be more restrictive than the Spaniards, after so many years when the boot was on the other foot.

The first full day with the border gates open saw a constant stream of people crossing, more into Gibraltar than in the opposite direction. Estimates for the first 24 hours put the total number of people going across at between 7,000 and 8,000, with the queue at one time during the late morning taking 45 minutes to get through the gates. One minor problem that the Gibraltarians encountered was that there was no official exchange rate for their currency, so they could not buy pesetas when they got into Spain.

One of the issues which had most concerned Spaniards from the Campo region, and from which they had suffered since the closure of the border, was the loss of employment opportunities in Gibraltar. Many of the unemployed from La Línea seized the first chance they had to find a job and were snapped up on the first day by the numerous employers who were anxious to fill vacancies for skilled workers or to replace absentee Moroccans. One of the attractions of workers from La Línea is that they did not need accommodation, whereas Moroccan workers lived in state hostels without their families, whom they went home to visit at week-ends.

The occasion of the opening of the border gave the Spanish press a fresh opportunity to reiterate Spanish claims and the need to find a permanent solution to the Gibraltar question. 'Spanish demands for the recovery of sovereignty over the Rock are protected by history and by International Law, and the interests and the rights of the inhabitants of Gibraltar can remain protected under a parliamentary monarchy similar to that of Britain and under a constitution which gives protection to autonomous governments', asserted a leading article in *El País* on 16 December. There is no longer any need or justification for Britain to retain the territory; the only real problem to be resolved is the healing of the wounds caused by the 'Castiella Curtain' which resulted in 13 years of isolation between Gibraltarians and neighbouring Spaniards due to a policy which has clearly been counterproductive.[5]

Meanwhile, more mundane problems needed to be solved; the replacement of the pre-democracy shield over the Customs shed with a new up-to-date one, and the removal of the Spanish soldiers' helmets (requested by the civil authorities), because they looked too much like German Second World War helmets. The former proved easier to secure than the latter.

The reopening of the border gates was a major step forward and marked the end of the Franco approach to the Gibraltar issue. Yet the opening of the frontier had only been partial and restrictions had been discriminatory. To the annoyance of Gibraltar businesses, Spaniards were not allowed to buy fresh produce in Gibraltar and take it back to Spain. The development of Gibraltar's tourist industry was hindered by the fact that tourists were not allowed to cross into Spain from Gibraltar. Britain wanted the frontier to be fully opened. Until that happened, further progress on negotiations was bound to be painstakingly slow.

Notes

1 *El País*, 29 October 1982, p. 15; 30 October 1982, p. 22.

2 Idem, 11 December 1982, p. 2.

3 'Normalisation' is perhaps the appropriate word rather than 're-establishment', since despite the closure of the border in 1969, by the time of its reopen-

ing Spain was already the third most important supplier of goods to Gibraltar after Britain and Morocco. See *El País*, 15 December 1982, p. 13.

4 Idem, 16 December 1982, p. 18.

5 Fernando María Castiella was Franco's Foreign Minister.

NINE
TOWARDS THE BRUSSELS DECLARATION
March 1983–November 1984

With the border gates between Spain and Gibraltar now open, the spring of 1983 was to be the time which saw a real start being made on the negotiations heralded by the Lisbon Agreement. The first opportunity for talks presented itself on 16 March, when (on the first visit made by a member of Felipe González's Government to Britain) Foreign Affairs Minister Fernando Morán went to London as part of a series of bilateral visits he was making to European Community countries. Gibraltar was not of course the exclusive—or even the main—item on the agenda, but it was there, and no doubt higher up on Sr Morán's list of topics than on that of Francis Pym or Mrs Thatcher.

The day before the talks, *El País* noted that although Britain had been very supportive since 1975 of Spain's desire to establish closer ties with the rest of Europe as far as defence and trade were concerned, an element of resentment at some of Spain's remarks during the Falklands/Malvinas crisis had appeared in British comments during the past year. This did not offer much encouragement to the Spanish visitors; the best that was hoped for was that working parties might be set up on the most contentious aspects of the Gibraltar question in order to prepare the ground for negotiations.

This was not the only factor which did not augur well for the talks. The correspondent of *El País* noted three reasons why little progress was likely. First, Francis Pym was being subjected to attacks from members of his own party (attacks, it was said, which had the support of the Prime Minister), and he was not therefore in a strong position to negotiate (especially not if such negotiations involved any concessions). Second, it was expected that Mrs Thatcher would call a general election by October at the latest, and little progress was likely in a pre-electoral period. Third, Mrs Thatcher had made clear her doctrine on decolonisation by stating in Parliament with reference to the Falklands/Malvinas that sovereignty would not be discussed as long as the islands' inhabitants did not wish it to be. Although it could be argued that Gibraltar was a different case, it was felt unlikely that on this particular question Britain would agree to talk about sovereignty in relation to one colony whilst refusing to do so in relation to another.[1] Certainly Mrs Thatcher had shown no interest in doing so.

As far as progress on Gibraltar was concerned, Sr Morán left London empty-handed. Britain was insisting that before talks could begin, the frontier between Spain and Gibraltar had to be open without restrictions. Spain at this stage refused to remove the restrictions without some concessions in return regarding the rights of Spaniards in Gibraltar and without some commitment to discuss the sovereignty issue. Consequently, no agreement was reached either on a date or on a framework for negotiations to implement the Lisbon Agreement. A statement issued at the end of the talks simply said that the two Foreign Ministers would maintain contact. As *The Times* put it on 19 March, 'once again, Gibraltar has prevented Anglo-Spanish relations from blossoming into a fully relaxed friendship'.

A few weeks later a storm blew up over a visit to the Rock by the Royal Navy, illustrating the extent of Spanish sensitivity over the issue at this time. The British Ambassador in Madrid, Sir Richard Parsons, informed the Spanish Government as a matter of courtesy that long-standing annual manoeuvres, called Spring Train, were due to take place in April in the North-East Atlantic and that these would involve some ships calling at Gibraltar.[2] To the great surprise of the Foreign Office in London and of the Government in Gibraltar, Sir Richard was summoned to the Spanish Foreign Ministry on 11 April (and again on the following day) to hear a statement of protest (although it was not officially described as such), and the Spanish Ambassador to NATO, Jaime de Ojeda, was instructed to protest in the same vein. Spain considered that the manoeuvres were 'unfriendly' and should have waited until the bilateral talks over Gibraltar had made some progress. In any case, it was felt that the

North-East Atlantic was sufficiently wide an area not to involve ships going anywhere near Gibraltar, and that the choice of waters had been deliberately designed to put psychological pressure on Spain.

The British fleet arrived off Gibraltar in the small hours of 13 April. In addition to three support ships, it consisted of 13 vessels, with the aircraft carrier *Invincible* as flagship, plus two destroyers, eight frigates and two submarines. The Spanish press did not fail to mention that all of the British ships had been used in the South Atlantic venture, and that on board the flagship was the Falklands/ Malvinas War-veteran Prince Andrew. It was also noted that reporters from the popular British press were more interested in finding the actress Koo Stark (who at that time was associated with Prince Andrew and was said to be in Gibraltar) than in the presence of British vessels.

When it learnt of the manoeuvres, the Spanish Foreign Ministry decided that it would send a Spanish naval presence to the Bay of Algeciras just outside the harbour of Gibraltar in order to demonstrate Spanish sovereignty over those waters. Apparently the Commander of the Spanish fleet initially opposed the idea, saying that not enough ships were ready, and that it would be more sensible to avoid any incidents. However, when the British fleet sailed into Gibraltar harbour, it did so under the watchful eye of the Spanish frigate *Cataluña*, the destroyer *Lángara* and the corvette *Infanta Elena*, which had dropped anchor in the bay.

The arrival of British naval vessels in Gibraltar was not an unusual event for the Gibraltarians—even the *Invincible* had called there twice before—and little fuss was made on the Rock. Consequently they were surprised at the attention being paid to the event on mainland Spain, which included a motion passed unanimously by the Spanish Upper House regretting the presence of units of the British fleet in Gibraltar 'which has resulted in a worsening of relations between two democratic states and has made negotiations over Gibraltar much more difficult'. Manuel Fraga, the Leader of the Opposition and former Spanish Ambassador in London, made political capital out of the incident by claiming that if he were Prime Minister he would revoke the Lisbon Agreement and send the Spanish navy to occupy what he claimed were Spanish waters.

Things got worse before they got better. Exercises involving combat planes, helicopters and rescue launches were held on 14 April. The same day, the Spanish Government sent a protest note to the International Civil Aviation Authority in Ottawa, claiming that the British manoeuvres were disrupting civil air traffic, although the real motive behind the protest note was contained in its closing words: 'The attitude of the British authorities shows a lack of sensitivity for Spanish feelings regarding the Gibraltar problem'. However, these Spanish protests assisted the Royal Navy in one sense; it was reported that some of the Gibraltarian dockers, who had organised a protest against the recently announced dock closures by the Ministry of Defence, decided that, as a response to the actions of the Spanish Government, they would call off their refusal to resupply the vessels.[3]

In Britain Spain's reaction, together with the fact that the border had only been partially opened, led to veiled hints that Spain's application to join the EC might be in jeopardy, and these were duly reported in the Spanish press. In a debate on 13 April in the House of Commons, Douglas Hurd, Minister of State at the Foreign Office, said that while the border restrictions remained Spain's entry was 'inconceivable', and from the Conservative backbenches Ivor Stanbrook called upon the British Government to oppose Spain's entry if Madrid was going to continue with its 'petty campaign' over Gibraltar.

At 9.00 am on 18 April, the British naval vessels left Gibraltar, leaving behind 2,000 men to reinforce the British garrison and a number of anti-aircraft Blowpipe missiles, which were among weapons used in the Falklands/Malvinas. The Foreign Office and the Ministry of Defence strongly denied a report in the *Sunday Telegraph* which had suggested that these men and weapons had been sent in case an attack was mounted to seize Gibraltar. Such a suggestion could only have been made in the sensitive atmosphere which was the legacy of the South Atlantic crisis.

The anger of the Spaniards at these naval exercises was generated not so much by the manoeuvres themselves as by a sense of frustration at not being able to move the negotiation process along. The feeling in Spain was that Britain was being obstructive by insisting that all obstacles to negotiations be removed, while at the same time refusing to allow Spaniards the same treatment in Gibraltar as Gibraltarians.[4] Whatever the motives for the protest, the outcome was that the implementation of the Lisbon Agreement suffered a further delay.

Over the ensuing months, no formal sessions were arranged specifically for bilateral discussions on Gibraltar to take place. Instead, the respective Foreign Ministers used meetings at which they were both present to have informal sessions together. Following Mrs Thatcher's second general election victory in June 1983, Sir Geoffrey Howe took over the reins at the Foreign Office. Sir Geoffrey met his Spanish counterpart, Fernando Morán, in Madrid for the first time on 7 September on the occasion of the summit of the Conference on Security and Cooperation in Europe (CSCE). The meeting had limited objectives, namely to improve the climate so that discussions could proceed, but afterwards spokesmen on both sides suggested that some changes to the interpretation of the Lisbon Agreement might be made in order to facilitate negotiations.

Later that month, the Howe-Morán dialogue was resumed at the 38th session of the United Nations in New York, where once again informal discussions took place. At a press conference given by Sr Morán on 30 September, he said that he felt that Britain was now more flexible about Gibraltar. He hoped that they would get over the 'trauma' of the Falklands/Malvinas and that a more balanced interpretation would be taken of the Lisbon Agreement, in which, he argued, the British view had so far prevailed.

Brussels was the scene of the third Howe-Morán encounter, at which the Spanish Foreign Minister addressed his fifteen counterparts on the Atlantic Council on 8 December. Sr Morán referred in his speech to the three issues which were at the top of Spain's foreign affairs priorities: entry into the EC, its relationship with NATO[5] and a solution to the Gibraltar problem. Few details were reported of the bilateral talks which took place between Sr Morán and Sir Geoffrey, but the hope seemed to be that the technical working groups which had been meeting behind the scenes would make sufficient progress to enable formal talks to get under way during 1984.

Before the end of 1983, however, an extraordinary situation of confusion occurred regarding the lifting of restrictions on those entitled to cross the frontier between Spain and Gibraltar. Marking the first anniversary of the reopening of the border, on the night of 13 December the Spanish Ministry of the Interior issued an order to the police at La Línea that for the Christmas period there were to be no restrictions on the nationalities of those entitled to cross the border. Instead of permission being confined to citizens of Gibraltar or British citizens resident in Gibraltar or Spanish citizens, the order allowed citizens of any nationality to cross the border in either direction.

However, on the afternoon of the following day, the Civil Governor of Cádiz, Salvador Domínguez, sent a telex to La Línea's police chief cancelling the original order which had been signed by the Director General of Police, Rafael del Río, and explaining that the only alterations to the current restrictions were that for the period 23 December to 6 January (a) the permitted categories of citizens allowed to cross the frontier could do so without being confined to one crossing per day, and (b) journalists of any nationality would be allowed to cross for professional reasons. Quite how the first telex came to be sent in the first place remains a mystery. Had its order been implemented, it could have broken the logjam on negotiations between Britain and Spain. But the reality was that the main restrictions remained in place for a further 14 months.[6]

Following Mrs Thatcher's visit to Peking in September 1982, early in 1984 Britain began to move towards a settlement with the Republic of China over the future of another British colony, Hong Kong. What aroused particular interest in Spain was the fact that Britain was conceding sovereignty to China over the whole of Hong Kong, including Victoria (also known as Hong Kong) Island and the Kowloon Peninsula (both of which had been ceded to Britain in perpetuity and were not subject to the 99-year lease under the Treaty of Nanking) in addition to the New Territories (which were). In a leading article in *El País* on 25 January, the writer concluded that Britain was for the first time recognising Chinese sovereignty over the whole territory, and that what must have changed Britain's mind was the fact that it recognised that its sovereignty over Victoria and Kowloon was based upon an outmoded colonial system, which now operated only in places like Hong Kong and Gibraltar. Echoing the parallels drawn during the South Atlantic crisis between Gibraltar and the Falklands/Malvinas, the opportunity was seized to draw two similarities between Gibraltar and Hong Kong. First, the British Government had renounced its sovereignty in Hong Kong over territory to which its claim was just as solid in juridical terms as that accorded to it by the Treaty of Utrecht over Gibraltar. Second, Britain had accepted the transfer of sovereignty despite the fact that the inhabitants had shown no indication that this was their preference. These were precisely the two arguments that Britain was using to reject Spanish sovereignty over Gibraltar, 'further proof that the British attitude in the Gibraltar dispute is not only ethically unsustainable but also that it is lacking in the most basic political logic'. The writer concluded that whilst it was important for democratic Spain to move closer to the people of Gibraltar in order to repair the damage done by the policies of the Franco regime, the Spanish Government should use the example of Britain's last colony in Asia to urge Britain to put an end to an unacceptable colonial situation in Europe.[7]

It was scarcely surprising that the Spanish press did not miss this chance to highlight what they saw as inconsistencies in British policy. What Spain chose not to mention here was the fact that Gibraltar had its own democratically-elected Assembly and, through its own constitution, a good deal of autonomy. Moreover, the people had voted in 1967 to express their wishes about their future. Neither of these applied to Hong Kong, even though following the events in Peking in June 1989 Britain came to regret the fact that it had not established democratic procedures in Hong Kong sooner. There was the additional factor that it would not have made sense for Britain to retain the territory in Hong Kong which was not covered by the Treaty of Nanking, because it was not viable on its own. The differences between the two colonies were significant, but that would not prevent Spaniards from drawing parallels again in the future.[8]

The other focus of Spanish attention early in 1984 was the General Election held in Gibraltar on 26 January, for the outcome could well influence the speed with which progress could be made on the Lisbon Agreement. The main issue was the future of the Royal Navy's dry docks, where 800 repair jobs were under threat. The British Government had offered the docks to Appledore International to manage a commercial operation. The Government was offering Appledore £28 million provided that the company obtained an agreement with the shipworkers' union, the TGWU, but Appledore was only offering a commitment to retain about half of the 800 jobs.

There was a three-way choice in the elections. Sir Joshua Hassan's Association for the Advancement of Civil Rights (AACR) recommended that the union reach an agreement with Appledore. The right-wing Democratic Party of British Gibraltar (DPBG) led by Peter Isola was seeking better conditions from Britain for the future viability of the shipyards. The left was represented by the Gibraltar Socialist Labour Party (GSLP), led by Joe Bossano, who had obtained wage-parity for Gibraltarian workers with those of the UK after Franco closed the border and who now rejected the British Government's solution to the shipyard issue as blackmail, because the workers would be forced to accept Appledore's conditions, including the loss of wage-parity. Bossano argued that if Britain wanted to keep Gibraltar as a vital NATO naval base, the British Government had a responsibility to convert the shipyard and to protect the interests of the workers, or alternatively it should give the Gibraltarians the £28 million to spend on the shipyard and on other improvements to the economy. Spain noted that the pro-Spain 'doves', who were routed in the previous elections, were not standing on this occasion, so that no-one in the campaign was arguing for a future closely linked with Spain. By contrast, there were three independent nationalist candidates calling for greater autonomy for Gibraltar.

The only poll taken during the campaign suggested that Bossano's GSLP would increase its seats from one to four or five, and that Sir Joshua Hassan's ruling AACR would win seven or eight out of the total of 15 up for election (a further two seats were appointed by Britain). It was predicted that the remainder would go to the right-wing DPBG. In the event, on a 74.5% turn-out (up from 65% in 1980), Sir Joshua retained his eight seats (the maximum possible under Gibraltar's election rules), with a one-seat majority over the seven gained by Joe Bossano's party and an increased percentage of the poll. The DPBG gained no representation at all.

Clearly, the threat of job losses in the shipyards had accounted for the major swing to the GSLP at the expense of the fanatically pro-British DPBG. The outcome held little by way of encouragement for Spain (Bossano had said that he did not want to be colonised by Spain any more than he did by Britain), although the fact that Hassan (who declared that this was to be his last period of office) was still in power at least meant that Gibraltar's policy in negotiations over the next four years would remain unchanged. Had Bossano's party won, that clearly would not have been the case, and Sir Geoffrey Howe and Sr Morán must have breathed a sigh of relief that Sir Joshua was still in charge. Spain's official response to the election result was that although everything that happens in Gibraltar is of great interest to Spain, negotiations would take place with London.

From April 1984 onwards, work continued behind the scenes as attempts were made to prepare the ground for negotiations on the implementation of the Lisbon Agreement. They began against the background of an interesting debate which took place in the pages of *El País* between a Professor of Logic, a leading politician from the Campo de Gibraltar and a Government foreign policy adviser.

The Professor of Logic, Jesús Mosterín from the University of Barcelona, published an article on 30 March entitled 'The pseudo-problem of Gibraltar'. In many ways his argument could not have been better put by a Gibraltarian, although it was clearly not his intention to argue their case for them, but rather to explore the logic of the arguments used by Spain for the return of sovereignty over the Rock. He suggested that from a variety of different standpoints Gibraltar was not a problem for Spain. It was not an historical problem, because just as Castille took Gibraltar by force in 1462 and held it for 242 years, so the British took it by force in 1704 and have held it legitimately (by virtue of the Treaty of Utrecht) ever since. It is not a geographical problem, because although it is part of the Iberian Peninsula, so too are the non-Spanish territories of Portugal and Andorra (while the Spanish possessions Ceuta, Melilla and the Canaries are not part of the Peninsula). It is not a problem of military strategy: Spain has no intention of trying to close the Strait; if Spain feels vulnerable with Gibraltar as a NATO base, the rest of the country is in NATO anyway, and even if Spain votes to withdraw from NATO, Portugal will still be a member; and in the event of a war the US base at Torrejón is far more dangerous for Spain than Gibraltar. It is not an economic or social problem: Spain would gain nothing from the incorporation of Gibraltar (except unwanted shipyards which require conversion investment). It is not a political problem: the Gibraltarians voted in 1967 to stay British and in the recent elections no-one voted for incorporation into Spain.

Commenting on the fact that Felipe González in his investiture speech could not refrain from mentioning Spain's well-worn claims to Gibraltar, Profesor Mosterín called upon political leaders to break with past rhetoric. 'Gibraltar does not cause us any bother, nor threaten us, nor hinder us, nor cost us a penny', he wrote. Spain should continue to open the border gates bit by bit (they were, he said, as shameful as the Berlin Wall), and enter the European Community, thereby guaranteeing the free movement of people and goods between the Rock and the rest of the Peninsula. 'As soon as we Spaniards stop threatening to annex the Gibraltarians, they will lose interest in continuing to be British and will simply be Gibraltarians, [in] a tiny autonomous town (like Andorra and San Marino) in a Europe without borders.'

Such an argument would no doubt have been echoed by most Gibraltarians, even though they would have had to admit that logic has had little to do with the resolution of most other disputes over sovereignty. One Spaniard who was clearly not impressed was Eduardo López Gil, mayor of San Roque in Cádiz, whose rejoinder to Professor Mosterín was published on 10 April under the title 'The problem of Gibraltar'.

Sr López Gil took each of the Professor's arguments in turn. He corrected him on his history and, reminding him that the mercenaries who took Gibraltar had also tried to take Barcelona, asked him how he would feel if Barcelona were now British. A glance at any map will answer the geographical issue. The strategic importance of Gibraltar is so great that it justifies Spain wanting to control it because 'it would give Spain world status'. Those who live near Gibraltar know that it is a social and economic problem because Gibraltar has turned the Campo into a second-class colony. It is also a political problem, because the UN discounted the 1967 referendum and does not recognise Gibraltar's right to self-determination. 'Spain does not want to turn Gibraltarians into Spaniards but to regain sovereignty over the territory', he concluded, before finally taking Professor Mosterín to task for damaging Spanish foreign policy by writing such an article.

What the Mayor of San Roque clearly demonstrated is that emotion is no answer to logic, but what both articles taken together demonstrate is that neither logic nor emotion is much use when it comes to persuading people to change their position.

Mariano Berdejo, Director General of European Policy at the

Ministry of Foreign Affairs and one of the participants in the technical talks which were taking place in Madrid and London, put the official Government position on 18 April in the third article entitled 'Gibraltar: the reality of a problem'. Like Sr López Gil, Sr Berdejo takes the headings of what he calls Professor Mosterín's 'emotional view', and puts great emphasis on the historical and legal aspects of the question. He gives four reasons why historically Gibraltar is an anachronism, including the fact that it is the last colony in Europe. As far as the legal aspects are concerned, he points to the limitations of the Treaty of Utrecht regarding territorial jurisdiction and the question of the isthmus, as well as the fact that self-determination by Gibraltarians is excluded by the Treaty (at least as a first option) and by UN resolution 2353 of 1968.

Ignoring the geographical aspects (perhaps because it avoided having to deal with Ceuta and Melilla), Sr Berdejo turned to the strategic issue and dismissed Professor Mosterín's conjectures about closing the Strait and nuclear war, pointing out instead that there is a foreign air and naval base installed in Gibraltar 'against our will and not subject to the control of the Spanish State', which is not the case with the US airbases. He also makes the point that British aircraft carriers and submarines which may be carrying nuclear warheads often cross Spanish waters en route to Gibraltar, in violation of Spanish policy. 'It is not difficult to conclude', he writes, 'that the existence of the base in its present form damages our security, devalues our strategic position, and breaks the Balearics-Strait-Canaries axis which is essential for the defence of Spanish territory'.

Whilst taking the now customary sideswipe at the damage done to the economy of the Campo de Gibraltar since 1969 by Franco's policy, Sr Berdejo claims that both smuggling and the militarisation of the region have damaged the economic development of the Campo area. On the political aspects of the question, Sr Berdejo quotes Felipe González's words in his investiture speech, that 'his Government will act in such a way that neither the people of Gibraltar nor of the Campo will be penalised, and that the final outcome of negotiations [with the United Kingdom] will respect the legitimate interests of the population'. He points out that the gates were erected unilaterally by the British in 1909 and that they have now been opened as part of the Spanish Government's policy to improve human contacts. Spain is not threatening the Gibraltarians with annexation, as Sr Mosterín put it, but 'encouraging respectfully and democratically their progressive integration with their natural surroundings'.

Sr Berdejo concludes his article by seizing upon the parallel with Hong Kong: 'Just as the United Kingdom has decolonised a large number of the territories of its empire, it can do the same with Gibraltar, and if it can hand back to China the sovereignty of the island of Hong Kong and the Kowloon Peninsula, [which were] ceded in perpetuity . . . it would not be rational to act differently with Spain'.

Sr Berdejo's rational and measured arguments provided an interesting counterbalance to those of Professor Mosterín and Sr López Gil, and also provided the British Foreign Office with a clear statement of Spain's current position and attitude. No doubt the British Government would have been prepared to concede some of the points that Sr Berdejo made. The one aspect which the Spanish Government's argument ignored, however, was that the *interests* of the Gibraltarians may not be the same as their *wishes*. There was little sign that rational arguments would make much headway on the latter in the near future.

During the summer and autumn of 1984 there were still no official bilateral meetings to discuss the Gibraltar issue, although as had been the case twelve months earlier, it was discussed when Sir Geoffrey Howe and Sr Morán met at the United Nations General Assembly in New York in September. Any substantive public pronouncements were awaiting progress in the 'technical talks' taking place behind the scenes, including those which were being held in relation to Spain's entry into the European Community. Sir Joshua Hassan went to Brussels in early October in order to plead Gibraltar's case for special treatment to soften the impact when Spain joined the EC, but these pleas were rejected by the European Commission. It was reported in Brussels, however, that encouraging results were emerging from the technical talks on such issues as communications between the Peninsula and the Rock, and the use of Gibraltar's airport.[9]

One sign that progress behind the scenes was being made was indicated in a leak reported in *The Sunday Times* on 4 November and picked up by *El País* the following day. The report indicated that

Britain had agreed that Spaniards could live and work on the Rock in anticipation of Spain's entry into the EC, in exchange for the lifting of restrictions at the border relating to goods, vehicles and people of all nationalities. What diplomatic sources said in Madrid on 5 November, however, was that Spaniards would be able to stay on the Rock overnight and also buy property there. As far as taking a job was concerned, in reality this would be difficult because few jobs were on offer and because Gibraltarian legislation on the subject had not been brought into line with EC legislation. Nevertheless, the progress which had clearly been made augured well for the next Howe-Morán encounter, due at the end of November in Brussels at a further session of negotiations on Spain's EC membership.

Prior to that meeting, however, *El País* picked up signs of what it described as 'an unusual climate of understanding within British diplomatic and political circles towards Spain's position on Gibraltar'. If such a climate existed, it was not likely to be a reflection of Government thinking, given that the source of the Spanish daily's observation seemed to be based on a leading article in *The Guardian*—hardly a voice of the British Government. What caught the eye of *El País* was the comment that 'the entry of Spain into the EC would create the absurd and unsustainable situation for the UK of occupying a territory broadly considered to be the legitimate property of another member state'. This was an extraordinarily bold statement by *The Guardian* which is open to extensive juridical and historical debate. But whoever might be indulging in such broad consideration, it certainly did not include Her Majesty's Government. *The Guardian* also picked up the analogy drawn by King Juan Carlos between Gibraltar and Hong Kong on the occasion of the visit to Madrid by the President of China, Li Xiannian, and described the King's comment as 'an entirely constitutional reflection of his Government's point of view'. In the British daily, at least, external factors and parallels were seen as a justification for highlighting the anomaly of Gibraltar's situation.

The eagerly awaited meeting of Sir Geoffrey Howe and Fernando Morán took place in Brussels on 27 November 1984. The negotiations which had been going on behind the scenes finally bore fruit in the agreement which they issued on that day and which has come to be known in Britain as the Brussels Declaration. Designed as a statement which committed both sides to apply the Lisbon Agreement of 1980, the two most significant aspects of the Brussels accord were that Spain would lift restrictions on Gibraltar by 15 February 1985 and that Britain would discuss the question of sovereignty.

At the same time that restrictions were lifted, Spaniards and Gibraltarians would enjoy reciprocity and equality of rights in their respective territories following the introduction of the necessary legislation on both sides. 'Lifting of restrictions' meant the free movement of people, vehicles and goods (although a customs post would remain, since Gibraltar did not belong to the customs union). It was made clear that, in all other respects, the rights of Spaniards and Gibraltarians in each other's territory anticipated Spain's membership of the EC. It was disagreement over the interpretation of the phrase 'the reciprocity and full equality of rights' in the Lisbon Agreement which had delayed the full opening of the border, and clarification of that issue now made it possible for Spain to remove the remaining border restrictions. Spaniards and Gibraltarians would also enjoy an advantage in each other's labour markets over nationals from non-EC countries, although there would be a transition period of seven years before full freedom of movement of labour came into effect. A negotiating process would be set up on the basis of working groups to resolve all differences between Spain and Britain over Gibraltar, and to promote cooperation in economic, cultural, touristic, aviation, military and environmental matters. The Declaration stated that 'both sides accept that the issues of sovereignty will be discussed in that process'.[10]

The fact that Britain was prepared explicitly to discuss the issues of sovereignty (of the territory ceded under the Treaty of Utrecht and, separately, of the isthmus) must have come as something of a surprise in Spain, given that barely two years earlier, in the wake of the Falklands/Malvinas conflict, Mrs Thatcher had explicitly said the opposite. Not surprisingly, Sr Morán was anxious to underscore the importance of the inclusion of such an explicit statement in the Declaration, for it represented a considerable diplomatic success. 'No Spanish Minister of Foreign Affairs can leave any ambiguity about the fact that the solution to the problem of Gibraltar lies in the return of its sovereignty to Spain', he said at a press conference.[11]

In return for the inclusion of the reference to sovereignty, the Spanish negotiators had conceded the omission of two statements originally included in the Lisbon Agreement. One referred to the commitment to solve the problem in accordance with the UN resolutions, which Spain said it was prepared to exclude in order to preserve the climate of cooperation which had been established. The significance of this from the British point of view should not be underestimated. It took the negotiations outside the context of decolonisation and bilateral Spanish talks (which is how the UN resolutions had viewed the problem) and allowed for the possibility of finding a solution which by-passed the restrictions of the Treaty of Utrecht (which required Spain to have first option if there were a change of sovereignty). In other words, it opened the way for a solution which would give Gibraltar autonomous status within a European context.

The other phrase omitted was the reference to the 're-establish-ment of the territorial integrity of Spain', but in order to distinguish between the land and the inhabitants, Sr Morán spoke now of integrating the territory but not its people, and envisaged a special status for Gibraltarians so that they could preserve their British nationality and their way of life. This would, however, be easier said than done, for the Declaration stated that 'the British Government will fully maintain its commitment to honour the wishes of the people of Gibraltar as set out in the Preamble to the 1969 Con-stitution'.

The inclusion of this statement was brought to the attention of the House of Commons when the Foreign Secretary spoke on the issue on 28 November. It also enabled Sir Joshua Hassan to express his satisfaction with the Declaration, despite the well-known reser-vations of the Gibraltarians on the question of sovereignty, although the leader of the opposition, Joe Bossano, saw it as a clear victory for Spanish diplomacy. He was also critical of the privileges given to Spaniards over workers from other countries, especially Moroccans, and of the fact that Britain was now going behind the backs of Gibraltarians to talk to Spain about their future.

One of the problems which was clearly accepted by both sides as requiring urgent solution was that of communications by air, for the Declaration made specific mention of the fact that 'the Spanish Government undertakes to take the early actions necessary to allow safe and effective air communications'. The problem was both one of allowing planes to fly over Spanish air space (Sr Morán described it as an issue of Spanish sovereignty), and of adjusting fare prices, since flights from Britain to Gibraltar were treated as internal and were thus cheaper than flights from Britain to nearby Spanish airports such as Málaga. The issue of air communications was to prove contentious and difficult to resolve. It became a substitute for discussions about territorial sovereignty which, although theoretically on the agenda, did not fit into the overall negotiating framework—there was no working group set up to study this issue—and which was studiously avoided by Britain when the Foreign Ministers had their annual meeting to review the progress of talks.

It was clear from the outset that the inclusion of the issue of sovereignty in the Declaration signified more a recognition of Spain's change of status than a change of attitude on Britain's part. Since 1980 that change of status had included substantial progress on negotiations for entry into the European Community and—even more significantly as far as Gibraltar was concerned—membership of NATO. But there was no clear indication as to how these new realities could be translated into a change from the status quo as far as sovereignty was concerned.

However, the more immediate concerns were preparation for the full opening of the border between Spain and Gibraltar and the establishment of the working groups on all the other issues to which the Brussels Declaration referred.[12]

Notes

1 *El País*, 16 March 1983, p. 15. As part of the attack on Francis Pym, the new Conservative Party Press Officer, journalist Anthony Shrimsley, published an article a few days before his appointment was announced, harshly criticising Pym for his policy towards Madrid on the Gibraltar issue.

2 It was reported (*El País*, 19 April 1983, p. 11) that the Admiral-in-Chief of the Spanish Naval Staff was informed of the manoeuvres by the Embassy in London on 30 March, but that the Spanish Foreign Office only found out from a Gibraltar television programme on 8 April.

3 Spain also saw an inconsistency in the British argument that the refusal by Spain to open fully the border between Spain and Gibraltar was harming the Gibraltarian tourist industry, while at the same time threatening the Gibraltarian economy with the closure of the shipyards which provide 4,000 jobs. See *El País*, 15 April 1983, p. 15.

4 Britain argued that this would require a change in Gibraltar's legislation, without mentioning the fact that the Governor of Gibraltar could initiate such

legislation as a sign of goodwill on Britain's part. See *El País*, 13 April 1983, p. 15.

5 The Spanish Government was committed by its election manifesto to hold a referendum on continued membership of NATO, and its intention was at this stage that such a referendum would be held in 1985.

6 A different type of confusion arose some six months later when changes to British passports meant that the bearer's place of residence was no longer indicated. This meant that Gibraltarians wanting to cross the border had to depend on the police either recognising them or being able to tell from their accent that they were Gibraltarians. See *El País*, 17 June 1984, p. 23.

7 *El País*, 25 January 1984, p. 8. Sr Morán took up the analogy between Gibraltar and Hong Kong in his meeting with Sir Geoffrey Howe in New York in September (see *The Times*, 27 September 1984).

8 See also below, pp. 112, 144–45.

9 The link between Gibraltar and Spain's relationship with NATO appeared once more in October when it was reported that Lord Carrington, who had taken up his appointment as Secretary General to NATO in June, had indicated his willingness in principle to mediate between Madrid and London over the Gibraltar dispute if the two NATO members were to ask him to do so. Lord Carrington's appointment to the NATO post had been warmly welcomed in Madrid, for as Foreign Secretary he had negotiated the Lisbon Agreement. See *El País*, 26 October 1984, p. 19.

10 For the full text of the Brussels Declaration, see Appendix 3.

11 *El País*, 28 November 1984, p. 13.

12 To these were later added social security and communications by sea.

TEN

THE BORDER IS FULLY OPENED: NEGOTIATIONS GET UNDER WAY
January–February 1985

In anticipation of the full opening of the border scheduled for early February 1985, thirty-six Spanish and Gibraltarian officials met on 10 and 11 January for preparatory talks to discuss practical matters relating to the re-establishment of communications, such as police control, customs, work permits and telecommunications.

The Gibraltar delegation was led by the Deputy Governor, John Broadley, while the Spanish group was headed by Francisco José Mayans, special adviser to the Spanish Foreign Affairs Minister, and both sides included representatives of several ministries concerned. The first day's meetings were held in La Línea, while on the second day they were held in Gibraltar itself, the first time that Spanish officials had come to the Rock since 1969.

Tact was very much in evidence in order to avoid any friction. The participants spoke in their own language and their contribution was then translated into the language of their interlocutors, despite the fact that practically all of the participants could speak both languages. For the first day's talks the Gibraltarians actually replaced one of their translators, a British subject who technically was not yet allowed to cross the border. The atmosphere in the talks was friendly, no doubt due to the fact that they were dealing with practical matters rather than political issues. The outcome was the publication in Madrid on 18 January of detailed regulations about the movement of people, goods and vehicles across the border. This augured well for the full opening of the border and for the Geneva meeting between the two Foreign Ministers to implement the Brussels Declaration, both of which had been set for 5 February.

Before that, however, on 16 January the Gibraltar House of Assembly gave approval to the law, proposed by the Brussels Declaration, which gave Spaniards and Gibraltarians reciprocal rights in each other's territory, in anticipation of Spain's membership of the European Community. The opposition Socialists, the GSLP, who opposed the signing of the Brussels Declaration, objected to the proposal, arguing that Gibraltar should have used the intervening period to protect Gibraltarians' rights in EC countries. In a dramatic gesture, the seven GSLP representatives walked out of the Assembly when the vote was being taken. One feature of the new situation was the fact that some 3,000 Spaniards who had worked in Gibraltar prior to the closure of the border were now eligible to receive a weekly pension which would cost Gibraltar's Exchequer a total of about £6 million per year.

Conscious of the criticism from many Gibraltarians that the Brussels Declaration represented a sell-out, Gibraltar's Chief Minister, Sir Joshua Hassan, took the opportunity at a press conference following talks with Sir Geoffrey Howe in London on 30 January to reiterate the desire of the people of Gibraltar to remain British. One of Sir Joshua's main objectives in the talks was no doubt to seek assurances from Sir Geoffrey that a firm position would be taken on the sovereignty issue in Geneva.

The following day, 31 January, the Spanish Cabinet took similar measures to those taken by the Gibraltarian Assembly in order to accord reciprocal rights. They also agreed to rescind Franco's decree of 11 July 1969 and to re-establish communications by land and sea. Meanwhile, the opposition in Gibraltar organised a demonstration of 2,500 people (*The Times* reported a figure of 1,300) against the Brussels Declaration and handed a ten thousand signature petition to the Governor. These gestures against the unstoppable process of negotiation and the numbers involved in them serve as a reminder of the Gibraltarians' impotence in the face of the internal and external pressures on Spain and the UK to resolve the differences between them as would-be fellow members of the European Community.

And so, on the stroke of midnight between 4 and 5 February 1985, the border gates which had been in place for 82 years and which had been closed on the Spanish side for the last 16, were finally fully opened.

The ceremony to open the gate on the Spanish side was carried out by the Civil Governor of the Province of Cádiz, Mariano Baquedano. Fortunately, a rehearsal had been carried out earlier in the day, which involved unlocking the padlock (in order to avoid any hitch during the real performance) and also, more significantly, the removal of a vertical bar which required the use of a pneumatic drill and which would otherwise have caused some embarrassment. Reports differed as to how the opening of the gates was received. *El País* reported that some 4,000 people had gathered on the Spanish side to witness the event, with somewhat fewer on the Gibraltar side, including about 40 rowdy youths shouting anti-Spanish slogans. Five cars, three Gibraltarian and two Spanish, were set alight. *The Times* referred to six cars (four Gibraltarian, one Spanish and one British) and mentioned about 600 Gibraltarians waving Union Jacks, with cheering on both sides. The first people across from the Spanish side were Jesús Malado, from Algeciras, on a Vespa scooter, and his pillion passenger María José Escarcena; in the opposite direction the claim to fame went to three young women who, although resident on the Rock, were not Gibraltarian but (perhaps significantly) French, Swiss and American.

During the day, some 300 vehicles crossed from Spain into Gibraltar, causing some traffic problems late in the afternoon, while about half that number went in the opposite direction.[1] Passport controls were still in force, thus slowing down the passage of visitors. The first commercial traffic into Gibraltar consisted of two car transporters bringing in Fiat vehicles which previously had had to depend on infrequent sea transport from Italy. The only problem was that the transporter drivers had not thought to bring passports with them, and had to be given temporary 24-hour entry permits.

Meanwhile, that same day British and Spanish delegations, led by their respective Foreign Ministers, met at the International Conference Centre in Geneva to discuss the implementation of the Brussels Declaration. It was the first occasion on which the two Foreign Ministers had arranged a formal encounter specifically to talk about Gibraltar. While the British delegation included, as usual, Sir Joshua Hassan and two other representatives from Gibraltar, the Spanish delegation included local government representatives from the Campo de Gibraltar for the first time.

The clear intention on the Spanish side was to lay the foundations for closer cooperation between the population of the Rock and the inhabitants of the Campo, in order to rebuild confidence lost during the years when the border was closed. One project designed to achieve this at a cost of four billion pesetas was the building of a commercial and leisure centre on the Spanish side to attract Gibraltarians.

But the principal business of the Geneva meeting was to establish the working groups which would have the task of tackling the separate aspects of cooperation. Clearly one of the most contentious was going to be the operation of the airport situated on the isthmus between Gibraltar and the mainland. Before the signing of the agreement in Brussels, Britain had suggested joint operation of the airport, a proposal which caused Spain some difficulties because it maintained that the isthmus was neutral territory.[2]

Whatever the problems over practical issues like air communications, however, these would pale into insignificance when compared with the thorny issue of sovereignty. Spain entered the negotiations with viewpoints that were markedly different from those of the British Government in two respects. The first was that 'history, international law and geopolitical realities allow no room for doubt that territorially Gibraltar belongs to Spanish sovereignty'.[3] Britain accepted very little of that; its position was rather that geopolitical realities alone required it to find some means of resolving the Gibraltar question. The second difference was that whereas Spain was prepared to protect the *interests* of the Gibraltarians, as required by the UN resolutions on the matter, the British Government interpreted these as being synonymous with their *wishes*, a point reiterated by Mrs Thatcher during Question Time in the House of Commons. Clearly this semantic distinction would be a far more difficult area to resolve.

In the plenary sessions in Geneva there were few surprises; Sr Morán went through the well-rehearsed reasons for Spain's claim to the sovereignty of the Rock which it had been giving for the previous 25 years. The surprises (although there had been some speculation along these lines prior to the talks) came in the private discussions between Sr Morán and Sir Geoffrey Howe before the plenary sessions, when the Spanish Foreign Minister proposed a range of ideas on the return of Gibraltar to Spanish sovereignty. Although they were not made public at the time, the proposals involved a new Treaty, through which Spain would regain sovereignty over the Rock, with a condominium or leaseback arrangement over a 15 to 20-year period. For an indefinite period the inhabitants would retain their nationality, political and labour rights, self-government and institutions.[4] The military base could also be the subject of a separate agreement. Sir Geoffrey asked for these proposals to be sent to him in writing for detailed study, no doubt as an effective means of pushing the sovereignty issue on to the back burner as quickly as possible and for as long as possible.[5] Sr Morán was encouraged by his British counterpart's response; the mere experience of discussing the sovereignty of Gibraltar must of itself have given any Spanish Foreign Minister *some* encouragement. Yet he was aware that the British Government was trying to play for time and consolidate the status quo.[6]

On practical matters, it was agreed that the working group on air traffic would get started later in February, with the groups on economic cooperation, culture, tourism, the environment and transport to follow. Military cooperation would be discussed at some future date. As far as sovereignty was concerned, this would not be dealt with by a special working group but through diplomatic channels. It was also agreed that the two Foreign Ministers would meet annually to discuss progress being made, in addition to any other encounters they might have in the normal course of events.

As for the Gibraltarians themselves, Sir Joshua Hassan managed to avoid giving a hostage to fortune when he refused to accede to a request at the press conference to answer a question in Spanish (which of course he was quite able to do, but which would no doubt have led many Spanish commentators to observe that most Gibraltarians were really as Spanish as they were). Sir Joshua had to be content with playing third string in the talks to Sir Geoffrey Howe and the British Ambassador in Madrid, although he made it clear that he would have preferred to be there as a third party, representing Gibraltar as an equal with Britain and Spain.

Meanwhile, his leading political opponent Joe Bossano was making waves by calling for independence for Gibraltar, citing in support the UN declaration on decolonisation. Such statements no doubt fuelled Spanish speculation that Britain's readiness to discuss sovereignty really meant that Britain might be using the opportunity to encourage Gibraltarians to become more independent without actually granting them independence.

But at least the process of negotiation was at last under way. On 5 February 1985 two important steps along the road towards a solution were taken, although the distance to be travelled remained unknown. The obstacles along the way were highlighted by the results of a survey published in the Gibraltar weekly magazine *Panorama*, which showed that 94% of Gibraltarians were opposed to any discussion of the question of sovereignty.[7] Little progress could be expected on that aspect of the issue for some considerable time.

Notes

1 Since the opening of the border to pedestrians in 1982, many Gibraltarians had transported their cars by boat from Tangiers to La Línea and left them parked there so that they could cross the border on foot, pick up their car and then drive along the Costa del Sol at will.

2 For a brief history of the dispute over the isthmus, see José Uxo Palasi, 'Gibraltar: el istmo', *Ejército*, August 1986, pp. 3–9.

3 *El País*, 5 February 1985, p. 8.

4 Fernando Morán, 'Las relaciones hispano-británicas', *Revista de Occidente*, No. 89 (October 1988), p. 17.

5 Leaseback had, of course, been considered by the British Government in relation to the Falklands/Malvinas between 1979 and 1980, prior to the Argentinian invasion in April 1982. The reaction to the idea from backbench Conservatives at that time would have made any Foreign Secretary think twice before allowing it currency in relation to Gibraltar. See Hugo Young, *One of Us* (Pan Books, 1990), pp. 259–60.

6 *Revista de Occidente*, No. 89 (October 1988), p. 17.

7 Other figures showed that 76% were in favour of the full opening of the gates, but 73% were opposed to the early concession to Spaniards of the same rights as citizens of other EC countries (see *El País*, 5 February 1985, p. 12). This was an early indicator, borne out by the elections in 1988, that the GSLP was more in tune with majority opinion in Gibraltar than the then ruling party, the AACR.

ELEVEN
OSMOSIS BEGINS
February–November 1985

In the weeks and months after 5 February 1985, business boomed from the new tourist trade to Gibraltar. Within the first week there were 45,000 visitors to the Rock, while during Easter week some 10,000 visitors per day followed the same path. After six months the number reached the one million mark, with 250,000 of them crossing the border in July alone. Vehicles were entering at the rate of 1,000 per day in July, and parking became a nightmare. By the summer, daily flights into Gibraltar from London had doubled, with tour operators offering packages combining the Costa del Sol and the Rock. Retail sales of food and clothing boomed, banks were busy, hotel bookings increased and pubs were overcrowded.

Initially, fears by the GSLP of Gibraltar being inundated by Spanish workers were unfounded. A fortnight after the gates had been opened, no work permits had been issued to Spaniards (even by June the figure was only 84), and newly created jobs had gone to unemployed Moroccans and Gibraltarian or EC nationals.

Traffic between the Rock and Spain was not, of course, all one way and many Gibraltarians crossed into the Campo, either at weekends to shop at the hypermarket Continente, or on Wednesdays for the market in La Línea.[1] One significant Gibraltarian who on 18 April made his first visit to the Campo after a 20-year interval was the Chief Minister, Sir Joshua Hassan. He was returning the official visit of the Chairman of the Councils of the Campo Region, Rafael Palomino, who went to Gibraltar on 22 March.

For the Spaniards of the Campo, the visit was an important step in re-establishing direct personal contacts, which they saw as an essential part of the process of 'osmosis' (as they called it) which would help to normalise relations between the Rock and the Campo. Topics discussed during the formal sessions covered the environment, protection of the Bay, and cultural, tourist and commercial exchanges.

Predictably, the visit drew criticism from the main Gibraltar opposition party, who saw it as part of the decolonisation process. But it was not long before the GSLP leader, Joe Bossano, was himself setting foot on Spanish soil, in his case after a 21-year gap. The purpose of his trip to Madrid on 10 May was to clarify his party's position regarding Spain's entry into the EC. He wanted to make it clear that their concern was not anti-Spanish, but anti-big-neighbour; as he put it, Gibraltar's membership of the EC since 1973 had only been theoretical, but once Spain joined and Gibraltar shared a border with a Community member, Gibraltar's relations with the EC would become a practical issue, and he wanted the PSOE Government to understand the threat that posed to Gibraltar.

Another long interval between visits came to an end when the Foreign Secretary, Sir Geoffrey Howe, arrived in Gibraltar on 7 June, the first visit by a British Foreign Secretary for 13 years. Despite the economic upturn on the Rock since February, which had resulted in the creation of 650 new jobs, local politicians were anxious to seek economic assistance from Britain. Specifically, they were asking for £18 million (half the total cost) for the development of the port area and other infrastructure projects, and also for Britain to foot the annual bill of £6 million for the pensions of former Spanish workers on the Rock.[2]

Opposition politicians were also anxious to know what Sr Morán had proposed in February in Geneva regarding Gibraltar's future sovereignty, since they felt they were being kept in the dark. Sir Geoffrey said that Sr Morán's proposals would be considered in detail at their first annual meeting in November. Joe Bossano took the opportunity in a meeting he had with Sir Geoffrey to push the idea of limited independence for Gibraltar (an idea which Sir Geoffrey rejected because of what the Treaty of Utrecht had to say on the matter), while the former Chief Minister Robert Peliza called for a referendum in Gibraltar on the sovereignty issue (which Sir Geoffrey thought was unlikely). The British Foreign Secretary's reaction to these proposals was well received in Madrid.

Sir Geoffrey had gone on to Gibraltar from the NATO foreign ministers meeting in Estoril. While in Portugal he had had bilateral talks with his Spanish counterpart on the Gibraltar issue. Sr Morán reported that they had discussed the progress of the Brussels Declaration. He also indicated that, as far as the resolution of the problem of Gibraltar was concerned, this was a long-term issue; when asked if 'long-term' meant the year 2050, he replied: 'Much less than that; less than half',[3] from which it can be deduced that the Spanish Foreign Minister was not expecting the Gibraltar question to be resolved definitively for about 25 years. Sir Geoffrey was not to be drawn on timescales.

Meanwhile, negotiations had begun in Madrid on the business of air communications between Gibraltar and the Spanish mainland. The group dealing with the airport issue first met on 4 March. Clearly, progress was not going to be easy: while Spain was seeking joint control of the airport, Britain wanted it to be opened up for use as a 'feeder' to Costa del Sol resorts, but this would mean Spain lifting restrictions on flights over the Bay of Algeciras. As a first step, and in the spirit of the Brussels Declaration to ensure safe and effective air communications, on 1 April Madrid issued new regulations allowing pilots more room to manoeuvre over the Bay when taking off and landing, but this applied to civil aircraft only. The question of overflying rights for British military planes was to remain a contentious issue for some time.

The main problem, however, was the use of the airport itself. Britain had established an airstrip in the 1930s on the isthmus, expanding it to a fully fledged airport following the outbreak of the Second World War. But as the isthmus is an area not covered by the Treaty of Utrecht, Spain claimed that the airport lay on Spanish territory. However, very sensibly neither side wanted to get bogged down on the aspect of territorial claims, so Britain did not ask Spain to renounce its claim to the isthmus, while Spain formally reserved its position on the matter.

By mid-June 1985 the proposal on joint use of the airport had taken broad shape. The idea was to model it on Basle, where passengers could disembark either into France or Switzerland. Passengers flying from Madrid would either enter the Campo de Gibraltar, or go through customs and passport control and enter Gibraltar. The Gibraltarians first learnt of this proposal, which was eventually discussed by the technical group on air traffic in London on 28 August, from a report in *El País* on 17 June, provoking an angry response from the GSLP both for the manner in which they learnt of the proposal and for the fact that it would mean recognition of Spain's superior rights to use the airport over those of any other country. They called for a debate in the Gibraltar Parliament preventing any agreement on the airport without prior parliamentary discussion, but in the debate Sir Joshua Hassan did not accept that the press report was accurate, and his amendment was passed to the effect that Spain had no jurisdiction over the airport, and that any proposal for practical cooperation would have to be for the benefit of both sides.

It was also reported in late June that the six-month-old shipyard company, Gibraltar Shiprepair (known as Gibrepair for short), which had received £28 million from the British Government, was in financial difficulties, having used half of this assistance in the first three months. The company wanted to employ Spanish workers, but had run into union opposition. In early July, it was announced that Britain was to spend £1.5 million on improvements to the naval base in an area known as Coaling Island.

Two other instances in June and July showed that collaboration between Spain and Gibraltar was increasing. It was revealed that the Gibraltar garrison had imported 3,000 tons of water from Spain because of a shortfall owing to leakage from underground reserves, while closer links of a different kind were agreed in July when the Gibraltar Broadcasting Corporation decided to transmit some TV programmes in Spanish for the first time. The idea was driven more by financial considerations than cultural ones, since such programmes would also attract advertising in Spanish and help to offset a heavy Government subsidy.

On the diplomatic front, the Gibraltar question re-emerged in the context of the final agreement on Spain's entry into the EC. The signing of the Treaty of Accession in Madrid on 12 June had provoked an exchange of notes between the British and Spanish Foreign Secretaries. Sr Morán's note sent on 13 June insisted that Spain's membership of the Community would in no way affect its claim to Gibraltar, while Sir Geoffrey Howe confirmed in his reply that Britain's position would not be affected either. Both agreed that they would continue to implement the Brussels Declaration.

The question of Gibraltar was raised by the Spanish Opposition when the Treaty was ratified by the Congress on 26 June. They argued that the Government had given no guarantee in the Organic

Law, by which the Treaty was being ratified, that the Gibraltar dispute would not be put on the back burner, but Sr Morán was able to point to the exchange of notes in his defence.

This was Sr Morán's last act as Foreign Minister on Gibraltar; on 5 July he was replaced by Francisco Fernández Ordóñez. Two months after leaving office, Sr Morán felt at liberty to reveal that in 1983 it had been suggested within the European Community that Spain should agree to withdraw its claims to Gibraltar in exchange for entry. Sr Morán said that he had taken the position that in that event Spain would have sacrificed joining the Community. He said that for over a year 'secret negotiations' had taken place with Britain before that particular threat was dropped. Surprisingly little was made of this revelation, no doubt because Spain was anxious for the other member countries to ratify the Treaty agreeing to Spain's membership in time for the entry date of 1 January 1986 to be met.[4]

The first encounter between Sr Morán's successor and his British counterpart took place in Helsinki on 31 July 1985. Although much of their discussion was taken up with other matters, including the official visit of the King and Queen of Spain to Britain planned for April 1986, the issue of Gibraltar was raised in their talks. It was confirmed that Sir Geoffrey Howe would visit Madrid in December, when it was hoped that Britain would respond to the 'ideas' (details of which had still not been officially released) put forward by Sr Morán in February. Naturally, there was continuing speculation as to what these 'ideas' might be, with a period of transition involving leaseback or shared sovereignty being seen as the most likely. As far as the timescale was concerned, Sr Morán was quoted as saying on 31 July that the beginning of the period of transition could be two or three years away and could last for two decades. He has been shown by events to have been over-optimistic with regard to the start of such a process, although had he suggested that the timescale might be longer it would scarcely have given the impression that the Spanish Government was pushing as hard as it could for a resolution to the dispute.

In the autumn of 1985 there were two brief reminders of the strong links made three-and-a-half years earlier between Gibraltar and the Falklands/Malvinas. The first came during a visit to Madrid by President Alfonsín of Argentina, who was attending a meeting of Liberal International, and who commented that 'long-lasting anachronisms in Gibraltar and the Malvinas which cause so much heartache for Spaniards and Argentinians will soon have to give way to rational solutions'.[5] The other reminder came with the announcement on 12 October that the British naval base in Gibraltar had been reinforced by the installation of the French-made Exocet missile system, which had been used to such devastating effect on the British navy in the Falklands/Malvinas conflict.

In early November Sir Joshua Hassan went to London for talks with the British Foreign Secretary. One of the subjects discussed was the question of the payment of pensions to Spanish workers, as it required a solution before Spain's entry into the Community the following January. But the main purpose was to agree their positions in the talks with Madrid due in December, the first occasion following the Brussels Declaration at which the subject of sovereignty would be formally under discussion.

Notes

1 Some residents of Gibraltar found it difficult to cross into Spain for many months after the full opening of the border, however. Members of the Indian community often had to travel to London to obtain a visa to enter Morocco and then travel to Morocco to obtain a visa to enter Spain. See *El País*, 8 July 1985, p. 17.

2 One of the consequences of an increase in the number of tourists to the Rock was the threat posed to the Gibraltar apes. On 5 June an incubator was made available to assist new-born apes, and in keeping with established custom, following Sir Geoffrey's visit it was expected that the next ape to be born would be called Geoffrey. See *El País*, 17 June 1985, p. 16.

3 *El País*, 8 June 1985, p. 15.

4 Such ratifications went through national parliaments throughout the Community, including in Gibraltar, where predictably the vote was eight to seven in favour following the debate on 29 November.

5 *El País*, 4 October 1985, p. 7.

TWELVE
SOVEREIGNTY AND SOVEREIGNS
December 1985–April 1986

Expectations were muted as the date approached of the first meeting between Sir Geoffrey Howe and Francisco Fernández Ordóñez to discuss the question of the future sovereignty of Gibraltar. Madrid's hopes were no doubt higher than those of London; whereas the former wanted a clear statement of the British position, the latter wanted to create a climate of confidence for the future.

It was seen as a difficult time for both governments. Madrid was under pressure because it had yet to hold the promised referendum on Spain's continuing membership of NATO. Britain's refusal to hold talks on the Falklands/Malvinas had been opposed at the UN (through a resolution supported by Spain) and the British Government was also coping with the aftermath of the signing of the Anglo-Irish agreement. It was not the time for the British Government to be seen to be making any concessions to Spain over Gibraltar. For this reason, rather than spend the talks exclusively exploring the question of sovereignty it was expected that Britain would prefer to discuss three areas in relation to the Gibraltar issue: first, to review the situation since the full opening of the border; second, to examine progress in the technical talks on air and sea communications and other areas of cooperation; and third, the question of sovereignty. In addition, the issue of pensions for former Spanish workers would have to be aired.

Sir Geoffrey arrived in Madrid on 5 December 1985 for two days of talks. On the first morning Gibraltar was the subject of editorials in both *El País* and *The Times*, a sure indication that this was seen as one of those historic moments in Anglo-Spanish diplomatic relations. The Spanish paper recognised that Britain was prepared to discuss the sovereignty of Gibraltar with Spain but not the sovereignty of the Falklands/Malvinas with Argentina for two principal reasons: the EC and NATO. Spain and Britain were to become more and more closely linked economically and militarily. But it was also recognised that the British Government's commitments to the Gibraltarians meant that a rapid solution was not possible. Moreover, a clear link was seen between Spain's membership of the European Community, NATO and the future of Gibraltar. Sir Geoffrey's visit was viewed as 'more symbolic than executive . . . the important thing was that contacts were taking place'. As for a solution to the Gibraltar issue, 'it is probably not a major question for Spanish national pride . . . Spanish society can live perfectly well, as it has done, without apparently being afflicted by the trauma of decolonisation . . .'. It was suggested that closer consideration should be given to the Gibraltar-NATO equation when Spain's integration with Europe was under general discussion. There is no doubt that by comparison with earlier such editorials, this was low-key stuff.

The Times editorial would have applauded such realism. Sir Geoffrey's response to the leaseback or condominium proposals was bound by the British Government's commitment to the 1969 Gibraltar Constitution. Confidence-building measures of cooperation in the region were the Spaniards' best hope if they were ever to persuade the Gibraltarians to accept the Spanish flag. The recent Anglo-Irish agreement suggested the additional possibility of bringing the Spanish Government into a consultative arrangement, although this might be seen as the thin end of the wedge by the Gibraltarians, and would not deter the Spaniards from their long-term ambitions. Agreements on the use of the airport seemed to offer more hope of success in the short term, although opposition to the implications of Iberia flying in from Madrid had led to the term 'Trojan plane' being coined. In conclusion, as in the *El País* editorial, the link was made between Gibraltar and NATO; some concessions by the Gibraltarians might help Felipe González to win the referendum vote on NATO membership, and this would be in the Gibraltarians' interests.[1]

Following the meetings held over two days, Sr Fernández Ordóñez informed journalists at a press conference that the question of the sovereignty of Gibraltar had occupied three-quarters of their time. But in the joint communiqué issued on 6 December, the sovereignty issue constituted only part of the second half of the one-page document, an indication that little progress of substance had been made. Both sides, said the communiqué, agreed to remit the question of sovereignty to normal diplomatic channels, and the text added that Sir Geoffrey emphasised that the British Government would fully maintain its commitment to respect the wishes of the Gibraltarians, as set out in the Preamble to the 1969 Constitution. The two Ministers said that they would continue to discuss the issue of Gibraltar in their regular encounters at meetings of the EC and NATO. The question of the joint use of the airport was also to be resolved through continuing discussions by the technical groups; the stumbling block seemed to be that the Gibraltarians were opposed to passengers embarking from Spanish airports being allowed to arrive in Gibraltar but not go through police controls. On the question of payment of pensions to Spaniards, agreement had been reached that they would be paid at the same level as Gibraltar-ians from 1 January 1986, although it was yet to be agreed whether Britain or Gibraltar would foot the bill.[2] Sir Joshua Hassan, as a member of the British delegation to the talks, was also at the press conference. In answer to a question on the issue of sovereignty he said (in English): 'I accept the Spanish position', although the British interpreter translated this into Spanish as 'I understand the Spanish position'. Spanish reporters tried to make something out of this distinction, for that was all they had to clutch at.

So the moment had come and gone. There must have been some disappointment on the Spanish side, although this was the first occasion when the British had not rejected outright a proposal which implied a Spanish future for Gibraltar. There must also have been some relief among Gibraltarians that the issue of sovereignty had remained unchanged. All the signs were that it was accepted that this was not a propitious moment to start discussing the issue of sovereignty in any depth, although cynics might have been forgiven for asking if there would *ever* be a good time to discuss it. It was clear that it was going to be a long haul.

Spain duly entered the European Community on 1 January 1986. Spaniards entering Gibraltar and Gibraltarians entering Spain had to continue to present their passports to police, whereas members of other EC countries entering Gibraltar only had to show their identity card. This was an arrangement agreed before the full opening of the frontier in February 1985, in order to keep out petty Spanish criminals, and the Gibraltarian authorities showed no sign of changing their position. There were no early tangible signs for Spaniards that EC membership had had any effect on their relations with the inhabitants of the Rock.

The next landmark was the first anniversary of the full opening of the border on 5 February. During that first year, there had been two million visitors to the Rock, compared with an annual average of 150,000 over the previous ten years. The economic benefits were substantial, not only for Gibraltarians but also for the neighbouring Spanish regions. Spanish exports to Gibraltar were worth between £20 million and £30 million, while it was estimated that Gibraltarians had spent about £15 million in Spain. Income from tourism in Gibraltar had doubled from £10 million to £20 million, and 400 jobs had been created. This would undoubtedly increase if the Spanish airline Iberia were allowed to use the airport. But not all Gibraltarians saw the issue exclusively—or even primarily—in economic terms.

Negotiators had a further meeting to discuss the airport question on 4 and 5 March in La Línea and Gibraltar. The Spanish delegation was headed by Fermín Prieto Castro, of the Foreign Affairs Ministry, while the British delegation was led by David Moss, of the UK Department of Transport—their departmental attachments reflecting an interesting difference in the perception of the issue from the two sides. On previous occasions the British delegation included a Gibraltarian, Joe Pitaluga, but this time he was absent because the Gibraltarian Administration did not want to be party to any agreement which gave concessions to Spain. Spain proposed the construction of a Spanish terminal on the north side of the airport in Spanish military territory, and the two delegations visited the site to consider the best location. Another thorny issue discussed was that of passenger and baggage handling, which Iberia wanted to undertake for its own services but which were so far exclusively operated by the Gibraltarian company Bland.

The main point of difference, however, continued to be the issue of customs and immigration control. On 23 March at the first meeting of the Gibraltarian House of Assembly to be held following the technical talks, the Opposition called for the Spanish proposals to be rejected. Clearly, the concern was that if any plane landing in

Gibraltar was allowed to be treated as if it were a domestic flight, this would constitute a de facto breach of Gibraltar's territorial integrity and a threat to its sovereignty. The details might have seemed petty; the underlying issue was fundamental.

Meanwhile, on 12 March, Spaniards took another step along the road of international responsibility by voting to stay in NATO (but to remain outside the military structure) in the long-awaited referendum. It was an unexpectedly comfortable margin of 51% to 41% on a 60% turnout, given that only a week before opinion polls were still forecasting a 'no' majority of 52 to 46. Clearly, Gibraltar was not a factor which weighed heavily in voters' minds; when asked if they thought that by staying in NATO Spain would be more likely to regain Gibraltar, only 26% said that they did. A much more decisive influence was the effect on Spain's political stability if the vote went against the Government. Despite the about-turn of the PSOE on the issue (they had campaigned in the 1982 elections to take Spain out of NATO), the referendum became as much a vote of confidence in Felipe González as a vote to stay in the Atlantic Alliance. The importance of the result as far as the Gibraltar problem was concerned was that a 'no' vote could have given Britain justification for maintaining the status quo on sovereignty because of Gibraltar's continuing military importance to NATO. This was one of many reasons for the Spanish Government to breathe a sigh of relief on the night of 12 March.

On 19 March the Spanish Foreign Minister paid his first visit to Portugal since both countries joined the European Community at the beginning of the year. At a meeting with foreign journalists, he indicated that he thought the Gibraltar issue would be easier to resolve now that Spain and Britain were both Community as well as NATO partners. He described Gibraltar 'as the only colony in Europe', a situation which was 'anachronistic' and 'morally intolerable'. *The Times'* leader writer on 24 March felt that Sr Fernández Ordóñez's remarks were not conducive to the confidence-building between Gibraltarians and neighbouring Spaniards, which Spain had hitherto recognised as essential. The taunt of 'colony', which in the case of Gibraltar was not denied, also provided the writer with the opportunity to draw the parallel once again between Gibraltar and the Spanish enclaves of Ceuta and Melilla. Spain would not of course accept that the two cases were comparable.

In April there occurred another of those incidents leading to a diplomatic protest which indicated the sensitivity of the Gibraltar issue. The problem arose this time from the British claim that the Spanish aircraft carrier *Dédalo* had entered British territorial waters in the Bay of Algeciras for some 20 minutes on the night of 20 March. The elapse of eleven days between the incident and the formal lodging of the protest on 2 April (a delay partly caused, it was explained, by Easter) suggested that the protest was undertaken rather as a matter of routine.

Not everyone in Britain treated the event with such equanimity, however. It was alleged that two Tory MPs, John Stokes and Albert McQuarrie (who was also Chairman of the Gibraltar Parliamentary Group) called for the cancellation of the royal visit to the UK (due to start in only three weeks) unless there was a formal apology from the Spanish Government.[3] This call was seen in Spanish diplomatic circles as a reflection of pressure exerted from Gibraltar itself, where many people were concerned about the significance of the rapprochement between the heads of state. The *Daily Express* claimed that the incident was an attempt by rebel Spanish naval officers to torpedo the royal visit, although the Foreign Office dismissed this as absurd. That they tried to play down the incident is indicated by the fact that the protest, in the form of an 'aide mémoire' sent to the Spanish Foreign Ministry in Madrid, was delivered by a British Embassy official and not by the Ambassador himself.

In the reply delivered on 3 April, Spain claimed that it was not possible for its ships to transgress British waters as accused because it does not recognise British jurisdiction over any waters outside the port of Gibraltar, in accordance with the Treaty of Utrecht.[4] And there the matter was allowed to rest. The British Government had made its point, and neither government wanted to cloud the atmosphere so close to the royal visit. In fact, on the same day as the protest was answered, the details of the royal visit were published.

Before that visit could take place, however, the strategic importance of Gibraltar was thrown into relief once again when US planes went into action over Libya on 15 April. Anti-terrorist and other security measures on the Rock were stepped up immediately, and over the following weekend surface-to-air Rapier missile batteries were installed in order to strengthen the air defences. Although there was no reason to suppose that Gibraltar might come under attack, the activity to prepare for such an eventuality was a sign of how important Gibraltar would be in circumstances involving a threat to NATO. For now, however, such activity proved to be something of a tourist attraction, and hundreds of Spaniards drove up the roads on the Rock itself to view the naval presence through their binoculars.

Fortunately, the situation in the Mediterranean was not suffi-ciently serious to threaten the royal visit of King Juan Carlos and Queen Sofía to Britain from 22 to 24 April. It was the first visit by a reigning Spanish monarch to the UK since Juan Carlos' grandfather, Alfonso XIII, visited in 1905. Queen Elizabeth (Juan Carlos' cousin through Alfonso's marriage to Queen Victoria's grand-daughter Victoria Eugenie) took whatever steps she could to indicate the close ties between her and her guests: inviting them to stay at Windsor Castle, for example, and sending Prince Charles to meet them at the airport.

Gibraltar was seen as the one 'issue' of the visit. Juan Carlos had, after all, made reference to Gibraltar in the very first speech he made as King in November 1975, and he and Queen Sofía had been obliged to refuse to attend the wedding of the Prince and Princess of Wales in 1981 because the honeymoon started from Gibraltar. Inevitably, therefore, reference to Gibraltar was made publicly by both Spanish and British monarchs. In a speech at the end of the banquet at Windsor Castle on the first evening of the visit, King Juan Carlos referred to some differences remaining between their nations, and expressed the hope that 'the two Governments will find, through the negotiating process which has already begun, the appropriate formulae for a solution to be reached which is satisfac-tory to all, so that the differences cease to be a point of conflict and become an element of harmony, understanding and cooperation between our two countries, for the direct benefit of the people concerned'.

Queen Elizabeth had earlier struck a similar note. It would be surprising, she said, if there were not differences between the two countries, but 'these differences are handled in a friendly and cooperative spirit, as befits close allies and partners, for we have so much in common that friendship between our two countries is assured'.

On the following day, 23 April, the Spanish King became the first foreign monarch to address a joint gathering of the two Houses of Parliament. Twice during the speech he made explicit reference to Gibraltar. He called for 'the early disappearance of the only problem that separates us', and later used a passage similar to that which he used at the previous night's banquet. Close observers of the King's words noted that reference to an early resolution to the problem went against his known view that it could not be rushed. But no doubt Spanish Government advisers, mindful of the fact that a general election was due later in the year, inserted the word 'early' to indicate that the Government was not going to let the problem slide.

The royal visit was by all accounts a great success. On a personal level the two royal families clearly got on well (the Prince and Princess of Wales and their children were invited to spend several days as guests of the Spanish royals in Mallorca in August). The visit cemented long-standing and recently reinforced ties between the two countries, and enabled the problem of Gibraltar to be put in perspective. The future of Spain and Britain was shown to be inextricably linked through membership of the EC and NATO, while the likeable personality of the Spanish monarch and his personal contribution to the restoration of democracy in Spain commended him to even the most ardent defender of the 'Britishness' of Gibraltar. At the same time the problem was not swept under the carpet, and reference to it by the Spanish head of state within the Palace of Westminster—unthinkable a decade earlier—ensured that efforts to find a solution would be continued.

Notes

1 Not surprisingly, the left-wing British MP Tony Benn, on a visit to Madrid in February 1986, took the opposing view that Spain's membership of NATO had nothing to do with the Gibraltar problem. Spain had been a member of NATO for four years, he said, and the problem had still not been resolved. See *El País*, 13 February 1986, p. 14.

2 Payments began in February 1986. By the time that an agreement was reached in 1989, whereby Britain would meet most of the cost of £15 million per year to be paid over 15 years, Britain had already paid £58 million.

3 Mr McQuarrie later denied that he had ever made such a statement. See *El País*, 14 April 1986, p. 15.

4 For a brief study of the dispute over territorial waters see José Uxo Palasi, 'Gibraltar: aguas y aeropuerto', *Ejército*, September 1986, pp. 3–9.

THIRTEEN
INTO FELIPE'S SECOND TERM: GUARDS AND GATES
June 1986–January 1987

Having won the referendum vote on NATO in March, Felipe González decided to call a General Election in June 1986, rather than run the full four-year term and wait until the autumn. An evaluation of the first PSOE government's foreign policy achievements would leave a question mark as far as NATO was concerned (largely because it was not clear what the Government's aims had been). But there could be no doubt that entry into the EC and the unblocking of the negotiations on Gibraltar had been the Government's two major successes.

Sr González comfortably won a second term, and just as he had done after his first victory, he included references to Gibraltar when presenting his new Government's programme in the Congress on 22 July. He expressed the hope that an agreement could be reached between Britain and Spain by 1990 on the decolonisation of Gibraltar. Setting a target date—a least for an agreement on procedures and a timetable, however long-term—at least gave the impression that the Government was determined not to let up the pressure on Britain. It would also give Felipe González the whole of his second term in which to achieve this objective and earn himself a place in the history books; he may perhaps have envisaged that a third successive term with himself at the helm could not be guaranteed. If that was the case, he was being over-optimistic about Gibraltar, although unduly pessimistic about his chances of continuing as Prime Minister into the following decade.

A sign of British concession soon came—though hardly enough to encourage Sr González that his target was likely to be met. It was decided to remove permanently the British military guard at the frontier post from 31 July. Britain argued that it was no longer appropriate to maintain such a military presence given that Britain and Spain were now both members of the EC and NATO. Although it was only a ceremonial presence and had become something of a tourist attraction since the opening of the gates, the withdrawal of the guard after some 250 years was inevitably viewed with some concern by the Gibraltarians. Sir Joshua Hassan, who had been informed in advance of the withdrawal, returned from his holiday on the Costa del Sol.

Two weeks later, in an attempt to make clear his opposition to the British move, Sir Joshua revealed that the British and Spanish Governments had been discussing the removal not just of the guard but of the gates themselves. He said that on 8 May he was informed that the Spanish Government had proposed that the gates be dismantled as a condition for the withdrawal of the Spanish military guard. Sir Joshua opposed this; the British Government expressed its disappointment at his reaction, agreed to put the issue of dismantling the gates aside for the time being and decided on the withdrawal of the British military guard without Spanish recipro-city. Despite this revelation, Sir Joshua gained little sympathy from the Gibraltarian opposition parties for the way in which the British Government had apparently treated him. They were united in condemning the unilateral withdrawal of the British guard, but whereas Sir Joshua would have been satisfied with a reciprocal Spanish withdrawal, the opposition parties would not.[1]

The discussions in May to which Sir Joshua referred (confirmed by the Spanish Foreign Ministry) prompted *El País* to consider the Gibraltar issue once again in an editorial. Recognising that the difficulty of the Gibraltar problem lay in reconciling the 'logical Spanish aspiration to recover its territorial integrity against the respectable wishes of the present inhabitants of the Rock to retain their British citizenship', the writer acknowledged the attraction of the so-called 'Andorrisation' proposal (first published in *The Economist*) under which Princes of the British and Spanish royal families could alternate as Governor-General of a Gibraltar under shared sovereignty. The Gibraltarians would in this way be able to retain their representative institutions, including their House of Assembly, with the likelihood that over time, through the process of 'natural osmosis', integration with Spain would evolve.[2] However impractical the details of the proposal might be, the Spanish press saw a welcome change in the readiness of the British Government to encourage a solution through measures such as the withdrawal of the guard.

The problem for many Gibraltarians was the fact that the territory in which the British guard had been mounted was part of the isthmus, territory not covered by the Treaty of Utrecht and which also includes the airport. Withdrawal of a British military presence from this sensitive area could therefore be seen as sending political messages which were encouraging to Spain and worrying for Gibraltarians. Eventually on 10 September, some six weeks after the British guard had been withdrawn, leading Gibraltarian politicians and community leaders from across the political spectrum sent a communiqué to Sir Geoffrey Howe on the issue. They protested at the withdrawal of the guard and asked the British Government not to remove the gates. They also rejected the Spanish policy of 'osmosis' because its ultimate objective was to drive them towards Spain, and requested that this be conveyed to Madrid.

Meanwhile, the technical talks progressed at a snail's pace. Those scheduled for early June were called off at Spain's request because it was felt that no progress had been made since the previous talks. David Radford, Head of the Southern Europe Department at the Foreign Office, met his Spanish counterpart Jesús Ezquerra, Head of European Foreign Policy at the Ministry of Foreign Affairs, on 18 July, and Mr Radford paid a lightning visit to Gibraltar at the end of August. The Civil Aviation Group met for talks on 10 September, prior to meetings on 18–19 September between Messrs Radford and Ezquerra, but continuing opposition in Gibraltar to the proposals on the joint use of the airport meant that little progress was made.

Perhaps prompted by the strongly-worded communiqué to which Sir Joshua Hassan had been the leading signatory, *El País* published an interview with the Chief Minister of Gibraltar on 21 September in which he made clear his concern to retain Gibraltar's own identity. When asked why Gibraltarians were so afraid of the question of sovereignty, Sir Joshua replied: 'Because we are an established community who have come from many parts of Europe but who today have an identity as a people; we are neither British nor Andalusian, but Gibraltarian. Let's say that we are British out of convenience . . . [We are] a combination of Mediterranean and

Anglo-Saxon cultures, which equals Gibraltarian'. He asserted that if Gibraltar was not so small they would already be independent: 'We are victims of geography, not history . . . Let's not talk of sovereignty; time and future generations will decide that . . . When there is European political union and frontiers have lost their present meaning, then there will be no problem . . .'.[3] Here was a clear indication that Sir Joshua and like-minded Gibraltarians saw their best hope in going along with negotiations between Britain and Spain, but delaying their progress wherever possible, in the expectation that political change within Europe would eventually allow Gibraltar a satisfactory degree of autonomy. Although the British Government would never have admitted it—and would certainly have rejected the objective of European political union—it is likely that they would have supported such a strategy.

Five months after his intervention on the Gibraltar issue in Britain, King Juan Carlos was again making a public statement about the need for an early solution and the reincorporation of Gibraltar into Spanish territory. This time his forum was the opening of the general debate on 22 September 1986 of the 41st session of the United Nations General Assembly in New York, where he was making his first official visit. He spoke on a range of issues, including reference to Gibraltar as an 'anachronism' and an 'unjust situation'.

In Gibraltar the Government rejected the validity of the terms used by the King; in the absence of Sir Joshua Hassan in London, his deputy Adolfo Canepa said that what was anachronistic was that a member of the EC was claiming territory which legally belonged to another member state, and that what would be unjust would be for Gibraltar and its people to have their sovereignty transferred against their wishes. Joe Bossano, the opposition leader, said that the King's speech marked a return to the Spanish position under Franco. But the fact that the King of Spain (widely respected for his role in the restoration of Spanish democracy and of Spain's full participation in international affairs) was making reference to Gibraltar before the United Nations (a forum whose principal success over the previous three decades had been to oversee the decolonisation process) was unlikely to have been lost on the British delegation at the UN which included the Foreign Secretary, Sir Geoffrey Howe.

On his return to London Sir Geoffrey hastened to reply to the communiqué sent to him on 10 September by leading Gibraltarians.

In a letter sent on 26 September he reaffirmed the British position that sovereignty extends over the whole territory of the Rock, and confirmed that the decision on the dismantling of the border gates would depend on the outcome of consultations going on in Gibraltar. He said that Britain was continuing to press the Spanish Government to remove the guard from its side of the border, and stated that 'Spain is entitled to raise issues relating to sovereignty ... but that these would be considered by Britain in the context of its commitments to the Gibraltarians'.[4] Gibraltarians could take some comfort from Sir Geoffrey's reply, although there is no indication that he was prepared to dissuade Madrid from following its 'osmosis' policy as requested, if for no other reason than that 'osmosis' helped the Gibraltarian economy, which in turn eased Britain's financial obligations to the colony.

As the end of the year approached, preparations were stepped up for the second annual encounter between the British and Spanish Foreign Ministers. Sir Joshua Hassan, together with the Military Governor, Sir Peter Terry, went to London for this purpose on 1 October. On his return to Gibraltar Sir Joshua expressed some concern about whether the meeting would actually take place because no date had yet been set, but the Foreign Office said that this was due to Sir Geoffrey Howe's busy diary. Britain currently held the Presidency of the European Community and the biannual summit was due to be held in London on 5 and 6 December. It came as no surprise, therefore, when in mid-November it was announced that the meeting would not be held until 13 and 14 January.

In the interim Gibraltar's role in NATO produced further discord over the visit to the Rock from 7 to 9 October by General Bernard Rogers, Supreme Allied Commander of NATO in Europe. The Spanish Government expressed its profound displeasure and submitted a formal protest to the Secretary-General, Lord Carrington, at the visit to GIBMED (the NATO naval command over the Straits situated in Gibraltar), especially since Madrid had made it clear in February that it did not recognise the jurisdiction of GIBMED.[5] The visit came at a sensitive time, since the USA and Spain were in the process of negotiating in Washington a reduction of the US military presence in Spain, which had been part of the Government's commitment in the NATO referendum campaign. General Rogers said that he understood Spain's objection to NATO bases in

Gibraltar, but that he lived in the real world and his visit to observe resources was essential. Spain's Ambassador to NATO, Jaime de Ojeda, said the visit was badly timed and ill-advised, and added that for Spain the main reality was Gibraltar's colonial status.

Another factor which had made the timing of General Rogers' visit so sensitive was that Spain was due to start discussions on 30 and 31 October in Brussels on its role within NATO—discussions which would inevitably be linked with those on reductions of US forces in Spain. The main difficulty envisaged for the Brussels talks (which were expected to take many months) was the implementation of coordination between Spain and NATO in Gibraltar through GIBMED, the command which Spain did not recognise but through which it would have to liaise. One solution would be on the basis of some diplomatic agreement between London and Madrid; another would involve Spain by-passing GIBMED (and the air command GIBAIR) and coordinating directly with AFSOUTH in Naples. Spain's concern, of course, was to ensure that any agreement that might be reached should not cast any doubts upon its claim for sovereignty over the Rock.

Spanish reaction to General Rogers' visit probably had something to do with the cancellation of the visit by Admiral Cesare Pellini, Chief of NATO naval forces in Southern Europe, which had been scheduled for 20 October. The official reason given by the British Navy in Gibraltar for the cancellation was 'operational reasons', whereas the reason given by a spokesman for the HQ of the Allied Forces in Southern Europe (AFSOUTH) in Naples was 'scheduling'. The Spanish Government interpreted the cancellation as being due to NATO not wishing to create further political turmoil in Spain, although his visit eventually took place on 6 January 1987 without any formal protest.

Felipe González made his first public comments on Gibraltar since starting his second term in an interview for BBC Radio on 10 October. He described the effect of Gibraltar on Anglo-Spanish relations as 'a stone in Spain's shoe' and felt that there was a pressing need to reach an agreement which would lead to an eventual resolution of the problem. His interviewer pressed him for a timescale, and Sr González stated that an agreement during his term of office would be 'reasonable'. But what annoyed Gibraltarians was his statement that they have 'no right to self-determination'.

Sir Joshua Hassan said that the Spanish Prime Minister's remarks 'went totally against the spirit of greater understanding in Anglo-Spanish contacts in recent years, and could contribute to a hardening of attitudes on all sides'.[6] Joe Bossano's reaction was that Felipe González's rejection of self-determination was totally unacceptable, and that an agreement on the problem was out of the question as long as he remained in power.

The Gibraltarian governing party's response to the Spanish Prime Minister was to consider in early November the possibility of changing the status of Gibraltar from a colony to a state in free association, like the Cook Islands in their relationship with New Zealand or Puerto Rico with the United States, with complete internal self-government excluding foreign relations and defence. However, the British Government's response was that such an idea was a non-starter, because it contravened Article 10 of the Treaty of Utrecht, although Sir Joshua Hassan's party argued that such an arrangement would not involve a change of sovereignty.[7]

These Gibraltarian reactions to the Spanish Prime Minister clearly indicated the continuing existence of a sizeable gulf in the perceptions of how negotiations should develop. The Foreign Office was not pleased with Sr González's utterances, particularly the pressure which a specific timescale implied, especially given the fact that the British guard had been withdrawn in what was intended as something more than just a symbolic gesture.

The British Government reacted to Prime Minister González's remarks by including reference to the maintenance of Britain's commitment to the people of Gibraltar in the Queen's Speech at the opening of the parliamentary session on 12 November. Although Gibraltar had been mentioned in the speech at the opening of the 1984 session, there had been no such reference in 1985 because of the visit of the King and Queen of Spain. Clearly, Mrs Thatcher was not at all pleased with her Spanish counterpart, especially given the fact that he had recently said that Spain would not recognise the 150-mile exclusion zone for fishing boats off the Falklands/Malvinas.

A further revival of the Malvinas/Gibraltar connection was made by Carlos Mendo at the beginning of December, following a further call by the UN (in a vote of 116 to 4) for the commencement of talks between Britain and Argentina. In fact, he threw in Hong Kong as well, for the point he was anxious to underline in his article 'La trinidad colonial británica' ('The trinity of British colonies') was the British Government's inconsistency in declaring the wishes of the Falklanders and of the Gibraltarians to be 'paramount', while rejecting the wishes of the inhabitants of Hong Kong not to become Chinese. Although the British argued that Hong Kong was different because of the expiry of the lease in 1997, Sr Mendo pointed out that that did not apply to the whole of Hong Kong, parts of which—like Gibraltar—had been handed over 'in perpetuity'.[8]

However, the logic was that geopolitical reality required Britain to react differently in the different circumstances of the three cases. Argentina, it could be argued, had no moral right to demand negotiations (whatever the UN might say), because it had attempted to take the Falklands/Malvinas by force. As far as Gibraltar was concerned, Britain was conscious of external pressures to move towards a solution, was disposed to make concessions to Spain of a practical nature and had agreed to discuss the question of sovereignty, but was clearly in no hurry to do so. With Hong Kong, the New Territories, which were on a 99-year leaseback and therefore had to be relinquished in 1997, constituted 92% of the territory of the colony, and Britain accepted that the remainder would be unviable as a separate entity. Besides, Britain felt that it could not afford *not* to be on good terms with China, and so it was not practicable to make the wishes of the Hong Kong people paramount (even those who held British passports). It was all very well for Sr Mendo to draw parallels, but it has to be remembered that parallels never actually meet.

In preparation for the talks between the two Foreign Ministers scheduled for January 1987, meetings were as usual held beforehand between officials, this time in London on 19 December. The leader of the Spanish delegation, Jesús Ezquerra, reported a sense of frustration over what they saw as British intransigence in refusing to discuss the sovereignty issue, as evidenced by the fact that nearly two years had elapsed since Spain put forward the leaseback or condominium proposals and Britain had yet to reply. There was further frustration at the lack of progress on the proposal for joint use of the airport, and the Gibraltarians themselves provided a timely reminder of their hostility to the idea by passing unanimously a motion in their House of Assembly on 17 December calling for the airport to remain under British and Gibraltarian control.

Further indications that the talks would not alleviate Spain's frustration occurred on 8 January when John Grant, a British Foreign Office spokesman, said in an interview for Spanish radio that 'our commitment to the people of Gibraltar is something which cannot be altered and we are not prepared to make any concession or any change on the question of sovereignty, nor to discuss proposals which may lead to changes in our position on sovereignty'. The Director of the Spanish Office for Diplomatic Information, Inocencio Arias, described the statement as 'unwonted and contradictory' and confirmed that 'Spain will broach the subject of the sovereignty of Gibraltar at all levels at the meeting in London on the 13th and 14th'.[9] The British position seemed to be that Spain was free to *discuss* sovereignty, but it should not expect anything to change as a consequence of such discussion. If that was the case, Spain's sense of frustration could well be understood.

Notes

1 It was not until September 1992 that Spain reciprocated and withdrew their ceremonial guard.

2 *El País*, 15 August 1986, p. 6. Although the writer recognised that one day a solution would also have to be found between Spain and Morocco over the Ceuta and Melilla problem, he also drew a distinction between Gibraltar and the Spanish enclaves, in that the Spanish inhabitants of Ceuta and Melilla would not be able to integrate with their human and geographical environment in the same way as the Gibraltarians could with theirs.

3 *El País*, 21 September 1986, Sunday supplement, pp. 8–9. It was reported that the interview caused a political storm in Gibraltar, and that Sir Joshua denied having said that the Gibraltarians were British out of convenience. See *El País*, 24 September 1986, p. 15; *Gibraltar Chronicle*, 24 September 1986.

4 *El País*, 27 September 1986, p. 16.

5 GIBMED comes under the control of AFSOUTH (Allied Forces Southern Europe) based in Naples, which is part of SACEUR (Supreme Allied Command Europe) near Brussels.

6 *El País*, 11 October 1986, p. 14.

7 Sir James Fawcett QC, former legal adviser to the Foreign Office, believed that free association for Gibraltar would not conflict with the Treaty of Utrecht. See *Gibraltar Chronicle*, 13 December 1987.

8 *Idem*, 1 December 1986, p. 12. In fact, Sr Mendo confused the New Territories with Hong Kong Island and Kowloon, saying that it was the former which were the parts ceded in perpetuity, whereas in fact it was the latter.

9 *Idem*, 9 January 1987, p. 13.

FOURTEEN
THE BATTLE OVER THE AIRPORT
January–December 1987

As if to prepare for the likelihood that the talks in London on 13 and 14 January 1987 at Foreign Minister level would produce little progress, the Spanish press noted that—once again—this was not an auspicious time for negotiations to take place. Elections were likely in Britain during the year, and were also scheduled in Gibraltar itself, and elections and concessions to foreign powers do not make good bedfellows. Britain's position on the sovereignty question was seen to have hardened in the light of the comments of the Foreign Office spokesman, John Grant, together with the fact that no response to Spain's specific proposals had been forthcoming.

The ongoing talks on the reduction of the US military presence in Spain (a reduction to which the USA was opposed) and the discussions on establishing Spain's role in NATO (two of whose military commands were established in Gibraltar) were other factors which clouded the issue. It was assumed in Madrid that no progress could be expected on the Gibraltar question until Spain's position on these matters had been clarified. Whilst that was probably true, it was also over-optimistic. For the fundamental difference between Britain and Spain was one of priorities, and these became quite clear when the talks got under way. The meeting on the afternoon of 14 January was described as tough and tense. There was even disagreement as to the nature of the meeting; the Spanish side saw it as a summit meeting on Gibraltar, whereas Britain viewed it as one of a series of meetings to discuss matters of mutual interest, including Gibraltar. Sr Fernández Ordóñez accused Britain of blocking the negotiating process by not responding to Spain's proposals on sovereignty. Sir Geoffrey Howe's position was that Spain had a lot more work to do in improving Spanish-Gibraltarian relations before the question of sovereignty could be considered.

On the following day, the two Foreign Ministers and their delegations met again, before Sr Fernández Ordóñez and Sir Geoffrey had a meeting with Mrs Thatcher. Sr Fernández Ordóñez argued that as long as the colonial anachronism of Gibraltar continued, the Rock would cast its shadow over bilateral and multilateral relations between Spain and Great Britain. But the British position remained that their priority was to respect the wishes of the Gibraltarians, although they did affirm that they had rejected the idea that Gibraltar might become a state of free association, and that any change in Gibraltar's status (if that should ever occur) would involve its transfer to Spain. That appeared a long way off, however, and satisfaction was expressed in Gibraltar at the outcome of the talks. In Britain it was suggested that one positive sign from the meetings was a determination to find an acceptable compromise on the use of the airport. In Spain they were not at the moment concerned with airports; the talks were described as a failure.

The Times' leader writer on 16 January blamed Madrid for being too impatient, but also ascribed some of the fault to London for allowing Spain to expect too much from the Brussels Declaration, which suffered from the weakness that it would always place the British Government in difficulty whenever the sovereignty issue was raised. However, any hope in London that Madrid's approach might change as a result of this round of talks had to be quickly abandoned. Felipe González, returning from an official visit to Egypt while the talks had been going on in London, said that Spain's line of negotiation on Gibraltar would not change at all.

Like it or not, Spain had to be satisfied with talks on the use of the airport as the next step, and further discussions at the Ezquerra-Radford coordinator level were held in Madrid on 26 March, but there was no announcement afterwards of any progress having been made. While the talks were proceeding, Gibraltar's Government announced a proposal to expand the air terminal at a cost of £2.5 million, as part of a total development package costing £20 million over four years up to 1990.

In January Sir Geoffrey Howe had put his weight behind progress on joint use of the airport—or allowing Spain to use the airport facilities, as he preferred to see it—because there would be mutual economic benefit from such an arrangement. The problem with the airport issue, of course, was that it too could be seen (and was seen by the Gibraltarians and the Spaniards) as a question of sovereignty because of its location on the disputed isthmus. Although they were prepared for Spanish civil airlines to use Gibraltar airport, Gibraltar saw any concession to Spain with regard to the establishment of their own terminal as the thin end of the wedge; Sir Joshua Hassan said as much on a visit to Seville on 6 May. However, progress on a different front was made earlier that month when Spain agreed to eliminate restrictions on the use of air space by British military aircraft over Gibraltar in exchange for Britain lifting its veto on Spanish membership of Eurocontrol, the European air traffic control body.

Meanwhile there was general agreement that Gibraltar's economy was booming. Prior to the opening of the border in February 1985 there were just under 2,000 companies established on the Rock, but by the end of 1986 there were 3,800. Part of the attraction was that, for companies registered in Gibraltar but not trading there, profits were largely exempt from tax. Financial services institutions had grown from four in 1980 to fifteen, including the Spanish banks Bilbao and Central, and many of their clients were resident in Spain. Bank deposits had increased by 68% during 1986.[1] Income tax and taxes on cars and car-parts had been reduced to make them more competitive with Spain. Goods were free from VAT and therefore a shopping visit remained an attractive proposition.

Imports from Spain had increased by 60% over the previous year, and now constituted 15% of total imports. Import duty revenue had increased from £4.4 million in 1984 to nearly £10 million in 1986.

The tourism sector was still booming and now provided nearly a quarter of Gibraltar's income. Since the beginning of 1985 more than five million visitors had arrived, and the rate had reached about 60,000 per week. The number of air passengers from London to Gibraltar in 1986 was 90,000, the highest level since 1968. Of these, 22,000 were heading for the Costa del Sol. Ambitious plans were in the pipeline for the development of Queensway Quay, a hotel, apartment and marina complex on the west side of the peninsula. Talks were held in March 1987 on tourism marketing which would involve the use of facilities on both sides of the border. Such collaborative ventures were essential if the Campo was to avoid feeling that all the advantages of the opening of the border had gone to Gibraltar. Of course there had been economic benefits to the Spanish side, but these were not as visible as they were on the two-and-a-quarter square miles of the Rock because they were not confined to the Campo region but were spread throughout Spain.

The Gibraltar issue affected a new element in Spain's relations with its EC partners on 25 May when Spain refused to sign two agreements during the first meeting of European Community Justice Ministers. The first agreement prevented the same person from being tried and found guilty of the same crime in two EC member states. The second agreement concerned abolishing the legalisation of commercial transactions. Spain's Justice Minister, Fernando Ledesma, said that he could not sign them because of the problem of applying them to Gibraltar.

But it was the issue of Gibraltar airport which took on a much more significant European dimension on 24 June at a meeting of EC Ministers of Transport in Luxembourg, when Spain threatened to refuse to agree to the deregulation of commercial air traffic. Agreement had been reached on the reduction of fare schedules (albeit hedged with an inordinate number of conditions) and the removal of the 50-50 agreement on the distribution of seat capacity between airlines. But there was also a 'market access' proposal to allow regular flights to major regional airports (so-called 'third category airports') from any member country using planes with a maximum seating capacity of 70 passengers. Spain argued that if Gibraltar were included in the agreement it would constitute implicit recognition of the airport as British and therefore recognition of British sovereignty over the isthmus. The issue was to dominate the rest of the year in Anglo-Spanish relations.

The negotiations on the deregulation of civil air traffic in the Community had been going on for almost a year, but it was not until 9 June that Spain decided to pose Gibraltar as an obstacle to its signing the agreement.[2] The question was raised in the form of a letter from the Spanish Transport Minister, Abel Caballero, to the European Commissioner for Transport Stanley Clinton-Davis, asking whether Gibraltar airport was included on the list of regional airports to benefit from deregulation. The letter was not formally answered; instead bilateral discussions between Sr Caballero and his British counterpart Paul Channon took place on 24 June. Spain hoped to persuade Britain to agree to exclude Gibraltar airport from the agreement, which had to be accepted by all member states. However, Britain (who had included Gibraltar in a list of airports submitted to the Commission in 1984) was unwilling to change its position.

Further negotiations on 25 June proved fruitless when a compromise, formulated by Spain but proposed by the Commission, failed to find acceptance. The Commission proposed that the directive be adopted, excluding its application to Gibraltar, while Spain and Britain would meet subsequently to find a solution to the Gibraltar airport issue, which they would then put to the Commission. Mr Channon said Britain would agree on condition that an agreement be reached within three months in order (so he said) not to delay work on the airport on which it wished to embark. But the Spanish delegation declined to accept this condition because they feared that an agreement would not be reached within such a timescale. Gibraltar airport would then be included in the directive and Britain would thereby establish through an EC directive what it had so far failed to establish in two years of bilateral talks. It was suggested (though not confirmed) that the British and Spanish Prime Ministers had communicated by telephone on the subject, but without altering their respective positions.

The Belgian President of the Council of Transport Ministers, Hermann de Croo, decided to reconvene the meeting on 30 June (to coincide with the meeting of Heads of Government in Brussels), in the hope that a compromise might be worked out in the interim. If this was not forthcoming, it was argued that the whole agreement (including reductions in fares) would be set back for months, possibly years, because under the Single European Act (due to come into force on 1 July) there would have to be a report from the European Parliament and the Economic and Social Committee which would take some time to produce. Britain no doubt hoped that Spain (who stood to gain from deregulation more than most other EC countries) would not be able to withstand the pressure which the remaining ten Community members would exert in order to produce an agreement on 30 June. If neither side gave way, they would have to hope that the other would be blamed for the failure.

Possible areas of compromise were explored during the weekend of 27 and 28 June, when Jesús Ezquerra (Head of Western Europe policy at the Spanish Ministry of Foreign Affairs) and David Hannay (permanent British representative to the EC) were seen separately by an official of the Belgian Foreign Affairs Ministry, Philippe de Schouthette. Spain requested (so Britain claimed) that these meetings be indirect (i.e. conducted through an intermediary) rather than bilateral, in the hope that such a formula would be more successful. It did not prove to be the case. On 29 June Belgium suggested a 12-month postponement before the agreement would apply to Gibraltar airport, but Spain rejected any time limit, while Britain said the time limit was too long and the implementation of the agreement would not thereafter be automatic. A face-to-face meeting between Ezquerra and Hannay only confirmed the distance between the two sides.[3]

It came as no surprise, therefore, that at the reconvened meeting of European Transport Ministers on 30 June in Luxembourg, no agreement was reached and deregulation was not adopted. Spain rejected the final proposal put forward by France—a verbal commitment by the ten other member states not to use Gibraltar while Britain and Spain resolved their differences—because it had no legal validity, although Spain's Transport Minister saw this move as a sign of support for his country's position. Britain saw Spain's position as inconsistent with having accepted the statute on Gibraltar when signing the Accession Treaty, and did not see that Spain's claim to Gibraltar or the bilateral talks were in any way threatened by their acceptance of the air transport directive.

The meeting broke up in the small hours of the morning of 1 July, by which time the Single European Act had come into force. Since one of the consequences of that was that certain proposals no longer needed unanimous agreement, Spain felt obliged to threaten to use a power of veto, still available to member states when they consider that vital national interests are at stake, called the 'Luxembourg compromise'.[4] This, Spain hoped, would be enough to deter the Commission from an early return to the proposal, although the Commissioner responsible for competition policy, Peter Sutherland, soon made it clear that they were unlikely to be deterred for long.

Meanwhile, in Brussels Mrs Thatcher, fresh from her third election victory three weeks earlier, had been undertaking her usual lone battle against the other member states, this time over the proposals for economic and social union in the so-called Delors Plan.

Spain was able to use the British Prime Minister's stubbornness there to gain some sympathy for the difficulties which Spain had to face on the airport issue, as well as to minimise the impact of the failure to reach an agreement on it.

The Times' leader writer on 2 July took a much more cynical view of the whole process. He accused Spain of thinking up the Gibraltar issue as a last minute wheeze to protect Iberia from competition, with the other governments feeling privately grateful that Spain had thought of a good way of scuppering the agreement so that they too could protect their national airlines. Whilst the extent of progress achieved since then goes some way to support this thesis, the fact is that in view of the stalemate in the bilateral talks on the joint use of Gibraltar airport because of what it might imply regarding sovereignty, Spain was hardly likely to agree to a European measure which had similar—if not greater—implications. It was inevitable that sooner or later the Gibraltar question would become a European issue, but the fact that in this instance it prevented the acceptance of a European directive which would have resulted in greater market freedom—the main *raison d'être* of the Community in Mrs Thatcher's view—will not have advanced Spain's cause on the Gibraltar issue in the eyes of the British Government.[5]

The whole incident left Anglo-Spanish relations—at least at governmental level—at a low ebb. Felipe González was as much irritated by the Luxembourg fracas as he was by Mrs Thatcher's intransigence in Brussels when he criticised Britain in a Spanish TV interview a week after the summit for 'believing least in European unity', and for being interested only in a free market by 1992, rather than a Europe 'of solidarity concerned with citizens' needs as a whole'. He added: 'I will oppose all steps to advance the internal market which are not accompanied directly by measures for solidarity'.[6] Given the tenor of such remarks, it was scarcely surprising that neither leader had visited the other during the five years they had both been in power. Even with interpreters, they were unlikely to understand each other's language.

Things went from bad to worse after an interview which Sir Geoffrey Howe gave to *El País*, published on 31 July. His insistence that Britain was obliged to respect the wishes of the Gibraltarians will have come as no surprise to Spain. His reiteration of the British position on the deregulation of air traffic was equally predictable, as was his conviction that moves on sovereignty will take a long time. But the Spanish Government will have been disturbed by the implication that Spain should not expect much in answer to the alternatives on sovereignty which it proposed in February 1985, because they do not make any provision for the Gibraltarians to have a say on the decisions affecting their future. Nor will they have liked the statement that the isthmus had been under exclusive British jurisdiction since at least 1838, and that Britain had no doubts about the legitimacy of its title.[7]

The response from the Spanish Foreign Ministry to these remarks was swift. The following day, 1 August, Francisco Fernández Ordóñez stated that Spain did not recognise Britain's 'occupation' of the isthmus. He went on to say that the issue was not just a legal one but a political problem relating to the decolonisation of the whole area, including the isthmus and the Rock. He reiterated Spain's position on the airport issue, claiming that Spain was prepared to accept the whole package as long as Gibraltar was excluded from the agreement, whereas Britain was prepared to scupper the whole proposal for the sake of including Gibraltar. Clearly, the airport issue had soured the negotiating climate considerably.

In his response Sr Fernández Ordóñez also took up the point that Sir Geoffrey had made about the paramountcy of the wishes of the Gibraltarians, saying that Spain was willing for them to keep their British nationality, their economic and taxation system, their cultural and linguistic identity and local self-government. Here was a clear attempt by the Spanish Government to make plain that their interest was in the territory and not the people. The irony was that Britain could probably have accepted all that, if only the Gibraltarians themselves were prepared to do so, too. An opinion poll published in Gibraltar on 4 August showed how unlikely that was. It indicated that Joe Bossano's GSLP, which had opposed the Brussels Declaration, had gained 7% since the elections of 1984 and was now in the lead—the first time in ten years of opinion polls that Sir Joshua Hassan's AACR was not ahead.

The 283rd anniversary of Admiral Rooke's occupation of Gibraltar occurred on 4 August, prompting another article in *El País* by Carlos Mendo entitled (in English) 'Rule Britannia'. He argued that Spain should have made its entry into NATO dependent upon a solution to the decolonisation of Gibraltar. He also picked up the parallel of Hong Kong once more, rejecting the distinction drawn by Sir Geoffrey Howe that Hong Kong was not viable without the New Territories by pointing out that, thanks to 'Spanish generosity or ingenuousness', Gibraltar is only viable with the isthmus and the open border. He quoted Lord Carrington as having said that 'the problem for Spain is that Gibraltar is in Europe (. . .) the issue would be settled, just like Rhodesia and Hong Kong, if the Spaniards were black or Chinese'.[8] Sir Joshua Hassan had claimed in his September 1986 interview that Gibraltar's problem was not historical but geographical because of its size, to which Lord Carrington had added the problem of its location.

Gibraltar became an issue at the European level for the third time in the year in mid-September, though in a very different way from the first two occasions. This time it involved a question of protocol during a visit by Sir Joshua Hassan and other leading Gibraltarians on 16 September to the European Parliament in Strasbourg at the invitation of Lord Bethell, a British Conservative MEP and Chairman of the Gibraltar in Europe Representation Group. The objective of the visit, to which Spanish representatives objected but which they could not prevent, was to provide the Gibraltarians with the opportunity to lobby MEPs on their right to determine their own future. Fernando Morán, former Foreign Minister and now a Euro-MP, expressed the concern of Spanish MEPs that Sir Joshua's visit should not be seen as official in any way, and in particular that he should not be received by the President of the Parliament, Lord Plumb.

When Lord Plumb switched a meeting with Sir Joshua and other Gibraltarians, including Joe Bossano, at the last minute from his parliamentary office to the residence of the British Ambassador to the Council of Europe, Sir Joshua went to the meeting only to stay long enough to say to Lord Plumb: 'I am very sorry you have submitted to Spanish pressure in this way. Thank you very much. Goodbye'. Lord Bethell, Sir Joshua and Mr Bossano gave a press conference the following morning, in which they denounced 'the dreadful manipulation by the Spaniards'.[9] Lord Plumb later explained to the press that he had not wanted to put the interests of the Parliament at risk, nor harm the European Democrats Group (the Euro-Parliament group which consisted mainly of British Conservatives and Spanish members of Alianza Popular and whose views on the subject of Gibraltar were, therefore, far from unanimous). He also argued that there was more room at the Ambassador's residence for such a large delegation. It is highly unlikely that the Gibraltarians will have found Lord Plumb's last explanation very convincing.

Meanwhile, bilateral negotiations on the airport, which should have taken place at the end of June, finally got under way again in London on 8 September. At the meeting Spain put forward a number of technical proposals, but there was otherwise no sign of progress. Pressure from the EC to work towards some agreement on the airport, so that the directive on the deregulation of air traffic could be implemented, resulted in an additional meeting being held on 5 October. The Spanish delegation was now headed by Fermín Zelada, who had replaced Jesús Ezquerra as Head of Western Europe policy at the Ministry of Foreign Affairs. The meeting was continued on the following day, but neither side showed any sign of willingness to shift its position.

The two sides agreed to meet again in London on 29 and 30 October. The six areas on which the discussions had centred involved access by Spaniards to the airport without having to go through border controls (which Britain and Gibraltar opposed); the building of another terminal (from which arriving passengers, whatever their point of departure, would directly enter Spain and which Britain accepted); Spanish involvement in the control of Gibraltarian airspace and the presence of Spanish air-traffic controllers in the control tower (both of which Britain rejected on miltary grounds, since the airport was still strictly an RAF base); the use by Iberia of airport facilities and their involvement in the running of the airport (which Britain was prepared to concede). But true to expectations, neither side announced any progress.

The chances of any agreement being reached before the next meeting at Foreign Minister level on 30 November were looking more and more remote. David Radford, the Under-Secretary at the Foreign Office heading the British delegation on the airport negotiations, went to Gibraltar on 10 November in an attempt to sound out local opinions on new proposals. But even before he went, Gibraltarian opinion was hardening. At the AGM of the Gibraltar Trades Council, a resolution was passed vigorously opposing any agreement on the airport which might adversely affect any aspect of

Gibraltarian sovereignty or any trade unionist. Other representative groups issued similar statements of opposition.

On 11 November 12,000 Gibraltarians, led by Sir Joshua Hassan and Joe Bossano, marched through the streets in what was one of the largest demonstrations ever held in the colony. Banners proclaimed 'British sovereignty is not negotiable' and 'The airport is ours, not Spain's', although ironically much of the shouting was done in Spanish. A 15,000-signature petition was presented to Mr Radford, calling on the British Government not to make any concessions to Spain over the airport. The following day Joe Bossano announced a motion to be debated by the Gibraltarian House of Assembly on 17 November endorsing the 'no concessions' demonstration.

Despite this show of opposition, Mr Radford went ahead and put the British Government's new proposals to the colony's political leaders. They involved the offer of the use of airport facilities to Spain in exchange for the lifting of Spain's veto on the deregulation of European air transport. It was argued that the facilities would not affect the question of sovereignty because they would only be take-off and landing facilities for air traffic generated by Spain for Spain.

When the Spanish and British negotiating teams had yet another pre-summit meeting on 16 November in Madrid, it was reported that some slight progress had been made, although no details were given. Sir Geoffrey Howe issued a statement in London indicating his desire to see an agreement reached, but once again Gibraltarian opposition was swift and unanimous. On 17 November the House of Assembly unanimously passed a motion calling on the British Government not to reach any agreement with Spain which would give them joint control of the airport. The Trades Council, representing 80% of the Gibraltarian workforce, announced their intention to block the implementation of any agreement. The response from the Spanish authorities was to tighten border controls, which caused long delays at the frontier.

Sir Geoffrey's statement was echoed a few days later on 20 November by Prime Minister González, who called for an extra effort to reach an agreement. With the imminence of the annual bilateral meeting of Foreign Ministers, which was due to be followed by a meeting of EC Transport Ministers a week later, a new round of talks at coordinator level was held in London on 23 November to try to establish some area of agreement.

On 26 November Sir Joshua Hassan travelled to London to discuss Britain's negotiating position with Sir Geoffrey Howe before going on to Madrid as part of the British delegation. On arrival in Madrid Sir Joshua made it quite clear that while flights from Spain to Gibraltar would be welcomed, he was totally opposed to any Spanish involvement in the control of the airport and any symbolic agreement which might appear to advance Spain's position regarding sovereignty over the isthmus.

The prospects that an agreement might be reached were in the balance as other negotiators gathered in Madrid for the meetings on 27 and 28 November. Accusations by Spanish Government officials that Britain appeared to make important concessions, but in reality only made proposals which were not acceptable to Spain, did not augur well. But in London it was felt that Britain's offer would be enough to persuade Spain to accept. In detail Britain was prepared to treat Spanish passengers flying to a Spanish airport (but not those with other destinations) as transit passengers, who would not therefore have to go through British passport and customs control. Britain was also prepared to allow the construction of an air terminal on the Spanish side of the airport for Spanish use, and the presence of a Spanish air-traffic controller provided that he was acting only as a link with Seville, on account of the military functions of Gibraltar airport.

For Britain the only danger was, as *The Times* put it on 26 November, that Gibraltarian demonstrations against such an agreement 'might awaken post-colonial sentries in the dustier corridors of Westminster'. But the real question was whether Spain would be prepared to accept the concessions which would allow it to use the airport facilities but not to exercise any control over them.

On his arrival in Madrid Sir Geoffrey Howe had a brief meeting with King Juan Carlos and Prime Minister González before getting down to talks with his Spanish counterpart in the afternoon and evening of 27 November. The four hours of talks were frequently interrupted while consultations were held with Downing Street and the Moncloa Palace. But a further six hours of talks the following day with the full delegations involved still proved insufficient for any agreement to be reached. The Gordian knot, it appeared, was whether Britain was willing to accept Spain's demand for a clause stating that the inclusion of Gibraltar airport in the deregulation of

European air-traffic did not indicate a recognition of Britain's sovereignty over the isthmus, nor in any way prejudice Spain's sovereignty claims. With the pressure still on to try and reach an agreement before the EC Transport Ministers' meeting on 7 December, the two sides decided to have further discussions in London on 2 December, the eleventh occasion since June that talks on the airport had been held.

With the threat of opprobrium by the rest of the EC hovering over the meeting, agreement was finally reached at 9.30 pm, after a further nine hours of hard bargaining between the negotiating teams, which included the respective Transport Ministers. The joint statement issued in the small hours of 3 December provided the details of the agreement, the main points of which were:

- Spain would decide which airlines would operate Spanish air services between Spain and Gibraltar;
- a new terminal would be built on the Spanish side of the airport, with direct access to and from Spain;
- the new terminal would be used for the arrival by air of any passengers of any nationality not intending to enter Gibraltar, or for passengers intending to depart from Spain to another country; passengers would be subject to customs and passport control in the appropriate terminal;
- a Committee would be set up under the supervision of the civil aviation working group to coordinate activities in the two civil transport terminals and their relationship with other airport services;
- there would be close collaboration on security measures;
- there would be continuing discussions on strengthening air safety and air traffic control in the region.

The declaration included a statement that the agreement was without prejudice to the respective legal positions of Spain and Britain in their dispute regarding sovereignty over the territory where the airport is situated. This was heralded by Spain as the first time since 1966 that Britain had conceded that Spain disputed British sovereignty over the isthmus.

As an indication that the bilateral talks did extend to matters other than the airport, in an annexe to the declaration there were also agreements to re-establish the ferry service between Algeciras and Gibraltar as soon as possible and to improve the flow of traffic through customs.

Predictable satisfaction was expressed by the European Commissioners for Transport and for Competition Policy on the agreement. Spain got its 'without prejudice' statement regarding the directive on the deregulation of air-traffic, and both sides would jointly inform the Commission that Gibraltar airport would be excluded from the directive until such time as the agreement was ready to be implemented.

Both the local governments in the Campo de Gibraltar and the Government in Madrid expressed satisfaction with the outcome. Spain had successfully prevented what would have been (as it saw things) the international legitimisation of a situation in which the sovereignty of the territory was in dispute. And although it would be some time before the agreement could be fully put into effect, Sr Fernández Ordóñez claimed that this was the first concrete and tangible step that Spain had taken in its sovereignty claim since the Rock had been occupied 283 years earlier. It was certainly the first tangible gain for Spain arising from the Brussels Declaration made three years before.

The British Government also seemed reasonably satisfied with the deal. Mrs Thatcher congratulated her Foreign Secretary during Prime Minister's Question Time on 3 December because the agreement, which she claimed would bring great benefits for the whole of Europe, was reached 'without any derogation from the sovereignty of Gibraltar, and gives the Gibraltarians the possibility of joining that agreement if they wish to do so'.[10] Sir Geoffrey Howe tried to sell the package to Gibraltar by reminding them of the economic advantages wider use of the airport would bring.

However, Gibraltarian leaders did not see it that way. The exclusion of Gibraltar airport from the deregulation package, together with the fact that once the Spanish terminal was built there would be an increase in the number of passengers entering Spain rather than Gibraltar, meant that there was very little in the agreement which was of advantage to Gibraltar. Since the agreement was also seen as the thin end of the wedge as far as Spanish encroachment was concerned, it was not surprising that the initial reaction from Gibraltar was less enthusiastic, although Sir Joshua

Hassan admitted that the agreement was the best that could be obtained, and both he and Joe Bossano welcomed the fact that Britain had given Gibraltarians the right to approve the necessary legislation to implement it. They interpreted this as a power of veto, although this interpretation was explicitly rejected by Spain and no doubt implicitly so by Britain. But there was no denying the fact that if they chose to do so, the Gibraltarians could delay the effect of the deregulation directive on their airport for some time.

Clearly, the saga of Gibraltar airport was far from over, but at least the agreement reached marked the end of the beginning. Both sides had carefully reserved their positions as far as sovereignty over the Rock was concerned, so no progress could be claimed in that direction.[11] However, the principal gain was not so much the specific outcome relating to the use of the airport or the knock-on effect it would have on air-traffic deregulation. Rather it was the fact that progress had been made within a European Community context. It had only happened because there was pressure for it to happen from the EC; the first step had taken 283 years because hitherto there had been no framework (*pace* the UN) outside the bilateral one to make it happen. It was that fact which should have given encouragement to both sides for progress in the long term. In the short term, there remained the problem of persuading the Gibraltarians themselves to accept the airport agreement.

Notes

1 An interesting historical footnote is that one of the first companies to make Gibraltar its international headquarters was Barlow Clowes. *The Times* reported on 26 March 1987 that 'Gibraltar has no intention of allowing its new-found status to become soiled by scandal and is keeping a close watch on its regulations to see whether there is scope for tightening its grip'. On 7 June 1988 joint liquidators were appointed to wind up Barlow Clowes International based in Gibraltar, and Peter Clowes was convicted on a number of charges of theft, conspiracy to steal and false accounting on 10 February 1992. This undoubtedly became a setback for the image of Gibraltar as an attractive international financial centre that the administration was trying to create.

2 Sr Fernández Ordóñez denied that the question of Gibraltar airport had only been raised on 9 June. He claimed that it had been discussed a year earlier with Sir Geoffrey Howe, but that Spain had not wished to make it public in order not to hinder the talks. See *El País*, 28 June 1987, p. 16.

3 In Gibraltar the leader of the opposition, Joe Bossano, tabled a motion to be debated in the House of Assembly in which Spain was accused of 'an attempt to deprive Gibraltar and its people of their rights as part of the European Community'. See *El País*, 30 June 1987, p. 17.

4 So called because it was first used in Luxembourg by France in 1966.

5 The Spanish Foreign Minister, Sr Fernández Ordóñez, began a two-day visit to Morocco on 4 July. It was felt in Spanish diplomatic circles that one advantage of the state of negotiations over Gibraltar was that Morocco would be unlikely to press for progress on its claims on Ceuta and Melilla.

6 *The Times*, 13 July 1987.

7 It was such a statement, first made by Britain in 1966, that led to the closure of the border by Franco.

8 *El País*, 4 August 1987, p. 7.

9 *The Times*, 18 September 1987. *El País*, reporting the same incident the same day (p. 13), quoted Sir Joshua as having said to Lord Plumb: 'I have no wish to be humiliated (. . .) you have insulted all Gibraltarians'.

10 *Hansard*, Vol. 123, No. 57, Col. 1102.

11 The editorial in *El País* on 10 December 1987, p. 12, tried to do so, however, by claiming that 'the logic of the agreement is to put into question the principle of British sovereignty over the Rock'.

FIFTEEN
GIBRALTARIANS VOTE TO RESIST
December 1987–March 1988

No sooner was the airport agreement reached than Sir Joshua Hassan dropped a political bombshell on the inhabitants of the Rock by announcing on 9 December 1987 that he would stand down as Chief Minister with immediate effect, and that he would not stand for re-election at the House of Assembly elections scheduled for February.

Sir Joshua had been leader of the Association for the Advancement of Civil Rights (AACR) party since 1947 and a member of the Gibraltarian legislature since 1950. He became Gibraltar's first Chief Minister following legislative changes in 1964, and apart from the years 1969–72 (when Robert Peliza, leader of the Integration with Britain Party held the post), he had acted in that capacity ever since. He had become almost a permanent fixture of Gibraltarian politics, but now at the age of 72 he had decided, in the catch-phrase of the late 1980s in British politics, to spend more time with his family.

Given the timing of his announcement, it was natural to assume that there was some connection between his decision and the outcome of the airport negotiations. However, Sir Joshua stressed that the decision had been taken some months before, and that he had waited until the airport negotiations had been concluded before making his decision public, although he conceded that if an agreement had not been reached he would have stayed on until it was. In a resignation statement, he called upon Gibraltarians to decide on the airport agreement with their heads and not with their hearts.

His successor as Chief Minister was Adolfo Canepa, aged 46 and former Deputy to Sir Joshua. A supporter of free association as the ultimate constitutional solution for Gibraltar, he was more hard-line than his predecessor towards Spain, although less so than the leader of the opposition, Joe Bossano, who saw the airport agreement as an unprecedented concession. Mr Canepa's first public pronouncement following Sir Joshua's announcement, to the effect that Gibraltar will not be Spanish even in 100 years' time, will not have won him many friends in Spain.

The new scenario brought about by Sir Joshua's resignation also produced a new political entity, the Independent Democratic Party, whose formation was announced on 10 December, and which was to be led by a close adviser to Sir Joshua, Joe Pitaluga. His intention was to stop a socialist election victory which he saw as likely in the vacuum caused by Sir Joshua's retirement, especially as three other ministers were expected to retire with him.

All the predictions, however, were that in view of the uncertain stance of the centre-right on the airport agreement, Joe Bossano was likely to win the elections. *El País* clearly thought so; on 21 December, ten days after the resignation of Sir Joshua Hassan, the Spanish paper chose to interview the leader of the opposition rather than the new Chief Minister Canepa.

Joe Bossano was evidently more unhappy about the airport agreement than had previously been reported in Spain or Britain. As a member of the EC since Britain joined in 1973, Gibraltar and its airport should, he argued, have been treated in the same way as any other EC airport included in the agreement. Instead, Gibraltar has been excluded, and when it is included it will be Spain who will decide which airlines can fly there, whereas if Spain wants to fly to any other British airport it has to ask Britain. He did not accept that there had been any real agreement on the airport, because the Gibraltarians had not accepted it all along. He did not envisage any particular relationship with Spain in the future, but simply a normal relationship between two neighbouring states within the European Community. In the forthcoming elections, he promised that if he won he would dissociate Gibraltar from the Brussels Declaration. This later prompted Lord Bethell, an MEP who headed the group which represented Gibraltar's interests in Europe, to suggest that under Bossano Gibraltar might try to become an independent state under the British crown, like Australia or Canada.

Whatever they thought of Mr Canepa, therefore, the Spanish Foreign Office must have wondered what they could do to assist him in preventing Joe Bossano from coming to office. The Foreign Minister, Sr Fernández Ordóñez, took the unprecedented step on 9 January 1988 of going to Algeciras to meet all the mayors of the Campo de Gibraltar region with a view to appointing a regional coordinator with the people of the Rock. The British Foreign Office saw this as a positive step, and Lynda Chalker, Minister of State, congratulated Sr Fernández Ordóñez on his visit when she was in Spain some ten days later.

Gibraltar and NATO came back on the agenda at this time when Spain informed the NATO Secretary General, Lord Carrington, of its decision regarding its contribution to NATO's military and operational activities. The letter which Spain's Ambassador to NATO, Jaime de Ojeda, handed to Lord Carrington on 18 January made clear that Spain would not participate in manoeuvres or operations which were under the command or control of military authorities in Gibraltar. Spain's objective was to highlight to its NATO allies the problem which would arise, as long as the Gibraltar issue remained unresolved, if, as Spain proposed, one of Spain's six contributions to NATO included a permanent naval presence under Spanish operational control stationed in and around the Straits.

The long-standing issue of pensions payable to the 6,000 retired Spaniards who worked in Gibraltar arose once again in the Gibraltarian House of Assembly on 22 January. The reason it came up again was because the original agreement between London and Gibraltar—that the UK Government would pay £16.5 million and the Gibraltarians would pay £4.5 million over three years—was due to expire at the end of 1988,[1] and the Gibraltarians felt that since they had actually paid out the equivalent of all of the pensioners' contributions plus interest, Britain and Spain should now work out a solution between them. The Chief Minister, however, felt that there was a moral obligation to continue to pay the pensions of those 500 Spaniards who had worked in Gibraltar but retired before 1969, at an annual cost of about £1 million. Joe Bossano did not agree that there was any such moral obligation. Here was yet more evidence that the Leader of the Opposition in Gibraltar took an even more uncompromising line towards Spain than the Chief Minister.

Cooperation with Spain was taking place, however, on a more mundane level. It was announced towards the end of January that the Gibraltarian authorities had reached agreement on the disposal of solid waste in a sewage plant on the Campo de Gibraltar side of the border; previously, solid waste had been dumped in the sea, to the annoyance of Spaniards in the region who complained at the effects on the environment and on public health. A consequence of the agreement made in Brussels in 1984, the plant was a further indication that on practical matters progress was possible.

In mid-February the date of the forthcoming elections in Gibraltar was set for 24 March, some weeks later than had been expected. Electioneering immediately gathered pace. On 1 February Joe Bossano had shaken the banking community by announcing that as part of his economic strategy he would set up a commercial bank with capital of £5 million, with half the amount raised by the Government and half from the private sector. While Bossano was tackling the banks, Adolfo Canepa was trying to take on the unions by threatening to introduce restrictive legislation if he were re-elected, as a response to the 25 strikes which Gibraltar had had over the previous two years. It quickly became clear that the main issues of the election would be the unions, the shipyard, housing and, above all, Gibraltar's relationship with Spain.

As far as the last-mentioned was concerned, the most immediate context in which it had arisen concerned the airport. The airport issue reappeared at the end of February when Adolfo Canepa and Joe Bossano both had to go to Basle, where they took the opportunity to visit the airport, as it had been cited as offering the kind of arrangement that was being proposed for Gibraltar.[2] On their return, there was unaccustomed coincidence in their view that the principal difference between the two cases was that in Basle there was no dispute over the sovereignty of the territory on which the airport had been constructed, whereas this was clearly not the case with Gibraltar. They both therefore indicated that Spanish acceptance of British sovereignty over the isthmus was essential before the Gibraltar House of Assembly would approve the agreement reached in December 1987 between London and Madrid. To all intents and purposes, that meant an indefinite postponement of the airport agreement.

On 6 March 1988 a good deal of unwanted publicity hit Gibraltar for reasons which were only indirectly connected with the dispute between Britain and Spain. Having entered Gibraltar from Spain, three unarmed IRA terrorists who were suspected of aiming to plant a car-bomb were shot by British troops and members of the British anti-terrorist squad.

There was hostile reaction in Spain to the action taken by the British security forces: the leading article in *El País* on 8 March described it as 'a grave violation not only of the moral codes of any civilised society but also of the legal basis which sustains them'. It condemned the principle apparently being applied that 'the only good terrorist is a dead one'. On the grounds that this incident took place 'on Spanish territory', the writer was drawn to make comparisons between the activity of ETA and the IRA, as well as with the British and Spanish Governments' methods of dealing with terrorism. He concluded than the two situations were in themselves very different, and also that the British militarisation of the problem meant that it had been made much more intractable that the problem in the Basque country.

The tone of moral superiority, together with the reference to 'Spanish territory', will not have pleased the British Foreign Office. However, the official Spanish Government position was stated by the Foreign Minister to the Congress on 16 March. He was speaking in reply to a representative from the Basque Community, who asked whether the Government was intending to make any formal diplomatic protest 'at the summary execution of three unarmed members of the IRA in territory which Spain claims as its own'. Sr Fernández Ordóñez neatly sidestepped the territorial aspect by answering that as the shootings occurred 'on territory whose jurisdiction is exercised by the United Kingdom', he had no intention of issuing a protest.

Sr Fernández Ordóñez's suggestion that what happened in Gibraltar had nothing to do with Spain was rejected in *El País* in a further leading article on 23 March, which claimed that since the Spanish authorities had not detained and extradited the three terrorists but allowed them to proceed to Gibraltar 'Spanish intervention in the incident was decisive'. Gibraltar's Chief Minister clearly agreed; he took the opportunity to thank the Spanish security forces for their role in ensuring that the terrorists did not carry out their planned operation.

It could well be that the Spanish Government, anxious not to jeopardise progress on the talks on Gibraltar, decided to collaborate with the British Government in helping them to track the IRA terrorists' movements. In any event, it is unlikely that the Spanish security forces would have known how the British forces intended to handle the situation once the terrorists reached Gibraltar; nor could they have made their collaboration contingent upon a 'no-shoot-to-kill' policy. The Spanish Government therefore played its hand well; it supported the British authorities and disclaimed any responsibility for what ultimately happened.

The political fall-out from the shootings was difficult to establish. The event does not appear to have had any effect on the ongoing bilateral talks on the implementation of the Brussels Declaration, because the British Government would have been quite satisfied with the cooperation it received from Spain.[3] As far as the Gibraltar elections are concerned, the polls were already indicating that the GSLP was likely to win in three weeks' time. However, one Gibraltarian journalist believed that the incident did have an effect on the people of the Rock because 'it broke the warmth and closeness that had existed between the military personnel of the colonising power and the people of the colony itself. After 1988, the MoD had to make new arrangements. Officers' quarters could no longer be in the town, and the troops could no longer go to the local pubs. Army and civilians became oil and water'.[4]

As the Gibraltar election drew closer and the two main parties published their manifestos, the differences between them on the central issue of sovereignty became more apparent. The position of Canepa's AACR party was that they were fully committed to turning Gibraltar into a state in free association with Britain, and would continue to support the Brussels Declaration on the understanding that Gibraltar would have the last word on any agreement affecting sovereignty. On the airport issue the AACR said it wanted to study the agreement further before making a decision on it.

By contrast, Bossano's GSLP called for self-determination; they stated that they were firmly opposed to their future and the sovereignty of their land being subject to negotiation between Britain and Spain, and they would resist the absorption of Gibraltar by Spain. They would withdraw from participation in the negotiations on the Brussels Declaration, although they would cooperate with their Spanish neighbours in the Campo. They were firmly opposed to accepting the agreement on the airport.

Three days before election day a poll gave Bossano's party 63%

of the vote. Not surprisingly, it was unofficially reported that the Spanish Government was seriously worried about the possible victory of the GSLP. In any event, they expected that as a consequence of the election campaign the agreement on the airport, as well as other projects involving local cooperation, would remain blocked for some time. All of the parties participating in the election had rejected the proposal made by the Spanish Foreign Minister during a visit to the Campo in January to offer grants and welfare benefits to inhabitants of the Rock. 'Offer them to people in La Línea; that's where they're needed', Joe Bossano is reported to have said.

On the day of the poll, 24 March, *El País* published an article by former Foreign Affairs Minister Fernando Morán. He stressed the importance of the elections for Spain as well as for Gibraltarians, noting that the main difference between the last elections in January 1984 and the present ones was that the question of relations with Spain was not previously so high on the agenda because the Brussels Declaration had yet to be signed. In particular, he observed that the platform of Joe Bossano, who had made great strides in 1984 on the strength of union concerns over the future of the shipyards, had changed from being 'social-populist' then to 'Gibraltar-populist' now. What made him different from the other leading politicians was that he rejected their 'British-isation' of Gibraltar—the endorsement of things British—but offered instead a psychological 'Gibraltar-isation'—the emancipation of Gibraltar from Britain. Sr Morán argued that whilst this was understandable, it was short-sighted and against the interests of the Gibraltarians themselves. 'History had created a disagreement for which there was only one solution', he wrote. His one solution was clearly that Gibraltar would become part of Spain. Neither Joe Bossano, nor the majority of Gibraltarians, was ready to accept that argument.

The outcome of the election was clear. On a turnout of 76% Joe Bossano's GSLP put an end to 40 years of Conservative domination in Gibraltar by winning the maximum possible eight of the 15 seats and 58% of the popular vote. Perhaps more significantly, Joe Bossano's personal vote of 8,128 was more than 4,000 votes higher than that of Adolfo Canepa, the leader of the AACR, which won the other seven seats. The candidates for Joe Pitaluga's Independent Democratic Party all came at the foot of the poll.

Although some observers saw Bossano's victory as a consequence of the absence of Sir Joshua Hassan and the comparatively weak opposition offered in personality terms by Canepa and Pitaluga, there was no doubt that the strength of the vote for the GSLP candidates, all of whom outpolled the opposition, was a reflection of the popularity, as well as the clarity, of the stance Bossano had taken on relations with Spain. Few people interpreted the outcome as a swing by the voters of Gibraltar from right to left, although some felt that the attraction of Joe Bossano was his blend of Gibraltarian identity and socialism.[5]

The leading article in *El País* on 26 March recognised the forces at work in Gibraltar which had led to Joe Bossano's election as Chief Minister. But the writer reminded him that he was in no position to reject the Brussels Declaration or the airport agreement, not only because it was not in the Gibraltarians' interests to do so, but also because Britain would if necessary remind Gibraltar of its colonial status. The writer welcomed Mr Bossano's more constructive awareness of the need to develop good working relations with his Spanish neighbours in the Campo region, concluding that 'Spain should talk to London about decolonisation and to Bossano about friendship and economic development'. The EC context was, however, once again seen as the way in which a solution to the problem would be found. The inexorable move towards political union in Europe 'would make abolition of the colony a simple administrative act appropriate to civilised nations', and, by implication, Gibraltar would become part of Spain.

Wisely, the writer did not mention a timescale. For even supposing that the future of Gibraltar might one day be determined at a European level, the inhabitants of the Rock still had to be persuaded that being part of Spain was a good idea, and by electing Joe Bossano as Chief Minister they had just indicated the exact opposite. He summed up his policy towards Spain by asserting that 'the Gibraltarian people do not want to integrate with Spain, but they do not feel any hostility towards Spain'.[6] Hence his willingness to assist in the development of the economy of La Línea and the Campo region.

But more significant was his strategy to exploit the impotence of Britain and Spain in implementing agreements reached over Gibraltar because of the Gibraltarians' intransigence, which led a *Sunday Times* reporter to remark prophetically on 27 March that 'unless

Spain and Britain make extravagant assurances to Bossano, any further talks on the territory's future are likely to stagnate over the next four years'. For the British Government, the Gibraltarians' attitude provided a ready justification for the slow pace of negotiations. But there were frustrations, too, as with the airport agreement, where the Gibraltarians' inflexibility threatened to impede the one aspect of European Community activity which Mrs Thatcher's Government unreservedly supported, namely the liberalisation of markets.

The Spanish Government—and the Spanish media—were steadfastly opposed to the notion that the Gibraltarians had any right to interfere with the negotiating process, although they accepted their influence upon it and the need to win their hearts and minds. But Joe Bossano's intention was to give himself greater status than Sir Joshua Hassan had ever had *vis-à-vis* Spain by talking on a bilateral basis with the Spanish Prime Minister, Felipe González. If that were accepted, it would fit well with his plan to enhance Gibraltar's position as a genuine third party in discussing the future of the Rock.

There was no doubt that the Gibraltar over which Joe Bossano now presided was very different from the pre-open border days. In 1987 the inhabitants of the Rock imported goods from Spain worth £15 million. To dispense the cash required for these purposes (and to provide the loans for the apartments for sale in Marbella which were advertised on Gibraltar TV) there were now 20 banks, including three Spanish ones, within its seven square kilometres, as compared with two 10 years earlier. In the shops pesetas and the Spanish language were as much in evidence as pounds and English. There were now over a thousand Spanish workers on the Rock, although this was still way below the 4,666 at the time the border was closed in 1969.

So in practical terms there was a creeping 'Spanish-isation' about day-to-day activity in Gibraltar. Osmosis was definitely at work. But the Gibraltarian voters had made it clear that they were seeking their own path for the future. The election of Joe Bossano as Chief Minister meant a clear change of attitude by the political leadership in Gibraltar towards the Anglo-Spanish negotiation process. As a consequence, the resolution of the Gibraltar problem was one step further away.

Notes

1 An interim agreement was reached on 10 August 1988 whereby the British Government would provide £2,360,000 (472 million pesetas) between mid-September (when Gibraltarian funds ran out) and 7 December (by which date a new agreement had to be reached). This new agreement was announced on 3 December.

2 See above, p. 93.

3 The incident was to re-emerge in March 1989. See below, Chapter 18.

4 Quoted in *The Guardian*, 9 November 1991.

5 Joe Bossano had acquired most of his early political experience as a trade unionist. Between 1958 and 1972 he spent a good deal of time in Britain, working first in the London docks and then as a merchant seaman. In Gibraltar he was a branch officer in the TGWU, turning it into the Rock's most powerful union. He also spent some further time in Britain studying at Birmingham University.

6 *El País*, 27 March 1988, p. 14.

SIXTEEN

FIRST VISITS BY FIRST LADIES
April–October 1988

In the autumn of 1988 Spain was due to receive first-time visits from both Queen Elizabeth and Mrs Thatcher. The visits were a sign that Britain felt comfortable about the way in which negotiations on Gibraltar were proceeding, and an indication that Spain accepted rapprochement at all levels as a necessary concomitant to those negotiations. The visits also served to demonstrate the determination on the part of the British Government that the message conveyed by the Gibraltarians through the election of Joe Bossano would not affect good relations between Britain and Spain and would not impede the continuation of the negotiation process.

Before these visits took place, however, there was earlier in the year another first visit, this time by General John Galvin, Supreme Commander of NATO in Europe and the first to visit Spain, where he arrived on 6 April 'to listen and to learn'. Inevitably, the question of Spain's contribution to NATO arose in connection with the visit, and as usual this involved consideration of the role of Gibraltar in NATO. Britain's informal reaction to Spain's position, which Spain had made clear in January[1] and which rejected any Spanish co-ordination with the GIBMED Command, was that any activities in Gibraltar involving Spanish forces would need to be coordinated from the Allied Forces Southern Europe Command (AFSOUTH) in Naples.[2] General Galvin let it be known that if Spain found this solution acceptable, NATO would support it. Here, too, there was a clear attempt on all sides to try to ensure that the Gibraltar issue did not impede the progress of good relations between Spain and its partners.

More tricky than General Galvin's position, however, was that of the Governor of Gibraltar, Air Marshall Peter Terry, who also tried to please all sides at the inauguration of the new Gibraltarian Assembly on 14 April. He reiterated the British Government's position of support for the Brussels Declaration, but also reaffirmed the pledge that 'the sovereignty of Gibraltar would never pass to another country against the freely and democratically expressed wishes of the people of Gibraltar'. To please the Spanish Government, he called the airport agreement 'sensible and acceptable'. But he also reassured the Gibraltarians that it in no way affected the sovereignty of any part of the territory, and conceded that it was for the Assembly to decide whether to accept the agreement or not. His address well demonstrated the balancing act that the British Government was trying to perform in order to keep all sides contented.

Mrs Thatcher got caught up in it, too. A major concern of the Spanish Government following the victory of the GSLP in the Gibraltar elections was the British Government's position with regard to Joe Bossano's preferred option of self-determination for Gibraltar. This was put to the test when Antonio Hernández Mancha, leader of Spain's main opposition party the Alianza Popular, visited London on 25 April for talks with Mrs Thatcher, who made it quite clear that autonomy or independence for Gibraltar was out of the question. This will clearly not have pleased Mr Bossano, who had already declared his intention to boycott the annual bilateral meetings of the two Foreign Ministers. But the Spanish Government will have been gratified to learn that Britain would not be influenced by Joe Bossano's stance, even though Britain's commitment to respect the Gibraltarians' wishes was a significant impediment to progress.

Joe Bossano soon demonstrated his intention to carve out a more independent path as Gibraltarian leader than his predecessor by making a visit to the Canary Islands on 5 and 6 May without reference to the British Foreign Office. Although technically there was no need for him to do so as it was a private visit, there was no doubt that the visit had a political motive, and Mr Bossano had talks with the CDS leader of the Government of the islands, Fernando Fernández Martín, which included discussion of a plan to link the Canaries and the Rock by sea. The visit did not pass without criticism, however, from the CDS's coalition partners in the islands, the Alianza Popular, who described Sr Fernández Martín's meeting with the Gibraltarian Chief Minister as 'a serious diplomatic error' because 'it legitimised the international contacts which Bossano might make in the future, to the detriment of Spanish interests' and because it 'threatened the unity of Spain'.[3]

The supposed threat to Spain posed at this time by Joe Bossano was not confined to the Canaries, however, for the Government decided to ban the broadcast of a debate on Spanish television on 20 May between the Chief Minister and the former Spanish Foreign Minister, Fernando Morán, for the same reasons. Not surprisingly (for when free speech is at issue one medium of communication always springs to the defence of another), the leader writer of *El País* that morning was scathing in his criticism of the Government for reverting to the Francoist ways of suppressing views which the Government did not want the Spanish people to hear. In his column entitled 'The policy of the ostrich', the writer contrasted the attitude of TVE in Spain with the BBC, which had resisted government pressure not to show the programme 'Death on the Rock'. He warned the Spanish Government that their attitude would only reinforce the views of Gibraltarians who were mistrustful of Spain's declared good intentions towards them.

Clearly, Spanish politicians had not fully worked out how to handle the new Chief Minister's approach to relations with Spain, and they fell back on old instincts from pre-democracy days. Sir Joshua Hassan was a devil whom they knew; by contrast Joe Bossano was treated rather like a terrorist who had to be declared a *persona non grata* if he tried to visit Spanish territory, or be denied the oxygen of publicity when it came to expressing his views over the air-waves.

One of Joe Bossano's declared intentions in his election platform was to make Gibraltar as economically self-sufficient as he could. A major step was taken in this direction when it was announced at the end of July 1988 that a land reclamation programme would begin in October in the port area. The objective, which had the support of the British Ministry of Defence, was to increase the Rock's land area by some 4% in order to provide building land for civil projects. When completed, the programme would no doubt delight the Gibraltarians who had voted for Mr Bossano, just as it would provide the Spanish authorities with further cause for concern about the future of the Rock. It would also provide a counter to the view expressed in a United Nations Decolonisation Committee working paper due for discussion by the Committee on 12 August, which indicated that industrial, commercial and service activity on the Rock was virtually limited to the needs of the civilian population and the remaining military garrison. If the development succeeded, it could make Gibraltar into an attractive off-shore centre for investors from all over the world.

Joe Bossano also started to undertake visits abroad in order to promote Gibraltar and to attract foreign investors. In early September he went to Washington and New York to try to secure US investments in the colony, as well as to persuade the US navy and merchant shipping companies to use Gibraltar's shipyards for repairs. Later the same month he went to the Commonwealth Conference in Cyprus and a conference organised by the IMF in Berlin. It was scarcely surprising, in view of the reaction to his visit to the Canaries, that he had still not been invited to visit Madrid.

The issue of the IRA terrorists came back into the frame on 6 September when the coroner's inquest into the killings began in Gibraltar. Security measures were stepped up several days beforehand, with armed soldiers in combat gear posted outside military installations and electronic screening of everyone entering the court. The Spanish press followed the event with interest: on the day that the inquest began the leader writer in *El País* took some pleasure in describing the fact that an inquest was being held at all as 'an important defeat for Margaret Thatcher's Government'.

Spain was largely a bystander in the month-long process. A report from the Spanish police concerning the location of the cars to be used in the attack was submitted as written evidence but was not used. Neither was a statement from a Spanish police officer from Málaga which provided crucial evidence about the tracking of the terrorists by the police in Spain. The officer was willing to appear in person at the inquest, but this offer was withdrawn under orders from his superiors without any clear explanation. Since they would be unable to question him, the lawyers in the case apparently agreed not to use the statement.

The main issue involving Spain concerned the fact that the SAS officer in command of the operation maintained to the inquest that the Spanish police did not inform the British security forces that the suspected terrorists had left Málaga for Gibraltar. Hence, the officer claimed, the SAS were taken by surprise when the terrorists appeared on the Rock and had to take impromptu action without clear information as to whether or not the suspects were armed. His evidence—delivered from behind a curtain which protected him and his fellow officers' identity from the public and the press—went against claims made by the Spanish police and by the Ulster lawyer, Patrick McGrory, representing the families of the three victims, but it was decisive in influencing the jury to bring in a verdict of lawful killing, which they did on 30 September.[4] As a consequence, the SAS officers involved did not have to stand trial. Given the evidence as reported by the media, there were many who were surprised by the verdict. But in Spain they were impressed by the legal process by which it was achieved: a coroner's inquest before a jury with the identity of witnesses (not accused) protected from public view was a complete novelty. The inquest served as a reminder of the different legal system in Gibraltar which would need to be respected if any future change in sovereignty were to occur.

By the time the inquest came to an end Mrs Thatcher had paid her first visit to Spain. On the eve of the visit on 22 September, Mrs Thatcher gave a press conference for Spanish correspondents in London. On the specific question of Gibraltar, she reminded Spain that they could not impose a solution against the wishes of the Gibraltarians, and she rejected parallels with Hong Kong because of the difference in the treaty arrangements governing the two colonies. She was determined to give the clear impression that Britain does not dictate to Gibraltar what it must do, either in matters of foreign policy or on issues such as the airport agreement.

Mrs Thatcher had put similar points in an interview broadcast on Spanish TV on 18 September. However, the Spanish Foreign Ministry did not accept these arguments. In an annoyed response they pointed out that the reason Britain was committed to respect the wishes of the Gibraltarians was because Britain had written such a statement into the Preamble to the 1969 Gibraltar Constitution. They argued that the difference between Gibraltar and Hong Kong was that Britain had chosen not to support Hong Kong in the same constitutional way.

The visit itself was described as both historic and difficult. Historic because, surprisingly, this was the first ever official visit by a British

Prime Minister to Spain.[5] It was seen as difficult for a number of reasons: Spain's role in NATO was not yet clear and it had not yet reached agreement on entry into the Western European Union (partly because it would have to accept the involvement of nuclear weapons); Britain and Spain (the latter due to take over the Presidency of the European Community for the first time in January 1989) did not agree on the right pace of progress towards closer EC involvement (Mrs Thatcher that week made her famous anti-EC Bruges speech). There was also the question of Spain's contribution to the development of the European Fighter Aircraft; the Spanish Government was considering reducing it from 13%, while Britain wanted them to keep to that figure.

Then there was the 'classic' problem of Gibraltar. A leading article in *El País* on 22 September, which paid tribute to Mrs Thatcher's support for Spain at the time of Tejero's attempted coup in 1981, and which played down the differences between the two countries, described 'the intractable Gibraltar problem' as the one which weighed down Anglo-Spanish relations. It was Gibraltar which made the front-page headline in the following day's issue: 'González tells Thatcher that talks on Gibraltar must produce results'. In fact, European union was the main topic of discussion on the first day of Mrs Thatcher's visit, but at a dinner at the Moncloa Palace Felipe González took the opportunity to say that on the Gibraltar question 'dialogue must not become an end in itself' and that they must work towards a 'concrete solution'. In reply, Mrs Thatcher said that it was not realistic to expect a rapid solution to their differences over Gibraltar, but gave assurances that 'Gibraltar will never be independent'.

An attempt to put the issue within its proper parameters was made in the same issue of *El País* on 23 September by Fernando Schwartz. He argued first that the Treaty of Utrecht only refers to what must happen to Gibraltar once Britain has decided to dispose of it; how Britain reached the decision to dispose of the colony was its prerogative, and it was quite within its rights to consult the Gibraltarian people. So Spanish arguments objecting to the 1969 Gibraltarian Constitution were invalid. Second, Britain was justified in dismissing parallels between Gibraltar and Hong Kong because the treaties relating to them were different, plus the practical fact that Madrid could not threaten or coerce in the same way as

Peking. Third, a solution to the problem would not come through discussions between governments and would not come quickly; it would come only when the Gibraltarians wanted it to, and this would only happen when there had been integration between Spaniards and Gibraltarians. To this end he advocated the establishment of an autonomous body to develop the Campo region through both Spanish and British investment. 'The only possible solution to the Gibraltar problem is the human one', he concluded.

Decisions to act in this way would, however, need to be taken at governmental level, and there was no sign that that was on the agenda on the second and final day of Mrs Thatcher's visit. The main conclusion to emerge from it on the Gibraltar issue, as reported on 24 September, was that Mrs Thatcher would endeavour to put pressure on Gibraltar's Chief Minister to accept the airport agreement of December 1987 on the grounds that it would be good for Gibraltar and for Spain.[6] At a joint press conference she insisted that the negotiations within the framework of the Brussels Declaration must go ahead, but admitted that 'we do not have a formula to resolve the differences between us'.[7] As far as the other differences were concerned, greatest progress seems to have been made on the entry of Spain into the WEU. On the idea of a 'social European space' which Felipe González wanted to introduce during his presidency of the European Community, Mrs Thatcher was quite dismissive, calling it 'the new jargon'. The Spanish Prime Minister did not rise to the bait, aware that within a month Spain would be welcoming Queen Elizabeth.

In terms of moving the Gibraltar issue forward, Mrs Thatcher's visit could scarcely be described as a great success. But only the diplomatically naive could have expected anything of substance to emerge. However, as a step in the post-Franco—and post Falklands/Malvinas—process of rapprochement, it was not only successful, but essential. Britain and Spain, as EC and NATO partners, had to demonstrate that despite the stumbling block of Gibraltar, they could conduct themselves properly in the normal niceties of official head of government visits. Restraint had to be shown on both sides, and that would have been no easy matter when one of the protagonists was Mrs Thatcher. With two visits from Britain's leading female figureheads following in quick succession, Spanish diplomats had a very taxing autumn in 1988. But there can be no doubt that the first of the two will have caused them to lose more sleep than the second, and they will have felt relieved to have it behind them.

Queen Elizabeth's visit to Spain in October was the return match, so to speak, of the one that King Juan Carlos made to Britain in 1986, and the first ever official visit by a British monarch. Now that Spain was comfortably settled as a constitutional monarchy, there was much admiration for nations with similar constitutional structures, and as one of the longest established and most stable, Britain came in for its share. Certainly that was the tone of the leading article in *El País* on 16 October on the eve of the Queen's arrival. There was no direct reference in the article to the Gibraltar problem, although the writer could not resist saying in the last sentence that the visit 'represents a victory for both countries, who today are rising above that which has separated them and continues to separate them'. Gibraltar was never far from the forefront when Anglo-Spanish relations were under consideration.

The Gibraltarian Government took the opportunity for some self-publicity and announced at the beginning of the royal visit that later in the year Gibraltar would issue its own currency, partly to bring income for its Treasury and partly 'to project Gibraltar's image in the world', in the words of the Gibraltarian Trade and Industry Minister, Michael Feetham.[8] Gibraltar's Chief Minister also arranged another of his visits (this time to the Far East, including Japan and Singapore) during the royal visit, to promote trade with Gibraltar. Such acts will have been seen in Spanish diplomatic circles as provocative, and part of Gibraltar's new strategy to promote its semi-independence from Britain. It is unthinkable that Sir Joshua Hassan would have done the same.

The royal visit—part official, part private—lasted seven days. In an endeavour to ensure that the subject of Gibraltar could not sour the visit in any way, it was reported that Spanish diplomatic sources had said not only that it would not be proper to broach specific political matters on a royal visit, but that the subject would not even be discussed when the two Foreign Ministers met on 17 October; their talks would concentrate on Spain's entry into the WEU.

However, for the first two days the reality was very different. In his speech at the dinner offered to the British royal visitors on 17 October, King Juan Carlos warned that Gibraltar 'could make full

cooperation difficult' between Spain and Britain. But he acknowledged that the dispute 'has now found an appropriate forum for
discussion'. 'Our Governments began a process of talks four years
ago', he said. 'They have been able to achieve some agreements
which, when implemented, will come to benefit the people most
directly affected'. He looked forward to a positive outcome: 'the
overcoming of the dispute through friendship in accordance with
the logic of history'. In reply Queen Elizabeth was more indirect,
saying that 'we are sure that our growing mutual understanding will
enable us to deal with the only remaining problem between us'.[9]

Not only did the royals bring the subject of Gibraltar into their
speeches; the two Foreign Ministers also discussed it when they met
for ninety minutes earlier in the day. The implementation of the
airport agreement—or rather the failure to implement it—was the
main topic of discussion, although no progress was reported.

The second day of the visit on 18 October involved two official
visits of a political nature—one to Parliament and the other to
Madrid City Hall—which offered further opportunities for reference
to the Gibraltar problem to be made, although there was clearly
much resistance against uttering the 'G' word itself. The President of
the Spanish Parliament, Félix Pons, made an oblique reference to 'a
page to be finished and a chapter to be closed', while the Mayor of
Madrid, Juan Barranco, spoke of the 'rivalries and disagreements of
the past'. In reply the Queen referred to the need 'to tackle areas of
historical misunderstanding' and to the recognition that 'often our
paths have not always been the same'.

Thereafter the royal visit followed a more conventional course,
and the Gibraltar issue moved off the agenda. But the important
thing was that the visit of the British Head of State had taken place,
immediately following that of the British Head of Government. The
acknowledgement during both visits that negotiations were under
way and would have to produce concrete solutions was interpreted
in Spain as a sign that something might emerge at the next annual
meeting between the two Foreign Ministers, scheduled for the turn
of the year for the express purpose of discussing the Gibraltar issue.
The same interpretation was not, however, made in Britain.

As the year closed Joe Bossano was once more ploughing his own
furrow, this time by making his first official visit to the Campo
region on 13 December for talks with José Carracao, the Chairman

of the Councils of the region. Gibraltar's Chief Minister proposed the establishment of industries in the region using capital from international companies based on the Rock, while Sr Carracao put forward proposals for cheaper drinking water for Gibraltar, a solid waste disposal system, and the sale of land in the Campo for industrial development. Cooperation was taking place on the ground, as Fernando Schwartz had advocated, as well as at head of government and head of state level. Would this encouraging situation carry over into the new year?

Notes

1 See above, Chapter 15, p. 132.

2 Spain's Defence Minister, Sr Narcís Serra, visited London on 21 April to discuss the proposal with his British counterpart, Sir George Young. An agreement was reached along the lines of the British proposal, but not identical to it. Narcís Serra's defence of Spain's position was that it avoided the NATO aspect of Gibraltar interfering with negotiations.

3 *El País*, 16 May 1993, p. 21.

4 For further discussion of the inquest, see below, Chapter 18.

5 Mrs Thatcher was also the last of the EC heads of state or government to visit Spain following Spanish entry in January 1986.

6 The pressure took the form of a request by Lynda Chalker, Minister of State at the Foreign Office, to Joe Bossano when he visited London at the end of September, that he should put in writing his objections to the airport agreement.

7 Fernando Morán, the former Foreign Affairs Minister, in a reflective article in *El País* on 25 September, warned of the danger of allowing Britain to think that it could live comfortably with Spain within the EC and NATO, without having to resolve the Gibraltar question. This could lead to Britain gradually giving way to demands within Gibraltar for more and more self-determination.

8 As a way of linking the Gibraltar issue with the royal visit, the news was juxtaposed in the 17 October issue of *El País* (p. 17) with the report of the Queen's visit.

9 According to a report in *El País*, 19 October 1988, p. 22, the Chief Minister of Gibraltar interpreted the Queen's comments as a clear indication of the British Government's respect for the Gibraltarians' right to determine their own future.

SEVENTEEN
THE BOSSANO STRATEGY
January–February 1989

There was certainly a positive note in the statements which emerged from the Spanish Foreign Ministry on 1 January 1989, and some good reasons for such a note to be struck. First, Joe Bossano—his reputation already established in Spain as more hard-line than his predecessor—had proposed a second visit to the Campo region on 10 January to continue with discussion of areas of cooperation, a move which was seen as both 'possible and desirable' by the Palacio de Santa Cruz. Second, it was felt that following the visits of Prime Minister Thatcher and Queen Elizabeth, there was a new climate which would lead to the British Government putting pressure on Gibraltar regarding joint use of the airport.[1] Third, the new line from the Spanish Foreign Ministry was to present a 'softer image'; an example was the Spanish Government's willingness not to create difficulties over land reclamation developments in the port area of Gibraltar Bay, on which it was planned to build some 1,200 dwellings.[2] And finally, Foreign Secretary Sir Geoffrey Howe, who was due to meet his counterpart on 6 February in their annual round of talks, had a new adviser on Gibraltar in the form of Richard Gozney, until recently a member of the British diplomatic mission in Madrid, and therefore seen in Spain as someone who understood the Spanish approach to the Gibraltar problem.

However, before the glow became too rosy, on 4 January the Municipal Council in Algeciras accused Gibraltar of contributing to dangerous pollution in the Bay of Algeciras through the disposal of solid waste in the sea. The major contributors to the pollution were in fact Spanish industries in the region, which produced high levels of metals and toxic waste, followed by local sewage, and then ships and oil-tankers cleaning out their tanks in the Bay. But Gibraltarians came in for a good deal of criticism, largely due to the fact that some untreated waste indentifiable as coming from Gibraltar had appeared while the main incinerator was out of service. This appeared to be a case of the pot calling the kettle black while finding a scapegoat, and the sensitivities in the region made the Gibraltarians an easy target.[3]

Relations between Gibraltar and the neighbouring Campo region were not enhanced by the publication of an interview given by Joe Bossano to the Gibraltar weekly *Panorama* on the eve of his visit to La Línea and reported in the Spanish press, which quoted him as saying that 'there was not the slightest possibility that we would accept the Anglo-Spanish agreement on the joint use of Gibraltar airport'.[4] He also said that he believed there was a new generation of Spaniards who were European, less insular and less sensitive about the Gibraltar issue. 'The day will come', he believed, 'when Gibraltar will not be an affront to the dignity and the virility of Spain which they have to avenge'.

Despite these hiccoughs, the process of osmosis initiated several years earlier took a major step forward when Joe Bossano made his first official visit to La Línea on 10 and 11 January. Mr Bossano's strategy to maintain an annual growth rate for the Gibraltarian economy of 12% included the establishment of an industrial sector in the neighbouring Campo region. Consequently, one of the main subjects under discussion during his four hours of talks with the mayor, Salvador Pagán, was the plan to set up a prefabrication factory in La Línea with Danish finance, which would create 50 jobs. Some 60% of the finished products would be used in Gibraltar, while the remainder would be exported from the Rock, and the company would be registered there for tax purposes. The main disadvantage for Gibraltar was the danger that Spanish customs might not give special treatment to the finished products when they were being transported to the Rock, and Mr Bossano was anxious to ensure that the Council in La Línea should negotiate such treatment with the Madrid authorities. Although Spain recognised that the motives for this collaboration were expediency on Gibraltar's part because of its limited room for industrial expansion, it was at least a move which was of benefit to both sides.

On 30 January Sir Geoffrey Howe visited Gibraltar for the first time since Joe Bossano's election victory on 24 March the previous year. He had been due to visit the Rock shortly after that date, but the official reason for the delay was due to the coroner's inquest into the shooting of the IRA suspects earlier that month.

The day before Sir Geoffrey's arrival, news was leaked that the Foreign Secretary would announce that Britain would withdraw its army presence from Gibraltar after the Royal Green Jackets (due to replace the Royal Anglian Regiment within a few months) had finished their two-year tour of duty. The intention was that they would gradually be replaced by a Gibraltar Regiment consisting of professionals rather than the mixture of professionals and volunteers who constituted it at the present time. Unlike the navy and the airforce, the British army in Gibraltar had no NATO role, but was there only to protect Gibraltar from its neighbour. With Spain itself now in NATO, Britain felt that there was no longer any such role for the army to play.

As expected, Sir Geoffrey Howe announced the withdrawal in his talks with Mr Bossano on 30 January. The three existing units—an infantry battalion, an artillery battery and a unit of Royal Engineers, totalling some 1,915 men—were to be cut by half by March 1991.[5] The news was greeted with concern in Gibraltar itself, not only because of what withdrawal represented politically, but also because the removal of over a thousand servicemen and their families could mean job losses and damaging economic consequences for Gibraltarians.

Publicly, however, Joe Bossano minimised the significance of the proposed withdrawal, and drew attention to the benefits for Gibraltar of being able to exploit land currently dedicated to military use.[6] While acknowledging that 'the defence of Gibraltar in 1990 did not require the same resources as in 1890', he reminded Sir Geoffrey of the commitments of the British Government to defend Gibraltar and of their 'political commitment to defend the right of the Gibraltarians to self-determination'.

The Secretary of State for Defence, George Younger, was quick to restate the first commitment, even if he avoided making reference to the second: 'Our commitment towards them is absolute and very clear. As long as the people of Gibraltar wish it, they will remain under the British flag, as the Prime Minister has said many times. The reduction of the military presence does not alter that, but if I have a limited number of battalions to deploy in the many tasks that we have, it is a luxury to have one of them stationed where it is not needed'. In general, the logic of this argument was accepted in Britain; some even wondered why it had taken the British Government so long to make a decision on withdrawal.

In Spain the decision was seen to have potentially more political than strategic significance, since it was recognised that the land army had little to do with the defence of the territory and even less to do with the control of the Straits, which could count on Rapier, Exocet and Harpoon missiles, as well as two permanently stationed warships and six Jaguar aircraft. But the Spanish Foreign Office decided not to exploit the subject in order not to undermine the 'softer image' which they were trying to cultivate.

The topic of the military withdrawal somewhat eclipsed the other main subject on the agenda for the Howe-Bossano meetings, namely the question of the joint use of Gibraltar airport. Nevertheless there were signs—both in a statement he made after the meeting on 30 January and in remarks made by the Gibraltarian Minister responsible for civil aviation, John Pilcher—that Mr Bossano was prepared to soften his opposition to joint use, although there was no indication as to when he might agree to do so. The agreement signed on 2 December 1987 was, as far as Gibraltar's Chief Minister was concerned, 'non-viable', but he said he was prepared to explore alternatives, including the possibility of negotiating a new agreement.[7] Whatever these alternatives might be, they would not involve sharing control of the airport: 'We are not prepared to buy peace at the expense of going back on the commitments for which we were elected'. He saw joint use of the airport as a part of Gibraltar's long-term strategy for economic development, which focused on cooperation with the Campo region.[8] However, he saw this collaboration developing in a European context: 'The economic future of Gibraltar depends on its potential within the European Community, and this must logically include Spain'.[9]

The idea that it must include Spain was pursued in an editorial in *El País* on 1 February. The fact that there seemed to be a shift in Joe Bossano's stance on the airport issue was welcomed as a sign of successful pressure having been exerted by the British Government. Even more significant, the article said, was Joe Bossano's recognition that Gibraltar has to cooperate with the neighbouring territory: 'His aspiration to modern development—which breaks with the 'mono-industry' of the military base—is unsustainable without integration with Spain as a whole'. The writer chided the Spanish Government for not being sufficiently active in trying to awaken in Gibraltarians the idea that they have a future in a democratic and decentralised Spain.

That was clearly not the future that Joe Bossano and the majority of Gibraltarians saw. Far from admitting defeat in pursuit of his objective, the strategy of Gibraltar's Chief Minister was to seek economic independence for Gibraltar as a means of maintaining political independence, and the removal of all trade barriers within the European Community from 1993 would provide Gibraltar with the opportunity to use its financial resources as a means to this end. To conceive of any other interpretation was to misunderstand Joe Bossano's game-plan.

Another sign of the different strategy adopted by Joe Bossano from that of his predecessor, Sir Joshua Hassan, was the fact that, whereas Sir Joshua had insisted on participating in the annual round of talks between the British and Spanish Foreign Ministers, Joe Bossano refused to do so in order to indicate his rejection of the Brussels Declaration. So it was that when Sir Geoffrey Howe and Sr Fernández Ordóñez met in London on 6 and 7 February[10] Mr Bossano was absent, whereas the Mayor of La Línea and the Chairman of the Local Councils of the Campo accompanied the Spanish Foreign Minister in order to demonstrate their desire to increase collaboration on either side of the border.

The two Foreign Ministers met on the evening of 6 February, and again the following day, when Sr Fernández Ordóñez also met Mrs Thatcher for 45 minutes. The British Prime Minister and her Foreign Secretary both stressed their desire and determination to persuade the Gibraltarians to implement the airport agreement. At a press conference Sr Fernández Ordóñez indicated that Mrs Thatcher had some ideas on how this might be achieved, although he declined to reveal what those ideas might be.

The question of sovereignty received its annual airing, with each side making predictable utterances; the British indicated their concern to respect the wishes of the Gibraltarian people, while the Spanish delegation repeated its wish to achieve territorial integrity, 'without in any way affecting the judicial, political, economic or any other aspect of the status of the population'. Sr Fernández Ordóñez again reminded the press that 'the UN voted overwhelmingly in favour of considering Gibraltar as a case for decolonisation'. The fact that the Spanish Foreign Minister could still wheel out such a statement nearly a quarter of a century after the first UN vote was taken was, in one sense, an indication of what little progress had been made, and what a gulf still remained to be bridged.

Diplomats on both sides were no doubt weary of hearing such well-worn arguments. But reaction to the current impasse took a different turn on this occasion, for the British press collectively rounded on the Gibraltarians for their 'obstructionism', their 'artificial semi-isolation', and their 'siege mentality which limits their vision and impedes progress'. Such criticism was amply quoted in the Spanish press on 8 February. One report they did not quote, however, was a brief item in *The Times* which suggested that with the EC discussing how all border controls might be dropped (except measures against terrorism and drugs-smuggling), 'the Gibraltar issue could "fade away" ' and 'create a climate of opinion in which few will care whether the Rock belongs to Gibraltar or Spain'. It is hard to imagine that anyone in Spain or Gibraltar would have agreed that this was a possibility in the near future.

The Spanish Government's official line was, however, one of 'active patience', as the Foreign Minister put it. For some Spaniards that patience was wearing a little thin. Carlos Mendo, in another of his articles for *El País* published on 14 February with the simple title 'Gibraltar', was convinced that British Prime Ministers and Foreign Secretaries had made a tape recording which said that 'we shall do nothing against the wishes of the Gibraltarian people', and switched it on whenever Spanish visitors raised the question of sovereignty. Yet they knew, he argued (recalling the British Government's rejection of the wishes of the people of Hong Kong) that the issue was really to do with territory, and not to do with citizens' political rights. It was all very well to establish a climate of confidence between Spain and Gibraltar, provided that it actually led to a solution; at the present rate the Union Jack would still be flying over Gibraltar in 2704, a thousand years after it was first planted there. He accused the British Government of apparently having given Joe Bossano the power of veto on the Anglo-Spanish airport agreement, while Spain made all the concessions. Even the reduction of British troops represented more of a financial saving to Britain than a move towards a solution to the problem, and Britain had the cheek to ask for 'a friendly gesture' in return, such as speeding up customs clearance at the border crossing. London, he said, was playing for time until 1992.

Then Sr Mendo's argument took a different turn. He cited a leading article recently published in the *Wall Street Journal* to suggest that Washington was also a player in the game. The American paper had stated that 'for a number of reasons Spanish trustworthiness continues to be suspect', the reasons ranging from the expulsion of the F-16s from the Torrejón airbase to the refusal to allow US planes to refuel in Spanish airspace en route to Libya. Sr Mendo suggested that Spain should try to get United States support for its aspirations towards Gibraltar by convincing the US that a Spanish Gibraltar would be as firm and stable as a British one. If the Spanish Government could achieve that, he argued, a solution to the problem would be that much nearer.

The thesis that the transfer of the sovereignty of Gibraltar depends on the United States requires further examination. Clearly, the strategic importance of Gibraltar for NATO meant that the USA had a close interest in the stability and commitment of the nation which controlled the military base; Sr Mendo had quoted the Spanish writer Salvador de Madariaga, who had said: 'Get rid of the base and you will get rid of the problem'. But such an interpretation of the situation contains two misapprehensions on the part of those whose view of the situation was the same as that of Sr Mendo.

In the first place the implication that Britain could be put under pressure by the USA to hand Gibraltar over to Spain over-estimated the Americans' willingness to get involved in European territorial disputes; they may have tried to play the role of broker in the Falklands/Malvinas crisis, but that was both globally destabilising and also involved a fellow member of the Organisation of American States.

Second, the assumption that Britain would not stand up to such US pressure had no foundation. Britain's relationship with the USA (or at least Mrs Thatcher's relationship with President Reagan) may have been caricatured as poodle-like, but when it came to protecting colonies under siege (again the Falklands/Malvinas situation is instructive) Britain's canine image is transformed into the more familiar bull-dog.

But there was also an earlier and more serious misapprehension in Sr Mendo's article, namely the assumption that Britain, like Spain, saw the Gibraltar issue as a territorial one. It is instructive that Sr Mendo again drew the analogy with Hong Kong. Such analogies, as has been suggested elsewhere,[11] are very misleading, not only because of the historical and juridical differences between the two colonies, but also, as Lord Carrington indicated, because Gibraltar is part of Europe.[12] Hong Kong may be a British Crown colony, but it is not almost British in the way that Gibraltar is. Whereas the Hong Kongese are mostly clearly of Chinese origin, the majority of Gibraltarians (despite their racial mixture) act and behave like British ex-patriates. Gibraltar is a corner of England in Southern Europe; for Britain to abandon its inhabitants against their wishes would be like casting its own cousins adrift. As Sr Mendo illustrated, Spaniards found that difficult to comprehend, perhaps because in the modern world, unlike Britain, Spain had never had a European colony.

While Britain therefore accepted the fact that Gibraltar was an anachronism in the context of the shape of modern Europe, it was quite happy to allow the colony to detach itself from the mother country at its own pace and in its own way, so that the wishes of the population could be met. The most accurate part of Sr Mendo's argument would seem to be that London was indeed playing for time.

Notes

1 The mayor of La Línea, Salvador Pagán, expressed the hope that Joe Bossano's idea of turning Gibraltar into the Hong Kong of the Mediterranean (see below, Chapter 19) would act as a further way of encouraging a move on the airport issue, as it would require the use of the airport to be extended.

2 One of the first acts of the Bossano administration was to establish the Gibraltar Land Reclamation Company which, during a nine-month period in 1988, increased building land in Gibraltar by one-sixth. It involved bringing 200,000 tons of rock from Spain, which were levelled off with 2.5 million cubic metres of sand.

3 A further incident occurred ten weeks later when a Gibraltarian barge, the *Rock Service*, was accused of discharging waste within Spanish waters.

4 The issue of the airport had also been picked up by the Governor, Sir Peter Terry, in his New Year message, when he referred to the British Government's desire to reach a solution on the airport issue. Mr Bossano replied, again rejecting any cooperation within the framework of the Brussels Declaration because it

represented 'a threat to the British sovereignty of Gibraltar and to the identity of the Gibraltarians'.

5 Further reductions were announced on 5 December 1989 in a written answer given by the Defence Minister, Archie Hamilton. These involved the withdrawal of the infantry battalion, the artillery battery, and the Air Defence Troop. This would leave the Navy as the largest of the three services, followed by the Royal Air Force. To counterbalance the reductions in army personnel, the permanent cadre of the Gibraltar Regiment would be increased from 63 to 150 men, with the number of volunteers also rising to 250.

6 With almost half of the usable land in the territory belonging to the Ministry of Defence, it was clear that some of it could be used to reduce the estimated shortfall of 2,000 dwellings.

7 The Chief Minister, Joe Bossano, was under some pressure not just from the British Foreign Office; the influential Gibraltar Chamber of Commerce wanted him to allow flights between Gibraltar and Madrid as a first step in order to improve commercial links with the Spanish capital.

8 Many Gibraltarians already had a vested interest in developing such cooperation. Over a thousand of them rented an apartment in the Campo region, while annually Gibraltarians were now spending some £15 million in Spain.

9 *El País*, 31 January 1989, p. 13; 1 February 1989, p. 14.

10 The meeting had been scheduled for mid-December 1988 but had been postponed due to Mikael Gorbachov's visit to Britain.

11 See above, Chapter 9, pp. 73–74.

12 See above, Chapter 14, p. 122.

EIGHTEEN
SPAIN'S ROLE IN DEATH ON THE ROCK
March–April 1989

One year after the incident involving the shooting of three IRA suspects in Gibraltar, and six months after the ending of the inquest, the issue suddenly re-emerged in a blaze of controversy.

On 15 March 1989, following a ceremony at which twenty-two Spanish policemen were given awards for their part in tracking the IRA activists, the Spanish police confirmed that they had in fact informed the British security forces on 6 March 1988 that the three suspects had left Torremolinos and were heading for Gibraltar but without arms or explosives. At the inquest the official British version had been that the Spanish police had failed to pass on this information, and that the SAS had not therefore known exactly when the terrorists would arrive on the Rock or whether they were armed. This version had been used to absolve the members of the SAS of unlawful killing at the inquest held during September 1988, although it was strongly contested by the solicitor representing the families of the victims.

A report in *The Sunday Times* on 2 April 1989, which was high-lighted in the Spanish press the following day, also suggested that two British army bomb-disposal experts had known that the car which was to have been used in the terrorist attack did not in fact contain a car-bomb, but they were over-ruled by a military adviser who was designated to testify at the inquest.

A further revelation of the report was that the British authorities had asked the Spanish police not to pursue the terrorists in order not to arouse suspicions. The British position at the inquest had been that the Spanish police had lost track of their Irish quarry; Spain said that they only lost track of them temporarily on 4 March for a few hours after their arrival at Málaga airport, and regained it long before the ambush in Gibraltar took place on 6 March. A report drawn up shortly after the events of March 1988 by the Spanish Interior Ministry's Comisaria General de Información (General Information Office), details of which were published in *El País* on 22 April 1989, indicates that the Spanish police knew the movements of the three suspects between Málaga, Fuengirola and Torremolinos on 4 March, and that the police informed the British authorities in Gibraltar.

It was also confirmed that a representative of the Spanish Foreign Information Service was prevented by the Spanish Interior Ministry from giving evidence at the inquest, and it was noted that Mrs Thatcher paid a visit to Spain during September in between the time that the Spanish police were called to appear at the inquest and the decision not to allow them to do so. At the time there were strong denials that the British Prime Minister had discussed the issue of the IRA killings during her visit. There were now suspicions that she had asked the Spanish Government to intervene and prevent the Spanish official from appearing at the inquest. However, a Spanish Government spokesman stated that the reason why the official was prevented from appearing was that Madrid had decided that his appearance would imply recognition of British sovereignty over Gibraltar. If the latter was the real reason, then the Gibraltar dispute had even been allowed to interfere in the proper pursuit of justice.

The way in which the whole terrorist incident had been handled by the British Government was put into question on 6 April in a report published by the National Council of Civil Liberties and the International League of Human Rights. In one part of the report, concern was expressed at the contradictions between the Spanish and British versions of the pursuit of the terrorists, and the fact that these discrepancies had not been revealed at the inquest. A further report on the incident issued later that month by Amnesty International referred to the absence of testimony at the inquest from Spanish police as one of its weaknesses. Whether the reason for their non-appearance was due to pressure from the British or Spanish authorities may never be known, but given the discrepancy in the account of the information which was passed to Gibraltar, it does suggest that there was some degree of collusion between Britain and Spain regarding the inquest, unless credence is given to the argument mentioned above that the issue of sovereignty was involved.

The re-emergence of issues relating to the terrorist incident had its effect on the Rock in a way that Britain and Northern Ireland in particular had long since got used to. On 3 April it was reported that British security forces in Gibraltar had received a telephone warning of a bomb threat on military installations. There was also a report that Spanish police had notified their British counterparts of the presence of two members of the IRA in Spain. Security precautions in Gibraltar were stepped up, especially since the Royal Green Jackets Regiment had just arrived to take up duties there. They were to be the last British regiment to do so.

NINETEEN
A EUROPEAN HONG KONG?
May–December 1989

By mid-April 1989 the IRA terrorist issue had receded, but as the year wore on there was little sign of progress on any of the major areas of disagreement. The British Government's desire to let sleeping dogs lie by not upsetting Madrid led to an angry statement by Chief Minister Bossano, when military manoeuvres scheduled to take place off Gibraltar on 13 May were cancelled in case the Spanish Government interpreted them as a provocation. The official reason given for their cancellation was that it was decided that the manoeuvres, involving commandos parachuting into waters close to Spain, were not militarily necessary. However, the decision to cancel came following Foreign Office advice to the Ministry of Defence. The British military involved were clearly none too pleased at having their activities interfered with for what they saw as political reasons, but their displeasure was matched by that of Joe Bossano, who issued an official communiqué stating that the Government of Gibraltar did not share London's opinion about Madrid's possible reaction, and that in any case such considerations should not interfere with matters involving the defence of Gibraltar. For its part, the Spanish Government refused to comment.

At the beginning of June 1989 comparisons between Gibraltar and Hong Kong re-emerged, although this time they were prompted by the Gibraltarians themselves rather than by Spaniards looking for parallels. The cause was the Tiananmen Square massacre in Peking, when the authorities put down the embryonic pro-democracy movement in China in brutal fashion. The future of Hong Kong after 1997 was uncertain in any case and was now further threatened by the events in Peking. But on the Rock they were seen as extremely helpful to Gibraltar's aim of making itself economically self-sufficient. Earlier in the year Joe Bossano had undertaken a promotional visit to the Far East and had opened a Gibraltar information office in Hong Kong. With Hong Kong capital now urgently looking for an alternative home Gibraltar was anxious to offer it one, and a further trip was planned by businessmen, bankers and politicians for September.

Capital deposited in Gibraltar banks was already growing at an annual rate of 70%, and the very Britishness of Gibraltar made it an attractive alternative for investments from Hong Kong. Although Joe Bossano was anxious to stress the differences between the two British colonies in political terms, there were attractions for Gibraltar in trying to emulate some of the attributes of its Far-Eastern sister, and there were plans to build a Hong Kong-style financial centre on land in the port area. If there was to be a mass exodus from Hong Kong over the ensuing eight years, it mattered little that Gibraltar was only seven square kilometres in size and that accommodation was at a premium; there were already more companies in Gibraltar than there were inhabitants (more than 26,000 new post office box companies had been established on the Rock during the previous two years), and many more would be attracted by Gibraltar's tax advantages to establish themselves as Gibraltarian companies without anyone having to set foot on the Rock.

Spanish banks had not been slow to seize opportunities to benefit from Gibraltar's business boom by setting up on the Rock. Indeed, one of the ironies of the situation was that the attractiveness of Gibraltar for investments, some of which were lodged with Spanish banks, would not have applied if Gibraltar had been part of Spain.

The desire by the Foreign Office not to upset Madrid manifested itself again in July. The cause this time was an order by a Gibraltarian court to apprehend four Spanish customs officials accused of illegal entry into Gibraltar and of illegal possession of arms. The officials, who had been part of an anti-smuggling operation,[1] had been arrested and released on bail but then failed to reappear at the hearing on 20 July after the Spanish Government had intervened because the arrest had taken place on the isthmus, which Spain does not recognise as British territory.[2] Meanwhile, the Spanish authorities responded by causing delays of up to three hours at the frontier crossing point between Spain and the Rock. In retaliation Gibraltar reduced the amount of assistance given to Spain in tackling smuggling.

A meeting was arranged in London for 29 July between the acting Governor of Gibraltar, William Quantrill, and the British Ambassador in Madrid, Nicholas Gordon Lennox, to discuss the deterioration in the relations between Gibraltar and Spain, although the Foreign Office described the meeting as routine. Gibraltarian leaders had called upon the British Government to intervene, but they declined to do so, arguing that the incident must not be allowed to interfere with the 'important work of both Governments in the fight against the activities of drug traffickers'.[3] The trouble with London's anxiety to stay on the right side of the Spanish Government was that it did not enhance relations between London and Gibraltar.

At the end of September 1989 an official visit to Spain by King Hassan II of Morocco prompted the editorial writer of *El País* on 1 October to draw parallels between Spain's North African enclaves and Gibraltar. What was notable about the column was the sense of realism about the future of Ceuta and Melilla which was usually absent whenever the Spanish territories were under discussion.

Although, as the writer observed, the subject had been studiously avoided during the royal visit, that did not mean that the problem had gone away. He noted that the Spanish Government's attitude seemed to be guided by two principles: to increase the ties between Spain and Morocco on the basis of shared interests which would make unilateral action undesirable and unlikely, and second, to gain time by putting the issue on ice. The writer approved of the first principle, and while he understood the second he considered it a risky strategy.

He then brought in the parallels with Gibraltar. In neither case, he argued, is the status quo a long-term option: 'the most likely outcome is that one day Britain will have to give up Gibraltar and Spain will have to give up Ceuta and Melilla. One day: perhaps in 20 years, perhaps before'. The writer suggested that the two issues should be seen as part of a common problem, since control of the Straits of Gibraltar has international implications, and that the three countries involved—the UK, Morocco and Spain—should set about creating the conditions which would have the least traumatic effect on the populations concerned. With 130,000 people in Ceuta and Melilla (more than four times as many as in Gibraltar), it was important for Spain to place the emphasis on 'the rights and interests of the population'. The writer noted that King Hassan had accepted that there was a connection between the problems of Gibraltar and the enclaves, and in the context of the King's idea of federal regionalism on the German model he concluded that shared sovereignty might be a possible solution.

It is doubtful whether the Spanish Government would have accepted these arguments in public at this stage, even if they were prepared to concede them in private. But it is interesting to note that the argument that Spanish writers usually used to distinguish between the two cases—that Gibraltar was a colony, while Ceuta and Melilla were part of Spanish territory—was now conspicuously absent. The possible timescale for a solution to be reached is a further indication of a growing realism in Spain regarding the Gibraltar issue.

The airport came back on to the agenda in October, when Gibraltar presented an appeal to the European Court of Justice to repeal Article 2.2 of the directive on the liberalisation of inter-regional flights which had been approved on 18 July.[4] The objective was to nullify the agreement signed between Spain and Britain in December 1987, which excluded Gibraltar's airport from the directive until there was a terminal available to Spain. The appeal was presented to the Court on 4 October, and although a response was normally delivered within a month, the issue dragged on for many more months before a decision was finally handed down. This delay—initially at least—suited the Spanish Government, which wanted to avoid the issue becoming embroiled in the General Election campaign which had been called for 29 October 1989. Spain was concerned that the British Government might be backing Gibraltar's position, thereby calling the 1987 agreement into question; alternatively, if Gibraltar had gone behind the Foreign Office's back, it made it difficult for Spain to know precisely who was in charge of foreign policy for Gibraltar.

Towards the end of December the Council of Ministers submitted its objections to the appeal, on the grounds that Gibraltar was not legally in a position to undertake action against a Community decision because of its special status within the EC which did not entitle it to make its own foreign policy.[5] In January 1990 the Spanish Government also submitted an objection to the appeal on the grounds that the airport was situated on disputed territory. When Madrid sought the British Government's support for its objection, it was duly given, and London also gave the assurance that if the Court decided to hear Gibraltar's appeal, a joint defence would be mounted.

This was the first time that Britain had agreed that it would take sides with Spain against Gibraltar, and a clear indication of its desire to keep on the right side of the Spanish Government. But the other side of the coin was that the Gibraltarians would only feel more isolated and therefore more determined to find other ways of increasing their economic independence.

Not only was there a new Government in Spain at the end of 1989, but there was also a new Governor in Gibraltar. At the investiture ceremony in the House of Assembly on 1 December, Admiral Derek Reffell called for closer cooperation with Spain. In his reply the Chief Minister said that Gibraltarians wanted friendship with their neighbours, based on fairness and justice, but without arousing false hopes regarding Spain's claims to the Rock. More than five years after the signing of the Brussels Declaration, there could be few Spaniards who had any hopes of an early resolution to the problem. It is true that there was internal criticism of the Gibraltar Government's position from opposition leaders such as Mr Canepa of the AACR, who claimed that there was no clear Government policy on relations with Spain, and Peter Montegriffo of the newly formed Gibraltar Social Democrats, who argued that Mr Bossano's boycott of the Brussels Declaration talks was damaging to Gibraltar's interests.[6] But there was no doubt that Joe Bossano's determined resistance to any modification to Gibraltar's sovereignty had overwhelming popular support, and that his stance on this issue was enough to enable him to ride any opposition for the foreseeable future.

Notes

1 Gibraltar had been excluded from an agreement on tackling contraband signed at the EC summit in Madrid three days before the incident occurred. It is estimated that 500 tons of hashish per year is brought across the Strait from Morocco and enters Europe either through Gibraltar or the Spanish Costa del Sol. It is also alleged that this has led to the laundering of drug money on the Rock, and that some of the thousands of new companies set up in Gibraltar were being used by drug traffickers to buy up Spanish property. Spain and Britain attempted

to improve cooperation on these matters through accords signed in February 1990 (see below, Chapter 20).

2 Charges were eventually quietly dropped by the Attorney General in Gibraltar in January 1990.

3 Some weeks later a right-wing Senator for Málaga, Enrique Bolín, was sentenced to four months' imprisonment in Gibraltar for possession of cocaine. He was released on medical grounds on 19 September after serving three weeks of his sentence following an appeal to the Gibraltarian Supreme Court. On release he claimed that the Gibraltarian authorities had 'wanted to show their teeth to Spain', and regretted the fact that the Spanish authorities had done nothing to help him. See *El País*, 20 September 1989, p. 20.

4 Earlier in the year it was reported that Gibraltarian Ministers were considering proposals to extend the airport on reclaimed land. They included a new terminal and a longer runway which would enable larger planes to land than the current Boeing 737s. It was seen as part of Gibraltar's plan to reject the agreement reached between London and Madrid on joint use of the airport, and to offer an alternative which would be acceptable to all parties concerned. At that stage (April 1989) the Gibraltar Government had not taken any decision on the proposals.

5 However, as Gibraltar's Chief Minister pointed out in a letter to *The Times* on 17 February 1990, the 1987 Agreement did give the people of Gibraltar or their elected representatives the right to decide whether or not to implement it, and they had chosen not to do so on numerous occasions.

6 Mr Montegriffo was calling for Gibraltar to be allowed to participate in the talks in their own right, and not just as part of the British delegation. There was no indication that Spain was likely to concede on this point.

TWENTY

TACKLING MONEY-LAUNDERING AND SMUGGLING
February–December 1990

Early in 1990 the Chief Minister of Gibraltar, Joe Bossano, had a meeting with one of the leaders of the Campo region, just as he had done at the beginning of the previous year. This time his interlocutor was the Chairman of the Association of Councils for the region, José Carracao, the venue was Joe Bossano's official residence, and the main subjects of their talks (held on 9 February) were the possibility of Gibraltar's water being supplied from southern Spain and the use by Gibraltar of the waste tip at Los Barrios when the incinerator on the Rock was out of commission. Mr Bossano was clearly intent on continuing to pursue his plan to collaborate with the Campo region for their mutual benefit but outside the framework of the Brussels Declaration.

However, the major meeting early in the year was the fifth annual encounter between the Spanish and British Foreign Ministers, Francisco Fernández Ordóñez and (for the first time) Douglas Hurd, who had replaced Sir Geoffrey Howe following his resignation the previous autumn. Their meeting had been scheduled for December 1989 and finally took place in Madrid on 26 February 1990. The run up to the meeting made it quite clear that there would be no progress on the current bone of contention—the implementation of the airport agreement—because the Chief Minister of Gibraltar had made it plain in an interview published in *Europa Sur* in January and reported in the Spanish press that he was still firmly opposed to it.[1] Furthermore, he emphasised that he was still firmly opposed to the spirit of the Brussels Declaration: 'When we have a single currency, the same passport with the same colour and can move around freely anywhere in Europe, how on earth will Spain be able to justify its historical claim? Spain is wasting its time if it thinks that it can tell Britain to force the Gibraltarians to become Spanish'.[2]

The principal outcome of the talks had been flagged in the Spanish press during the preceding few weeks: a decision to include Gibraltar in two existing bilateral agreements—the 1985 extradition treaty and the 1989 anti-smuggling agreement (it was the exclusion of Gibraltar from this which had led to the diplomatic confrontation in July 1989). This was the first time that Britain had extended an agreement held with Spain to cover Gibraltar. The ministers also signed a new agreement to tackle money-laundering, and Britain agreed to include Gibraltar in the Naples Convention of 1967 on mutual customs assistance.

That something needed to be done on cross-border crime was blatantly evident. Money-laundering had become one of the fastest growing industries in the region. By early 1990 border crossings in each direction totalled over 160,000 pedestrians and nearly 110,000 cars per month. More than half of the vehicles bore number plates from Málaga or Cádiz; many of them crossed several times in one day, carrying each time the maximum currency allowed of 120,000 pesetas (£600) plus 300,000 pesetas (£1,500) in foreign exchange. Five such trips could involve the outflow of over 2 million pesetas (£10,000) per person per day, and those who risked taking out more than the limit on one trip stood only a 2% chance of getting caught. The banks in Gibraltar asked no questions when an account was opened and money was deposited.[3] The money could be used to set up an off-shore company, with the owner's name concealed from public scrutiny by use of a nominee as share-holder. The company's assets could then be used to buy property in Spain, with the company benefiting from tax concessions available to foreign investors. Small wonder that since the opening of the border some 30,000 companies had been established on the Rock, with deposits conservatively estimated at £1.85 billion (370,000 million pesetas), and that much of their capital had been used to buy property on the Costa del Sol. The only consolation for Spain was that at least a good deal of it was Spanish money being reinvested in the country, but the loss to the Spanish Exchequer in tax revenue was substantial.[4]

The smuggling industry was equally thriving. In 1989 the

Customs Detection Service (Servicio de Vigilancia Aduanera) for the Province of Cádiz alone seized 1,355 crates of cigarettes arriving from Gibraltar, containing some 677,500 packets. The total number of packets smuggled into Spain on an annual basis was estimated to be in the region of 100 million. Smugglers would buy the cigarettes at 60 pesetas per packet on the Rock and ship them to the Campo by speedboat for resale at 225 pesetas.[5] In addition, 70 kilos of cocaine and 3,900 kilos of cannabis were seized. Clearly, only the tip of the iceberg came into the authorities' hands.

Joe Bossano saw the move to extend the anti-money-laundering agreement to Gibraltar as a means whereby Spain could restrict Gibraltar's economic growth. This had indeed been spectacular in the last couple of years, and the last thing Spain wanted was for Gibraltar to demonstrate its ability to acquire financial independence. From the British point of view, although the agreements could be seen as a sop to Spain in lieu of progress on more substantive issues, it was also the case that it gave Spain a lever by which it could argue that if Britain could impose a decision on Gibraltar on these accords, then it could do the same with regard to the airport agreement.

At the press conference after the meeting, Mr Hurd claimed that there was a difference between these agreements—which were part of Gibraltar's external relations and which the Gibraltar Government welcomed—and the airport agreement, which was partly an internal matter for Gibraltar. Sr Fernández Ordóñez reiterated Spain's growing impatience at the lack of progress on the airport issue by referring to the possibility of establishing a Spanish airport on the Campo side of the border. On the question of sovereignty he made the customary assertions that 'a colonised territory has no place in a united Europe' and that 'there will be no progress on Gibraltar until sovereignty is returned to Spain'. Douglas Hurd gave the traditional response that Britain had 'a constitutional commitment' to the Gibraltarians.

The tone of the editorial published in *El País* on 1 March was more conciliatory towards Gibraltar than it was towards London. Negotiations take place between Madrid and London, but the writer acknowledged that the solution to the problem depends upon the Gibraltarians being persuaded that it is in their interests to become part of Spain, and this is a long-term process. Where the writer is critical is in relation to those responsibilities which are exercised by London in theory but not in practice, exemplified by regulations to prevent money-laundering and the implementation of the airport agreement. The writer concludes by suggesting that Joe Bossano should be invited to Madrid for civilised discussions.

The problem with that suggestion was that all along the Spanish Government had wanted to avoid enhancing the status of Gibraltar's Chief Minister. While Sir Joshua Hassan had been accepted as a member of the British delegation during post-Brussels Declaration discussions, there was never any question of bilateral talks between him and Spanish ministers. Joe Bossano could, of course, have participated as a member of the post-Brussels British team, but he was implacably opposed to the Brussels process and had rejected any and every opportunity to take part. The British Government had hoped that Mr Bossano would change his mind, for as a participant he would have been giving Gibraltarian consent to any agreements between London and Madrid. But after three successive refusals to do so, there was little likelihood of any change of approach or change of strategy by the Chief Minister.

Following the meeting of the two Foreign Ministers, concern about Gibraltar's connections with tobacco-smuggling, drug-running and money-laundering continued in the Spanish press. It was scarcely surprising, given the impasse on the major issue of the airport and on talks on sovereignty, that much should be made in Spain of those issues which highlighted dubious activities and criminality, for they cast both the British and the Gibraltarians in a bad light and threatened to undermine Gibraltar's pretensions as an off-shore financial centre. As a consequence, the British Ambassador in Madrid, Sir Robin Fearn, felt obliged to defend them both in an article published in *El País* on 24 March entitled 'A Rock free from all suspicion'. Some in Spain might have felt that he protested too much.

An important contact between the Rock and the Campo was re-established at Governor level when on 11 May Admiral Derek Reffell, the Governor of Gibraltar, paid the first official visit for 25 years to the Governor of the Campo, General Carlos López Poza. But this was a diplomatic formality which had more of a symbolic than a practical impact.

The agreement to tackle the smuggling—particularly drugs and tobacco—and related money-laundering problems bore fruit later in the year with the establishment of two joint working groups, one to try to combat the money-laundering involving the twenty-five international banks which had by then been established in Gibraltar, the other to tackle the use of speedboats to bring cannabis across the Strait, many of which were alleged to operate out of Gibraltar (following a ban in Spain from September 1989 on the use of speedboats over a certain size and capacity). The meeting to establish the working groups was held in Madrid on 23 and 24 July, and was attended by the Head of Britain's National Drugs Intelligence Unit, two liaison officers from Scotland Yard, Gibraltar's police commissioner, the Director-General of Spain's judicial police, a Guardia Civil colonel and officials of the Spanish Foreign Ministry. According to a joint statement issued at the end of the meeting, the two sides agreed to meet regularly 'to study measures necessary to confront the problem of drug trafficking' in an area of the Campo de Gibraltar extending both to the east and to the west of the Rock itself. Although the problem was clearly not confined to Gibraltar, the fact that joint measures were to be taken was an indication that the lack of progress on more substantive matters did not prevent the implementation of action on practical issues which affected both sides.

The latter part of the year saw dramatic international events unfold as the Cold War came to an end and profound changes began to take shape in Central Europe. One of the main diplomatic events in that process was the meeting of thirty-four Heads of State and Heads of Government in Paris in November at the summit of the Conference on Security and Cooperation in Europe (CSCE). Each national representative had the opportunity to address the Conference, and when it was the turn of the Spanish Prime Minister on 20 November he could not resist such an opportunity to remind the leaders of so many governments of the fact that his country still had a problem to resolve with Britain. It was only a paragraph, it was moderate in tone, and in order not to cross swords with the British Government the Spanish delegation informed them beforehand that Sr González intended to refer to Gibraltar. 'We cannot', he said, 'allow the continued existence of anachronistic relics. I am confident that through the process of negotiation we can resolve the problem of Gibraltar'.

Of the other leaders present, there was one—Mrs Thatcher—whom Sr González hoped was listening most attentively to his remarks. However, it is highly likely that her mind was on other matters, for (leaving aside the fact that the Conference was dealing with far more momentous issues than that of Gibraltar) back in London Conservative MPs were in the process of stabbing her in the back. Two days later Mrs Thatcher resigned. The Spanish Prime Minister would have to catch the ear of a new British counterpart.

The resignation of Margaret Thatcher as Prime Minister and leader of the Conservative Party on 22 November was given full coverage in the Spanish press the next day. *El País* made it the front-page story and devoted five further pages to it, plus an editorial. Mrs Thatcher was Prime Minister at the time the Lisbon Agreement was signed in 1980, and had been in power ever since. She had therefore been the ultimate arbiter of British policy on Gibraltar for the past decade, and the pace of progress on the implementation of the Lisbon and Brussels accords had been determined by her policies. The story of the resignation and the résumé of her career printed by the Spanish paper contained no reference to her stance on Gibraltar—there were too many other dramas and highlights with which to fill the allotted space. But reference to the Rock was contained in a related story, for it so happened that on 27 and 28 November Felipe González was scheduled to make the first official visit to Britain since 1982 by a Spanish Prime Minister, a visit which in the circumstances he decided to postpone. He let it be known that—not surprisingly—he had intended to raise the issue of Gibraltar in his talks in London. Sr González would not have bet on any change to the status quo as a consequence of his doing so, but for those who believed that diplomatic pressure at the highest level was an essential ingredient in the process of change, the timing of the British Prime Minister's resignation could not have been more frustrating. Joe Bossano's comment on the resignation—'a change of leader does not mean a change in the basic position'—was, however, a realistic assessment, as the immediate future was to prove.

Despite postponement of Sr González's visit, *The Observer* went ahead with an interview with him which it published on 25 November and which was duly reported in the Spanish press the following day. In his most outspoken statement on the Gibraltar issue since becoming Prime Minister in 1982, Sr González was quoted as saying that he thought Britain's claim to sovereignty over Gibraltar was 'at least doubtful', and that in his view, by allowing Gibraltar to block the implementation of the airport agreement for three years 'the United Kingdom had, de facto, forfeited sovereignty over Gibraltar'. No doubt there was a certain amount of power-play about the Spanish Prime Minister's remarks, which were designed to remind the new British Prime Minister of the Spanish Government's resolve not to slacken the pressure on the resolution of the Gibraltar question.

The year drew to a close with a return to an issue which had been left on the shelf since May 1986. It concerned the complete removal of the border gates and railings between Gibraltar and Spain, and it was raised on 27 December at a meeting with the Spanish Foreign Minister, Sr Fernández Ordóñez, by Tristan Garel-Jones, Minister of State at the Foreign Office, who was in Spain for Christmas with his Spanish-born wife. Their thirty-minute meeting was held at Mr Garel-Jones' request to sound out Spanish reactions prior to the next bilateral meeting of Foreign Ministers scheduled for February 1991. The British Minister proposed the replacement of the gates and railings by boundary stones or flower-beds, and they also discussed a Japanese plan to build a new airport in Gibraltar elsewhere on the isthmus. The Spanish response was that they would support the replacement of the border 'in a Europe in which walls were being brought down;' on the airport question, they insisted on the implementation of the agreement on joint use.[6]

So another year drew to a close with the position on Gibraltar much the same as it was when the year began. However, the new year was to reveal that events which had occurred in 1940 might have made things very different.

Notes

1 According to the results of a survey published in *Panorama*, 78% of Gibraltarians were also opposed to the European directive on joint use of the airport.

2 *ABC*, 21 January 1990, p. 37.

3 In June 1991 a Financial Services Commission was established to regulate all financial companies. One of the measures introduced to combat money-laundering was to restrict cash deposits to £10,000 (two million pesetas) in all Gibraltarian banks, and to investigate the origins of those over £5,000.

4 By early 1992 the amount of investment in Spain originating from Gibraltar exceeded 37,000 million pesetas (over £185 million) per year. An Income Tax Reform Law introduced in Spain in January 1992 made such companies subject to Spanish taxation through the Impuesto Especial sobre Sociedades (the Special Company Tax). In anticipation, during the course of 1990 and 1991 many of these Gibraltarian companies transferred to other countries, particularly to Holland, where the tax system was less rigid than in Spain and with whom Spain had an agreement to avoid double taxation in such cases.

5 In a parliamentary reply to Jerónimo Andreu in November 1990 this 'loop-hole'—whereby speedboats could operate out of Gibraltar—was blamed by the Spanish Government for the failure of their anti-smuggling measures passed in September 1989. In August 1989 a memorandum from the Guardia Civil to the Treasury accused the Gibraltarian authorities of aiding and abetting tobacco-smuggling.

6 In mid-December Gibraltar offered to open its airport to Spanish planes, but the offer was turned down by the Spanish Government on the grounds that it was outside the 1987 agreement.

TWENTY-ONE
FELIPE VISITS LONDON
January–May 1991

As is customary, British Cabinet papers for 1960 were released to the Public Record Office on the first day of 1991 under the thirty-year rule, together with other papers previously held back because of their continuing sensitivity. Amongst the latter should have been minutes of Second World War cabinet discussions from 18 and 19 June 1940, which revealed that the British Government had considered handing Gibraltar to Spain after the war in return for guarantees from General Franco that Spain would remain neutral during the remainder of the war. Because it was felt that placing these minutes in the public domain might damage Britain's current negotiating position with Spain, it was decided by the Whitehall 'weeders' (presumably under instruction from the Foreign Office) to extend the delay on their release.

However, the minutes and their contents had already been released by mistake, and reference to them had been made in a book which had already been published.[1] This reference was reported by *The Guardian* and picked up by the Spanish press. The Foreign Office was surely not amused at Whitehall's error. The last thing that the British Government wanted Spain to know was that they had long since viewed Gibraltar as expendable, and that they had even been prepared to hand the Rock over to a dictator against the wishes of the Gibraltarian people.

Joe Bossano was more concerned with what Britain planned to do about the colony in the future than with what it might have done in the past, and he continued to try to shape those plans through dialogue and collaboration with leaders in the Campo region. On 12 January he had further talks, this time in Algeciras, with José Carracao, the Chairman of the Association of Councils of the Campo region. Sr Carracao made it clear to the press that his approach to good relations was to consider their usefulness to the region, not to deal with 'philosophical' questions (as he put it) like sovereignty.[2] He pointed out that of the 1,000 jobs created on the Rock over the previous four years, 800 had been taken up by Spaniards and that 20% of the colony's workforce now came from the Campo region. The use of the airport was discussed in the talks, but Mr Bossano's position remained that 'Gibraltar airport belongs to the people of Gibraltar and we shall decide who uses it'.[3]

The strategic importance of Gibraltar was highlighted once more when the UN ultimatum to Iraq to withdraw from Kuwait expired on 15 January and hostilities in the Gulf became inevitable. Gibraltar immediately suspended all air and sea communications with Morocco and Tunisia in case of a terrorist attack because of Britain's participation in the crisis, and Gibraltarians were advised by the British Foreign Office not to travel to North Africa. On 22 January anti-terrorist exercises were carried out by the military and civil police, the Royal Navy and the RAF.[4] Gibraltar's police were armed for the first time and North Africans were subject to identity checks and detention. Military installations were sandbagged and troops were placed on a high degree of alert. Heavily armed soldiers patrolled the airport, where 18 fighter planes had recently arrived. Sniffer dogs were used at the frontier crossing point and there were fears that it might be closed. Moroccan passport-holders required visas. Such precautionary activities, despite the distance between Gibraltar and the theatre of operations, served as a reminder of the sensitivity of Gibraltar's position whenever a military crisis arose.

With the Gulf crisis still in the balance—the land offensive against Iraqi forces had yet to take place—the annual encounter on 12 February in London between British and Spanish Foreign Ministers to discuss the Gibraltar issue went almost unnoticed. The briefest of press reports since the annual meetings began indicated that Sr Fernández Ordóñez was still calling for the return of sovereignty to Spain, but that with the Single European Market now less than two years away the argument had increasingly to be placed in a European context. Describing the position of Gibraltar as 'an anachronism', the Spanish Foreign Minister said that 'since the fall of the Berlin Wall, Gibraltar is the last remnant of an absurd situation'. But with attention focused on the Middle East, it was scarcely surprising that no progress on the Gibraltar question was made at this juncture.

The following month, despite the recent heightened awareness of the strategic importance of the Rock, Britain went ahead with the withdrawal of British troops which had been announced by Sir Geoffrey Howe two years earlier. On 19 March the last English battalion to serve on the Rock, the 3rd Battalion Royal Green Jackets, lowered its flag for the last time and handed over the Lathbury Barracks to the Gibraltar Regiment. The only remaining British forces, once the Green Jackets' withdrawal was complete, would be 530 men of the Royal Navy and 390 of the RAF. So ended 287 years of British infantry presence in Gibraltar. The message being sent to Spain was clearly that Britain was prepared to withdraw; what was not so clear was what kind of future for Gibraltar was envisaged.

Joe Bossano, Gibraltar's Chief Minister, played down the significance of the withdrawal, suggesting that Britain no longer needed to defend Gibraltar from possible Spanish invasion ('no-one thinks that Spain will do with Gibraltar what Iraq did with Kuwait'), and that this was all part of a reduction in British defence spending made possible by the easing of tension between Eastern and Western Europe.

Although it might have reacted differently some years earlier, Spain did not read much more than this into the withdrawal, either. It was self-evident that the British troops were no longer needed for defence purposes. Whilst it might have been possible to draw some parallels between Saddam Hussein and General Franco, no-one would have contemplated doing so between the Iraqi leader and King Juan Carlos or his Prime Minister Felipe González. What the removal of the British infantry showed was British confidence in the stability of Spanish political institutions and in Spain's commitment to its international obligations. But it made no difference to the impasse on the implementation of the Brussels Declaration; Britain was no closer to handing the Rock over to Spain than before. The main effect was not a political but an economic one; about 25% of Gibraltar's income came from defence spending, representing some £40 million a year, and although the Gibraltar Regiment's numbers were increased to 400 men, the withdrawal of the Green Jackets represented a loss of the spending power of 500 men and their 750 dependents. The Gibraltarian economy would have to find some way of compensating for the financial loss.

Spain's low-key reaction to the withdrawal of the British troops reflected the fact that the Spanish Government was coming to terms with the impossibility of a straight political solution to the question of sovereignty (although in diplomatic encounters they would continue to demand it), and was adjusting to the idea that a more realistic approach was indeed through the reduction of a British presence in Gibraltar as a military base. Spain was still undergoing the process of negotiating with NATO the six basic missions or general directives which it had assumed on membership. By April 1991 four of these had been concluded—air defence and operations in the Eastern Atlantic in May 1990, air and sea operations in the Western Atlantic in January 1991, and most recently the defence of Spanish territory on 12 April 1991. The two remaining agreements concerned the complicated issue of logistical support to be provided by Spain and the control of the Strait of Gibraltar.

What Spain was seeking in relation to this last agreement was for the defence of the Strait to be principally under Spanish control. Spain could not get rid of GIBMED (the NATO command held in Gibraltar) because the country was not part of NATO's military structure, but Spain's objective was to reduce GIBMED's importance substantially by assuming all its powers. Spain based its argument on the strategic point that Gibraltar was boxed in geographically and that the Strait could be better defended from the Spanish naval base at Rota, in the Province of Cádiz. The weakness of the Spanish case (although plans were already in hand to remedy it) was that Spain's communications system was far inferior to the British system installed in Gibraltar which acted as a link between AFSOUTH, the NATO command responsible for the Mediterranean based in Naples, and the SACLANT command covering the Atlantic and based in Norfolk, Virginia. According to a Spanish Foreign Affairs Ministry source, an agreement giving Spain the responsibility for control of the Strait would offer 'a legal process to a difficult problem, the solution to which will require that Gibraltar ceases to be a British base'. Once that was achieved, the Spanish Government would have a stronger case to argue for a political solution. Britain, however, wanted to lose neither responsibility for GIBMED nor, as a consequence, control of the coastal waters around the base. Inevitably, the outcome agreed in July was a compromise whereby Spain and Britain would jointly but separately exercise control over the Strait, with each having access via the commands at Lisbon and Naples to information generated by the other. Control of operations would be exercised by whichever country contributed more troops. Thus the key question of who had the main responsibility over the Strait remained unresolved.

Nevertheless the dual thrust of Spain's approach to the Gibraltar problem continued to be that the demands of the EC and of joint membership of NATO required a solution to the dispute to be achieved sooner rather than later. That was still the case when, accompanied by the Minister for Foreign Affairs, Sr Fernández Ordóñez, and the Finance Minister, Carlos Solchaga, Felipe González paid his first official visit to London for two days of talks on 7 and 8 May.[5] This was the visit the Spanish Prime Minister would have made in November 1990 had Mrs Thatcher not resigned. He had visited the other major countries of the EC four or fives times during his nine years in office. There was never any suggestion that he had preferred to avoid a meeting with Mrs Thatcher for personal reasons—clearly, the Gibraltar problem was the reason why this was his first visit during that time—but there can be no doubt that he was more likely to establish a good working relationship with John Major (who was close in age, who regularly spent his summer holiday in Spain, and whose style is less abrasive) than with the new British Prime Minister's predecessor.[6]

On 26 April, just before the visit took place, there was a minor diplomatic incident which resulted in a protest by the Foreign Affairs Ministry to the British Embassy in Madrid. Two super-tankers—one Liberian, the other Iranian, with a combined total of 525,000 tonnes of oil on board—had dropped anchor in the Bay of Algeciras awaiting instructions from their owners and had refused to leave, despite the request of a Spanish patrol vessel acting in accordance with a ministerial order of 18 April restricting the mooring in Spanish waters of vessels carrying dangerous cargoes. The problem arose from the fact that the ships claimed they were in Gibraltarian territorial waters because, although such issues were not covered by the Treaty of Utrecht, the British Government argued that juridical title to the coastline gave it sovereignty over the territorial waters. The Spanish diplomatic approach—they denied it was a protest—was made on environmental rather than on juridical grounds. With the Heads of Government meeting so close, the British Embassy's response was that they would 'move in the direction requested by Spain'. Once again it was notable that the temperature in such an incident was kept far cooler than would have been the case in the recent past.

There were several important subjects on the agenda for discussion in London; Gibraltar was inevitably one of them. There was never any likelihood of any shift by the British Government, especially since the Foreign Office position was, according to one source reported in *El País*, 'not to resolve the problem, but to dissolve it' through closer collaboration with the Campo de Gibraltar and, as far as possible, to place the issue within an EC framework.

At the dinner held in 10 Downing Street on 7 May Sr González said in his speech that the Gibraltar problem was an 'historical anachronism' which affected bilateral, European Community and multilateral relations, and he called for an imaginative response (with which Spain was willing to assist) by the British Government to find a solution which was not solely based upon the wishes of the Gibraltarians. At the press conference following the talks, the Spanish Prime Minister indicated that he had made some 'imaginative proposals', upon which he declined to elaborate. There was some confusion as to whether these proposals included joint sovereignty. According to the Spanish Foreign Minister they did not (a position which he reiterated in an interview a month later in the *Gibraltar Chronicle*), but a report in *The Independent* on 9 May indicated that Sr González had suggested a plan which would involve the two monarchs as joint heads of state with virtual autonomy for the Gibraltarians. Neither side was prepared to comment publicly. If this was indeed a Spanish proposal, it marked a concession on Spain's part because hitherto the demand had always been for the *transfer* of sovereignty. But for Britain to accept it, it too would have to make the major concession of discounting the wishes of the Gibraltarian people. Although it was reported that Mr Major had 'an open mind' on the Spanish proposal, there was little likelihood that it would be taken up. The official line was that 'Britain would continue to work through the established framework' (shorthand for the Brussels Declaration process) and that nothing would be done without the agreement of the Gibraltarians.

The Foreign Office position was that 'joint sovereignty is not something that we are considering'.

With Britain seeking allies amongst its EC partners on the questions of monetary, economic and political union, it is likely that Sr González saw this as a propitious time to press for some movement on the Gibraltar issue in return for Spanish support. That, together with the fact that he had to be seen to be reiterating Spain's claim to Gibraltar on his first visit to Britain, is why he gave it a high profile in the talks and the press conference. But he was realistic enough to recognise that a reminder of Spain's ability to jeopardise Gibraltar's growing economic self-sufficiency was more likely to have an impact on the impasse in negotiations than were proposals on joint sovereignty. Sr González reiterated, therefore, the suggestion made by his Foreign Minister fifteen months earlier, that if Gibraltar persisted in refusing to allow joint use of the airport, Spain would build another one on the Spanish side of the border in order to force the issue, although in an interview with *The Financial Times* on 9 May he did describe the situation as 'absolutely irrational that while we are building a Community I am obliged to build an airport 20 kilometres away from one that already exists'. With major airports at Málaga and Jérez de la Frontera as well as Gibraltar, any decision to build one near La Línea would clearly be a political rather than an economic one.

There was still clearly both a difference in British and Spanish attitudes towards the Gibraltar problem, and a difference in the strategy each adopted to deal with it. Felipe González, in the interview with *The Financial Times*, neatly summed up the difference in attitudes: 'For the British, Gibraltar is a visit to the dentist once a year when we meet to talk about it. For us, it is a stone in the shoe all day long'. As far as strategy is concerned, Spain tried a combination of the carrot of different models of sovereignty, all with a high degree of autonomy for the Gibraltarians, and the stick of threatening economic warfare through a rival airport. Britain's strategy was not to try to solve the problem, but to continue to seek to 'dissolve it within the EC', as the Minister of State at the Foreign Office, Tristan Garel-Jones, put it.[7]

The editorial writer on 9 May in *El País* was not impressed with the way the Gibraltar issue was being handled. In a column headed 'Empty words' the writer rejected Felipe González's suggestion that

Gibraltar was interfering with good Anglo-Spanish relations, saying that they had never been better. Spain had behaved perfectly correctly over its claim, and the blame for the failure to resolve the issue lay with Britain, caught in its own trap of having to act in accordance with the wishes of the Gibraltarians. But, the writer suggested, the Spanish Government ought at least to be insisting on the implementation of the airport agreement, otherwise there was no point in having signed it. It did not seem to have a realistic plan, but preferred to avoid any fundamental analysis of the problem.

In an attempt to show an understanding of how Spaniards must feel about Gibraltar, a leading article on the same day in *The Independent* was certain that if the Germans had acquired a few square miles on the tip of Cornwall by force of arms a couple of centuries earlier the British would resent their continuing presence. The writer therefore welcomed the joint sovereignty proposal as the planting of a seed which deserved to be nurtured. Both statements drew dissenting letters from correspondents which were published on 10 May. One asked why Spain's presence in Ceuta and Melilla is not mentioned when British intransigence over Gibraltar is being criticised; another asked why joint sovereignty is right for Gibraltar but not for Northern Ireland; a third, from the Director of the European Movement, criticised the concept of national sovereignty as an outmoded notion, and called for Gibraltar's position within the EC to be clarified so that it could acquire self-determination within the new European framework.

The correspondence did not stop there. On 14 May Sir Anthony Kershaw, a former Chairman of the House of Commons Select Committee on Foreign Affairs, called for the British Government to scrap the Preamble to the 1969 Gibraltar Constitution and to consider a change to an arrangement like that of the condominium between France and Spain in Andorra. 'Twenty thousand Gibraltarians ought not to have a veto on British policy', he wrote. 'I hope that Her Majesty's Government will stop sitting on its hands, and will agree to modify the Treaty of Utrecht'.

The riposte was swift and in triplicate. In a letter published on 16 May John Crookshank, a former ADC to the Governor of Gibraltar, rejected Sir Anthony's claim that Gibraltar no longer had any military value, and pointed to the role that the Rock had played in the recently concluded Gulf War. Rather than the analogy with

Andorra, he preferred one with the North African enclaves, and suggested that 'a solution will evolve through commercial imperatives'.

The second letter came from a Charles Gomez from Gibraltar, who argued on 20 May that Gibraltar could not enjoy its existing legislative, judicial and fiscal freedom under the Spanish Constitution, as Sir Anthony had implied, and called on politicians on all sides to 'give the topic a rest and allow the situation to resolve itself in a natural way'. Some in Spain would no doubt say that this was close to the British Government's current position.

The third correspondent to reply to Sir Anthony was none other than Gibraltar's Chief Minister himself. Mr Bossano's letter on 16 May accused him of being 'in dismissive contempt of the people of Gibraltar' by suggesting the scrapping of the Preamble, and reminded Sir Anthony that the co-princes (as they are called) of Andorra, President Mitterand and the Bishop of Urgel, recently recognised that sovereignty resided with the Andorran people. He concluded: 'Sir Anthony does a great disservice to the traditions and principles of British democracy and to the aspirations of a new diverse European family of peoples by trampling on, and negating, the rights of the people of Gibraltar to decide how they wish to live in their own homeland in harmony with their neighbours'.[8]

There was clearly no shift in the position of Gibraltar's Chief Minister, and if either Britain or Spain were to push the idea of joint sovereignty it would clearly not get very far. Whether or not he was still fully in touch with popular opinion on the Rock was, however, put in some doubt when a poll conducted by the *Gibraltar Chronicle* and the Gibraltar Broadcasting Corporation (and reported in *The Times* on 13 May) indicated that 60% of Gibraltar's eligible voters wanted Gibraltar to resume participation in the Brussels Declaration negotiations,[9] which Gibraltar's Government had boycotted since Bossano came to power in 1988. Since elections were due in January 1992, the voters would soon have the opportunity to indicate whether this was of such overriding importance that a change of Chief Minister was desirable.

Notes

1 The book concerned was by Clive Ponting who, in his *1940: Myth and Reality*, records that Sir Samuel Hoare, Britain's Ambassador in Madrid, suggested that Britain should offer to discuss the future of the Rock with Spain if General Franco guaranteed to remain neutral, and that Churchill vetoed the suggestion. John Costello, whose book *Ten Days that Saved the West* (Bantam Press, 1991) was published after the New Year revelations in the press, puts it slightly differently: he shows (p. 359) that Sir Anthony Eden, the Foreign Secretary, had instructed Sir Samuel to tell General Franco that 'we should be ready to discuss after the war any matter of common interest to Spain and ourselves', but without making specific reference to Gibraltar. The Cabinet minute indicated that even as long ago as 1940 the British Government considered the view that 'Gibraltar was probably far less valuable than in the past owing to the development of air power'.

2 This position was totally contradicted later in the year by the General Secretary of the right-wing Partido Popular in Spain, Francisco Alvarez Cascos. On 3 May, speaking in Algeciras, he said that the Spanish Government should never have opened the border, arguing that 'any surrender of the Spanish position on Gibraltar should be rejected if it does not contribute to the advancement of the recovery of sovereignty, even though there may be favourable economic reasons to do so'.

3 Gibraltar's Chief Minister was also in discussion with the mayor of Jerez, Pedro Pacheco, and on 15 January returned the latter's visit to the Rock made in August 1990.

4 United States air and naval forces used Gibraltar for an anti-terrorist exercise simulating the rescue of diplomatic personnel on 9 February. British troops were not involved. Whereas at one time such activities would have provoked Spanish protests, there were none on this occasion.

5 Several British newspapers claimed that this was the first visit to Britain by a Spanish Prime Minister. In fact, Leopoldo Calvo Sotelo had visited Britain as Prime Minister in January 1982.

6 Mrs Thatcher had, of course, visited Spain in September 1988 (see above, Chapter 16) and as heads of government Felipe González and Margaret Thatcher would have encountered each other on many occasions. The fact that they probably did not find much to say to each other is indicated by a report of the dinner held in Versailles on 20 November 1990 at the CSCE summit. The Prime Ministers of Spain and Britain were seated next to each other, but when asked, Sr González said that he did not speak to Mrs Thatcher 'because I don't speak English and there wasn't an interpreter'. If they had really wished to do so, they could have communicated in French.

7 In an Adjournment Debate, 15 July 1991, (see *Hansard*, Vol. 195, No. 145, Col. 202). Mr Garel-Jones reiterated the Government's position that they rejected Spain's territorial claim over Gibraltar but accepted that 'independence for Gibraltar is not an option' (Col. 200).

8 Mr Bossano had also written to *The Financial Times* on 15 May, accusing the Spanish Prime Minister of misrepresenting the position over the airport question, and reiterating the arguments he had used in December 1987 for Gibraltar airport to be treated as a British regional airport.

9 However, according to the Chairman of the British Gibraltar Group in the House of Commons, Michael Colvin, those polled were not asked whether sovereignty should be part of the negotiations. See *Hansard*, Vol. 195, No. 145, Col. 198.

TWENTY-TWO

FOUR MORE YEARS FOR JOE BOSSANO
May 1991–January 1992

Joe Bossano continued to plough his own furrow. To underline his view that the solution to the Gibraltar problem lay in self-determination in a European context, the Gibraltar Government issued a gold coin on 27 May with a face value of £50 or 70 ecus. Unlike other ecu coins issued for collectors but without the status of legal tender, the Gibraltar coins were the first which were intended for circulation.[1] One side showed a mounted knight in full armour, said to represent Charlemagne, the European Emperor par excellence. The obverse bore Queen Elizabeth's head, and the edge of the coin had twelve stars, representing the EC nations, with a thirteenth star on the knight's shield to represent Gibraltar. It may have been highly symbolic, but it sent a clear message of Gibraltar's commitment to an independent future under both a British and a European umbrella.

A new aspect of Gibraltar's identity had come into play in April 1991 when the International Federation of Association Football (FIFA) rejected an application for membership from Gibraltar because, according to a spokesman, 'it could create political problems between Britain and Spain'. The rejection, in which Gibraltar was described by a sports writer lacking in diplomatic finesse as 'a Spanish territory dependent on the United Kingdom', was reported in *El País* on 27 April. The Spanish Football Federation had indicated that it would object to the admission of the Gibraltar Federation, using Article 1, Paragraph 4, of the FIFA statutes, which requires countries to be independent states. The Government of Gibraltar accused FIFA of politicising their application.

Worse was to follow in the sporting field in June when the International Olympic Committee, meeting in Britain for the first time since 1948, found on its agenda an application from Gibraltar for IOC recognition so that it could compete in the next Olympic Games in July 1992. The complicating factors were that these Games were scheduled to take place in Barcelona, and that the President of the IOC since 1980 was a Spaniard—albeit a Catalan—Juan Antonio Samaranch. Gibraltar's prospective National Olympic Committee feared that attempts would be made by Spain to delay or obstruct their application. They based their fears on a copy of a directive from Spain's Foreign Ministry to its sports organisers, which they claimed to possess and which instructed the organisers to stop Gibraltar from participating in the Barcelona Games.

The fears of Gibraltar's Committee were not without foundation, for the IOC postponed taking a decision on their claims until after the Barcelona Olympics. The IOC President did admit that Gibraltar was a 'delicate problem' but gave as one reason for the decision the fact that there was no more room in the Olympic Village. Gibraltar argued that Spain had being trying to deny them Olympic recognition for 30 years, although the IOC were able to exercise a degree of even-handedness on this occasion by postponing a decision on Cataluña at the same time, as well as Lithuania and Latvia. Gibraltar was entitled to feel aggrieved because, unlike the other supplicants, they had already established the minumum of five international federations required for membership. Gibraltar promised to be back in 1993, but even if recognition were to be granted in time for the 1996 Games, the impact would clearly be much less significant in Atlanta than it would have been in Barcelona. The Spanish Olympic Association clearly contravened the Olympic Charter by observing its Government's directive when the Charter specifically rules otherwise, but it no doubt felt that it was the lesser of two evils. The road to the Barcelona Olympics would no doubt have enough problems without the IOC granting Gibraltar's application at a meeting in Britain (of all places), while at the same time rejecting one from—of all places—Cataluña.

But what the two episodes of FIFA and the IOC showed was that the issue of Gibraltar's sovereignty touched all aspects of the colony's life. It did not just affect its constitutional and legal position, but spheres as diverse as the judicial process (as suggested earlier in connection with the inquest on the IRA terrorists) and the activities of its sportsmen and women.[2]

The Gibraltar issue also became a stumbling block once more to EC agreement. On 26 June the twelve Ministers of the Interior (including Britain's Home Secretary Kenneth Baker and José Luis Corcuera from Spain), were in Luxembourg to prepare an agreement on the crossing of external EC frontiers, in anticipation of the free movement of goods and people within the Community from 1 January 1993. Britain had certain reservations about non-EC citizens legally living in an EC country being able to move freely around the Community, because Britain's borders are simultaneously internal and external borders. Britain therefore succeeded in having words added to the agreement indicating that the recognition of external frontiers had no implications for the recognition of internal frontiers. It was thought that this formula would also satisfy Spain. Initially, Spain was concerned that if it signed the document it could compromise its claim to Gibraltar on the grounds that unless its frontier with Gibraltar were officially recognised in the agreement as an external boundary, with mention made of Gibraltar's special status within the EC, Spain would be deemed to have ceded its claim to sovereignty. Felipe González therefore made it clear on 29 June that Spain would not add its signature to the document while the Gibraltar question remained unresolved.

The date scheduled for the signing of the document was put back to 19 July to allow for agreement between Britain and Spain to be reached, but was eventually postponed indefinitely. For although the problem of the sovereignty issue had been dealt with by Britain agreeing to the inclusion in the document of Spanish concerns in this regard, the real difficulty lay in Spain's insistence that there should be joint control at Gibraltar's external entry points (the port and airport) for foreign visitors before Spain would agree to the removal of the gates at the internal border with Spain.

Spain had tried to persuade Britain to accept by the inclusion in Article 30 that the agreement would only apply to Gibraltar when there had been a bilateral agreement between Britain and Spain. In addition, Spain proposed that in Article 1 the definition of external frontiers should exclude 'foreign territories whose international relations are in the hands of another member State'. Britain would not accept joint control of external entry points; hence the impasse. Once again the Gibraltar dispute was obstructing the process of harmonising EC policies. The patience of other members of the EC was being sorely tested.

Whether as a result of this latest delay in EC negotiations, or whether simply because August is the political silly season, the notion emerged that a solution to the issue of Gibraltarian sovereignty might be to transfer it to the EC. On 29 July *The Times* reported briefly that the Minister of State at the Foreign Office, Tristan Garel-Jones, had rejected such an idea and urged Gibraltarians to come up with realistic proposals.

Despite his reaction, the idea reappeared two weeks later when *The Observer* of 11 August reported that Spanish ministers had welcomed the imaginative idea in principle, and that the two Prime Ministers would discuss it in the autumn. However, *The Independent* the following day reported that both the Spanish Foreign Ministry and the British Foreign Office insisted that the idea of Gibraltarian independence, with the EC holding responsibility for defence and foreign affairs, had not been discussed.

The most likely origin of such a proposal is Gibraltar itself; a survey published on 5 August showed that 52% of Gibraltarians favoured independence, the first time that a majority had called for an end to the link with Britain. It is possible that the British Minister was informed of the poll result, but the idea that the proposal had been explored further was probably pure speculation. Although several leading figures in the dispute had envisaged a solution emerging in an EC context, until the EC developed as a political entity endowed with the capacity to formulate defence and foreign policy, the idea was unlikely to make any progress, even if—and it was a big if—both Spain and Britain thought it was a good one.

Later in the year the Gibraltar issue re-emerged at the United Nations, almost thirty years after the UN Special Committee on Colonialism had first discussed it and with a solution satisfactory to Spain no nearer. The occasion was a speech by King Juan Carlos to the UN General Assembly on 7 October 1991, the second time he had spoken at that forum (the first was in September 1986). The thirty-minute speech was wide-ranging, but included a reminder to the Assembly that Gibraltar was 'a colonial problem which had still not been resolved, which affects Spain's territorial integrity, and which . . . is particularly sensitive for all Spaniards'. The King expressed the hope that the ongoing negotiation process would succeed in reaching a solution 'in tune with the times in which we live'. It would have been interesting to know what the King had in mind by that phrase, and what it implied regarding the future sovereignty of the Rock. Within an EC context, it could be argued that the pooling of sovereignty was more in tune with the times than its transfer. Perhaps the King would urge his Ministers to explore such a possibility.

The question of external frontier controls had remained in abeyance since negotiations broke down in July. Spain had also suspended cooperation with Britain on the control of tobacco and drug smuggling between the Rock and Spain, although it was hard to see what advantage it hoped to gain. Frontier control talks were renewed on a bilateral basis when a British delegation went to Madrid on 14 October. In the interim the issue had become a struggle between the Spanish Interior and Foreign Ministries. The British Home Secretary, Kenneth Baker, had proposed to his Spanish counterpart, José Luis Corcuera, that the agreement should allow Spanish control at the Gibraltar-Spain border to be maintained. The Spanish Interior Minister was inclined to accept the proposal, but the Foreign Ministry argued that it would contradict both the requirement of the Single European Act to suppress internal borders and Article 1 of the proposed agreement which does not allow two consecutive external entry points (in this case Gibraltar and Spain) to be maintained. There was a suspicion in Spain that because of the overlap between Interior Ministry responsibility for border controls and Foreign Ministry responsibility for (as they saw it) a decolonisation issue, Britain had deliberately tried to reach an agreement with the Interior Ministry to which it knew the Foreign Ministry would object. The meeting on 14 October made little progress and was more of an introductory meeting between the newly appointed Director for European Affairs at the Spanish Foreign Ministry, Carmen Rico, and her British counterpart, David Greenstock.[3]

A new figure in Anglo-Spanish discussions on Gibraltar made his appearance at the end of October. José María Aznar, leader of the right-wing Partido Popular, visited London for talks with Conservative colleagues on issues of mutual interest. On 28 October he discussed drug-trafficking and money-laundering between Gibraltar and Spain with the Home Secretary, Kenneth Baker. According to reports of their talks, each pointed to the degree of responsibility held by the other country for these problems. When Sr Aznar met John Major the following day, their discussion on Gibraltar was described as a dialogue of the deaf.

If the talks proved anything, it was that the British line on Gibraltar when talking to Spanish politicians of the right was the same as when they talked to those of the left. The same could not be said of the Partido Popular when talking of Gibraltar on the one hand and Ceuta and Melilla on the other. For while Sr Aznar was arguing to John Major that 'it is quite illogical for such a tiny colony to be a constant tooth-ache for 40 million Spaniards', in a debate in the Spanish Parliament held on the same day (29 October) his party was arguing (and losing the vote) that the North African enclaves of Ceuta and Melilla should be established as autonomous communities like the rest of Spain on the grounds of their Spanishness, and that the Socialist and Izquierda Unida (United Left) Groups, who opposed the proposal on the grounds that the timing was inappropriate, were acting more in the interests of Morocco than of Spain.

Ominously for both Britain and Spain, on the same day as Sr Aznar's meeting with the British Prime Minister was reported, news appeared of the formation of a new political party in Gibraltar, the Gibraltar National Party, which planned to fight for 'the indisputable right of the Gibraltarian people to self-determination'. Certainly the growing activity on the Rock, with new office space and improved telecommunications, was boosting Gibraltarians' confidence in their ability to go it alone financially. In November a further boost was provided, ironically, by Spain's largest bank, the Bilbao Vizcaya, which used the Rock in preference to Luxembourg to raise capital (£167.5 million, equivalent to nearly 33,500 million pesetas) for the largest placement of preference shares on the US stock market by a non-US bank. The founders of the GNP only had to wait until 16 January 1992 to find out whether they had accurately judged the mood of the voters.

In the run-up to the election, the polls gave Joe Bossano and the GSLP a substantial lead, predicting that his party would get 70% of the vote. With the pre-1988 governing party the AACR having collapsed, the main opposition came from the Gibraltar Social Democrats led by a barrister, Peter Caruana.

The election was fought on the issue of Gibraltar's relationship with Britain. The GSD believed that Gibraltar's leaders should participate in the Brussels Declaration negotiations with a view to influencing their outcome. Joe Bossano, who accused the GSD of being 'soft on Spain', hoped that a crushing defeat of the Social Democrats would make Britain and Spain think again about the Brussels Declaration process. His argument was that Gibraltar was now virtually financially independent from Britain (support now came only in the form of Ministry of Defence spending, and this accounted for only 15% of Gibraltar's income), and that it was ready for a new, non-colonial relationship with Britain and other members of the European Union in the post-Maastricht context of pooled sovereignty.

In a 71.7% turnout (5% lower than in 1988) Joe Bossano obtained an overwhelming 75.3% of the vote, 17 points higher than four years previously. The GSD obtained just over 20% and the new GNP 3%, while the leading Independent candidate, Reginald Valerino, came close to taking a seat off the GSD. For the British and Spanish Foreign Ministries, the result of the election could not have been a much harder slap in the face. Mr Bossano's call for a change in Gibraltar's status had clearly been given a boost. He described the result as 'an expression of the self-determination of the people of Gibraltar', and said that if there is to be dialogue with Spain, he has to be the one to speak for Gibraltar, not the British Foreign Office.

The leader writer in *El País* on 22 January recognised that such an overwhelming victory could not be ignored. The answer to a vote for Gibraltarian independence had to be pragmatic and practical. The only way to convince the Gibraltarians, he wrote, that their future lay with Spain was to establish a single tax regime, get rid of smuggling, invest large amounts of money in the whole of the Campo area, set up a joint Campo-Gibraltar Council, build a new airport in Algeciras, and finally invite Joe Bossano to Algeciras, Seville and Madrid for talks about the interests of the people he represents.

Some of these proposals were clearly more realistic than others. But the irony is that although the article was clearly hostile to the notion of Gibraltarian independence which Joe Bossano so firmly advocated, within a week the Chief Minister had actually implemented one of the proposals, for on 29 January, thirteen days after his election victory, he went outside the terms of the Brussels accord and signed an agreement to form a joint economic coordination council with the Mayor of Algeciras, Patricio González. With that, and with Britain's continued willingness to let Gibraltar have the final word on any agreement with Spain, the Brussels Declaration was virtually dead in the water.

Notes

1 On 28 December 1991 Harrods became the first British retail store to accept Gibraltar ecus, in anticipation of ecu coins to be minted elsewhere.

2 The boot was on the other foot just over a year later when in July 1992 the International Cricket Council was asked to consider an application from Spain for affiliate membership. Gibraltar, with five cricket grounds on the Rock, played in the ICC Trophy tournament as an associate member of the Council, and viewed Spain's application with some apprehension.

3 However, an EC agreement was reached at the end of October on the mutual recognition of tourist visas for visitors from third countries. The agreement did not mention border controls and the Gibraltar dispute did not therefore affect it.

TWENTY-THREE
THE EXTERNAL FRONTIER ISSUE REMAINS UNRESOLVED
February–November 1992

Early in 1992 Britain was rudely reminded of the hazards of maintaining a virtually autonomous colony which operates at arm's length from the Foreign Office but for which the Foreign Office holds ultimate responsibility. When things go wrong, the mother country takes the blame.

On 3 February the Joint Council for the Welfare of Immigrants published a report accusing the Governor of Gibraltar of inflicting 'inhuman and degrading treatment' on thousands of Moroccans who came to work in Gibraltar after General Franco closed the border with Spain in 1969. The drafting of some 5,600 workers (all but 600 were Moroccans) to the Rock during the 1970s enabled Gibraltar in general—and its military bases in particular—to survive the blockade. Problems arose largely because the situation was viewed as being temporary, but in fact lasted for 16 years, by which time the guest workers had put down roots and did not wish to return to Morocco. The men were given temporary resident permits, conditional upon their having a job, on the assumption that they would return to North Africa when things returned to normal. Most left their families behind; they had to live in overcrowded, squalid hostels. Some men were deported because they no longer had a job, and when wives and children came to visit and tried to stay, they, too, were deported on the grounds of being unemployed. Some 2,500 Moroccans remain on the Rock; if any of them are laid off, they are liable to be deported, too.

Lawyers were therefore planning to present a series of cases against the Foreign Office at the European Court of Human Rights in Strasbourg and at the European Court of Justice in Luxembourg. But to make matters worse for the immigrants, under EU regulations which came into force on 1 January 1992 Europeans were to be given preference for any new jobs which became available. It was often ordinary Gibraltarians—who were conscious of the valuable role played by the Moroccans during the 16 years of siege—who came to the defence of immigrants threatened with deportation for being unemployed. And ironically, it was often Spaniards—whose Government had been responsible for the siege—who now came to take the jobs on the Rock's new construction sites for which Moroccans and other non-Europeans were not eligible.

The attitude towards the Moroccans in Gibraltar was, however, only a reflection of an increasingly circumspect, not to say hostile attitude towards non-Union citizens which was being manifested across Europe as the questions of external frontiers, immigration and refugees became a major EU preoccupation. In fact, it was Spain itself which was seen as one of Europe's most vulnerable entry points for illegal immigrants from North Africa.

Given that the British Government was having to accept the blame for the treatment of the Moroccans at the hands of Gibraltarian administrators, there will have been some in the Foreign Office who will have wondered whether there was not some way in which Britain could respond positively to what Joe Bossano had to say at the opening session of the new Gibraltar Parliament on 14 February. The Chief Minister took the opportunity to make plain his intention to seek a change in Gibraltar's constitution and status by transferring responsibility for Gibraltar's defence and foreign affairs to the EU, while Britain retained sovereignty and the Rock had autonomy in all other matters. In this way, because there was to be no transfer of sovereignty, change could be effected without contravening the Treaty of Utrecht provision that if sovereignty were to be transferred Spain would have first option. Mr Bossano set a timetable of four years for these reforms to be agreed. With Madrid, to say the least, unlikely to take kindly to the proposal and with talks between the Chief Minister and the Foreign Secretary Douglas Hurd due to take place in London on 20 February, the Foreign Office response to Mr Bossano's remarks was non-committal and restrained.

Such utterances as that of Mr Bossano tend to bring out Spain's sensitivity on the Gibraltar question, and this manifested itself on 2 March when the British Ambassador in Madrid, Sir Robin Fearn, was summoned to the Spanish Foreign Ministry to explain why 44 members of the Gibraltar Regiment had been on a military exercise in the Sierra Nevada. Their presence in Spain had come to light when one of the officers was killed in an avalanche on 20 February. The British Ministry of Defence explanation was that the exercise, called Operation Snowfox, was an annual adventure training event, not a military exercise. The explanation was eventually accepted, but the fact that one was called for in the first place—and at ambassadorial level—is a reflection of the fact that the unresolved Gibraltar problem still represented an irritant in Madrid. The Spanish Foreign Minister described the incident as having 'little importance', although three weeks later British troops were banned from exercises in Spain.[1]

Just prior to the Snowfox incident, Carlos Mendo published one of his periodic fulminations on the Gibraltar situation, entitled 'Two colonies, two attitudes', in the 14 February edition of *El País*. He was particularly concerned about Joe Bossano's use of European institutions to try to protect or further Gibraltar's position.[2] He was critical of the fact that the Spanish Government permitted the border to be opened in 1985 and thereby lost the only negotiating card it had. He lamented the fact that the Crown is the only Spanish institution not to have relegated Spain's claim to Gibraltar to a low priority. Finally, he picked up the parallel with Hong Kong once again, pointing out that Britain's argument that Hong Kong Island could not survive without the New Territories was exactly the same as the case of Gibraltar, which could not survive without the Campo. Yet Britain was prepared to sacrifice the inhabitants of one against their wishes, but not those of the other. He concluded by observing that there were signs that the off-shore banking system of Hong Kong was thinking of moving to Gibraltar, and that it would be ironical if Lord Carrington's remarks—that the problem for Spain is that it is not populated by blacks or Chinese—proved to be prophetic. Sr Mendo's complaint at his own Government's inactivity on the Gibraltar issue stemmed from a sense of frustration that all the huffing and puffing which led to the Brussels Declaration now seemed to have achieved nothing. Sr Mendo himself had said it all before.

Following the Snowfox incident, another previous contributor to the Gibraltar debate,[3] Fernando Schwartz, suggested in an article in *El País* on 5 March that the whole issue was in a cul-de-sac and going nowhere. Having decided that they can do nothing without the prior agreement of the Gibraltarians, he wrote, the British merely complain about Spain's obstinacy. Spain looks for solutions such as sharing sovereignty or running up the Spanish flag on the Rock because 'although the problem leaves the majority of its citizens indifferent, paradoxically they would not tolerate any concessions which could be described as appeasement'. The result is a 'dialogue of the deaf'. Schwartz quotes Fernando Morán, the former Foreign Minister, as having made the only contribution to the Gibraltar issue in the last fifty years which is worthy of mention: 'If Britain were to hand us Gibraltar on a plate, but against the will of its inhabitants, we would not want it'. Hence any solution has to start with the premise that the Gibraltarians agree to it. Therefore, Spain was not going to get anywhere through negotiation with London. The person to negotiate with was Joe Bossano, and what was needed from London was support for such negotiations.

Schwartz described his proposal as pragmatic, and felt that it was pragmatism which would lead to a solution to the problem, not declarations of principles or a search by Britain or Spain for the most glorious way to wrap themselves in their respective flags. The trouble with his proposal was that neither Britain nor Spain could agree to grant the colony the status of a negotiator. Britain could not do so for several reasons: because colonial powers simply do not deal with decolonisation processes in this way, because the outcome could not be guaranteed, and because, constitutionally, Gibraltar's external relations were the responsibility of the British Government. And it was out of the question for Spain because it would have signified recognition of Gibraltar as an independent entity, rather than as it had always been viewed: a long-lost part of national territory 'stolen' by a former enemy as part of the spoils of war.

This certainly appeared to be the official view of the Partido Popular (PP), according to a draft manifesto of foreign policy which was published at the end of April and described in *El País* on 2 May. The PP called the Government's policy on Gibraltar 'a resounding failure', and reproached them for their 'concessions and blandishments', which have done nothing to bring a solution any nearer. In government, the document argued, the Partido Popular would denounce the British Government to the EU and to NATO for the 'passive complicity' which they have shown with regard to solving the problem, and they would demand the opening of negotiations with Britain which would have as their sole objective the return to Spain of sovereignty over the Rock. They would put pressure on Britain by strengthening border controls and progressively restricting border-crossing facilities, even to the point, if necessary, of closing the land-border completely and imposing a blockade. It was a predictably right-wing, reactionary appeal to Spanish chauvinism, and ignored the similarity of this approach to the failed strategy of General Franco. But although the Government would have dismissed the PP's criticisms as unjustified and their proposals as impractical in the context of Spain's modern role, they would have accepted that the PP were also reflecting the growing frustration with the post-Brussels process, a frustration which they themselves shared.[4]

The imminence of a General Election in Britain had been responsible for the postponement of the annual talks between Foreign Ministers which last occurred in February 1991. With the Conservative Party re-elected for a fourth consecutive term of office on 9 April, it was still Douglas Hurd as Foreign Secretary who met his Spanish counterpart Francisco Fernández Ordóñez in Madrid on 4 May, following Mr Hurd's visit to Expo 92 in Seville. With the implementation of the Maastricht agreement and the war in former Yugoslavia their major preoccupations, and with Britain due to take over the Presidency of the European Union in July, the two Foreign Ministers spent very little of their time discussing the Gibraltar problem. In their press conference they merely announced that officials would be meeting shortly in order to prepare for a ministerial session in the autunm. It was looking increasingly unlikely, therefore, that an agreement would be reached on external frontiers in time for its implementation at the beginning of 1993.

The brevity of their remarks did not deter the leader writer on *The Times* on 5 May from devoting a column to the Gibraltar issue and his counterpart on *El País* from doing the same. *The Times'* writer called for an end to the avoidance of the question of sovereignty, particularly in view of the case on the airport agreement which Gibraltar had brought before the European Court. With Britain and

Spain both claiming that Gibraltar had no competence to bring the case, he argued that 'the judgment on the admissibility of the hearing goes to the heart of the constitutional position and the campaign by Joe Bossano's government for Gibraltar's self-government within Europe'.

The writer in *El País* could see no political solution in the short-term, because of the known positions of the protagonists; Spain would never agree to some kind of Union statute for Gibraltar, he asserted. A better chance lay in seeking collaboration; rather pointedly, the writer suggested that Gibraltar's economic situation was not exactly booming and that they needed finance and development based on something more solid than the establishment of tax havens (whether orthodox ones or those based on tobacco-smuggling). Integration for Gibraltar in the EU had to come through Britain or Spain, he argued, and this is what the two Foreign Ministers should be discussing, together with Union officials.

However, there has been no sign of any enthusiasm for such an approach, and in any case the Union has been preoccupied with other matters. Agreement on the external frontier issue still has to be resolved, and there is little sign of that happening either. The Secretary of the Gibraltar National Party, Joe Garcia, wrote a forceful letter to the Prime Minister, John Major, a copy of which was published by *The Times* on 8 May. Mr Garcia foresaw a time when, through the process of European integration, 'there will be no Britain, no Spain and no Gibraltar. We will all be Europeans', and as enthusiastic Europeans, he argued, it would be a betrayal for Gibraltarians to be 'sacrificed at the altar of political expediency' on the external frontiers issue.

The British Prime Minister will certainly not have accepted the kind of Europe of the future that Mr Garcia described, but in his reply, made public on 11 May, John Major made it clear that he would not allow Gibraltar to be excluded from the Convention on External Frontiers. The week before, Sr Fernández Ordóñez had confirmed his Government's position that Spain would not accept the inclusion in the Convention of Gibraltar as an external frontier of the Union unless the application of the Convention was subject to a bilateral agreement, involving joint police and customs control at the port and airport. Spain, in other words, hoped to secure with Britain the same kind of accord on the external frontier issue as it had on the airport question in December 1987. On this occasion, however, the British Government was being less compliant, arguing that the exclusion from the agreement would marginalise Gibraltar from the advantages of the Single Market.

Discussions continued, with Spanish and British delegations meeting outside Lisbon on 1 June to discuss the frontier question. They came up with the proposal that passports of travellers entering Gibraltar would be read by Spanish immigration officers in La Línea via an optical reader, and that permission for entry would have to be granted by an official in both locations. It was formally presented to the British and Spanish Prime Ministers on 3 June in a letter from their Portuguese counterpart Anibal Cavaco Silva, who was anxious to unblock the External Frontiers issue during the Portuguese presidency of the Union which was due to end later that month. The proposal was discussed over the following weekend by Tristan Garel-Jones and his Spanish counterpart, Carlos Westendorp. Felipe González rejected it not on the grounds of expense or impracticality (such machines were already in operation in three Spanish airports), but because it would only further delay a solution to the airport agreement which Spain had been seeking for four-and-a-half years.[5]

Spain was making more progress on another front in relation to Gibraltar, namely its participation in NATO. In May 1992 it completed the negotiations on the two remaining basic missions of its contribution to NATO—the use of Spanish territory for logistics and support, and the control of the Strait—and these were confirmed on 24 June.[6]

It was the second of these missions which had a direct bearing on Gibraltar. On 22 June it was announced that in 1993 Spain would participate for the first time in the 'Open Gate' manoeuvres in the Strait. This would also be the first occasion on which Gibraltarian forces would not be taking part. Hitherto, Spanish forces had been excluded from participation in NATO operations in the area. Now there was the possibility that GIBMED (the NATO command in Gibraltar) would disappear in a restructuring exercise, leaving the way open for Spain to assume control—together with French, Italian, and US participation—of the Strait on NATO's behalf. It remained Spain's hope that the weakening of Gibraltar as a military base would open the way to progress on the political aspect of the problem.

However, political progress (at least in a direction which Spain would find acceptable) had become increasingly unlikely as long as Gibraltarians supported political parties which encouraged the concept of self-determination. Even more worrying for Spain was the fact that it was not only Joe Bossano's GSLP which adopted such a position, but also the main opposition party, the Gibraltar Social Democrats, and on 10 September the leadership of both parties headed a demonstration of over a thousand people who marched on the Governor's residence calling for self-determination for Gibraltar. Later in the year a group calling itself the Self-Determination for Gibraltar Group emerged. They got little encouragement from the British Government, but made their feelings clear about the Brussels Declaration by ceremoniously burning a copy of it on 27 November, the eighth anniversary of its signing.

With the British Government fully occupied with the presidency of the European Union in the second half of 1992, the meeting of Foreign Ministers scheduled for the autumn was further postponed. British and Spanish officials met in London on 15 September to set up the talks, against the background of a European Commission report issued earlier in the month which not only criticised Britain for its stance on border control checks from 1 January 1993, but which also called for Britain and Spain to resolve the sovereignty dispute over Gibraltar. The plan was that they would agree an agenda and a date for the meeting between Douglas Hurd and the new Spanish Foreign Minister, Javier Solana, who had taken over from Francisco Fernández Ordóñez in June following the latter's resignation on grounds of ill health. There were rumours, mentioned in the British press, that Spain would press for a response to Spain's leaseback or power-sharing proposals which Britain had never formally answered.

The month of November had been mentioned as a possibility for the meeting, and in anticipation of that Salomón Seruya, a former Minister of the Economy and Tourism for Gibraltar, published an article in *El País* on 7 October calling for a constructive policy for Gibraltar. It consisted of nine points: recognition that Gibraltar was within the external borders of the EU; acceptance in principle by Gibraltar of the 1987 airport agreement; the removal by Spain of restrictions on Gibraltarian air traffic; the re-establishment of communications with the Rock by sea; measures to speed up the flow at traffic at the border; the use of red and green channels in customs; the removal of import duties on articles for personal use; the establishment of a Spanish-Gibraltarian border commission to deal with practical problems; and the acceptance of EU identity cards instead of passports at the border.

All of these practical measures seemed eminently sensible steps to take in themselves. The problem underlying all of them was the issue of sovereignty, and the implications that acceptance of any of them might have upon it. To ignore the issue of sovereignty when trying to improve economic cooperation was like trying to ignore earthquake tremors when considering the purchase of an apartment in a high-rise tower block.

It was unlikely that Mr Seruya was highly confident that his nine-point plan would be taken up. He could not even place a safe bet on his assumption that the meeting between the Foreign Ministers would be held in November, for once again pressure on Britain from its tenure of the Union presidency meant that the meeting was put back until March 1993. That was probably just as well from the British point of view, because relations between the Gibraltar Government and the Foreign Office in London were somewhat strained in the closing months of 1992. Indeed, there were suspicions in Spain that this was the real reason for the delay. In October Britain had to remind Gibraltar that as an EU member state Britain was responsible for the implementation of EU decisions on the Rock, and that as a crown colony Gibraltar could not decide for itself not to implement certain EU regulations just because they might undermine its aspirations as an off-shore financial centre. Joe Bossano had a direct confrontation over the issue with the Foreign Secretary in London on 12 November, when Douglas Hurd reminded Gibraltar's Chief Minister that the Rock is only in the Union because it is a British colony, and that there is no mileage in Gibraltar's pretensions to be the 13th EU member. Mr Bossano's argument was that Gibraltar's House of Assembly had already implemented EU directives under its own initiative and that it could therefore claim to have acted as an independent member of the Union.

Clearly, there was no way that Britain was going to accept Gibraltar's position, but with Gibraltar already an EU problem in two respects—the airport agreement and the external frontiers convention—Britain was anxious to avoid a confrontation with its Union partners on the question of the implementation of EU directives. Spain might view Gibraltar as a stone in its shoe; under Joe Bossano's leadership Gibraltar was increasingly becoming a thorn in Britain's side.

Perhaps it was because of such a feeling on Britain's part that when the encounter between the two Foreign Ministers finally took place in Madrid one year late on 1 March 1993, there was an implicit recognition that the Brussels process was leading nowhere and that a new approach was required. Exactly what that approach might be was not made fully clear when Douglas Hurd and Javier Solana appeared at a press conference after their meeting. There was talk of the drafting of a new constitution for Gibraltar, in which Spain might be involved, although given Mr Hurd's comment that he had 'not put forward any new proposals on sovereignty' it was unlikely that it would imply any Spanish involvement in the running of Gibraltar's affairs thereafter.

Mr Hurd gave no indication that he was prepared to force Gibraltar to budge on the airport issue, despite a specific Spanish request that he should do so, and insisted upon the well-worn formula of continuing to 'respect the wishes of the Gibraltarian people'. Sr Solana, while inviting Gibraltarian leaders to rejoin the negotiating process as part of the British delegation (an invitation which Joe Bossano was certain to continue to reject), secured Douglas Hurd's agreement that self-determination for Gibraltar was out of the question. He recognised that the Gibraltarians had to normalise their relations with Spain; that would partly be done by persuasion—including a 3,000 million peseta (£15 million) investment by the Spanish Government in the Campo de Gibraltar, plus a bid for EU regional development funds. But Sr Solana indicated that it would also partly be done by economic pressure, and he repeated the threat of building a second airport on the Spanish side of the border—a threat which was wearing somewhat thin three years after it had first been made, and with the Spanish economy clearly in the grip of recession.

Whatever the details of the new proposal, the fact that both sides agreed to meet again before the end of the year was an indication of the importance they attached to it. However, after nine relatively unrewarding years of the Brussels process, no-one was convinced that a solution to the problem of Gibraltar was in reality any closer.

Notes

1 By contrast an incident at the end of January, in which two Gibraltar-based Harrier fighters intercepted an Aviaco Fokker 27 flying from Melilla to Málaga, provoked no reaction at all from the Spanish authorities.

2 On 22 January Mr Bossano tried to voice his views on air transport in the Union at an open session of the Transport Commission of the European Parliament, but two Spanish MEPs prevented him from doing so. Later, in early May, Gibraltar's case on the airport question was dealt with by the European Court of Justice in Luxembourg; Britain and Spain joined forces in opposing Gibraltar's right to present its case.

3 See above, pp. 145–46.

4 An opposition motion calling on the Spanish Government to insist upon the implementation of the 1987 airport agreement in Gibraltar was defeated in the Spanish Parliament on 19 May.

5 Despite a good deal of pressure being applied by other member states during May 1992, Britain was able to use the fact that the signing of the External Borders Convention was being held up as a means of insisting upon immigration checks for all travellers even after the Single European Act came into effect at the beginning of 1993.

6 See above, Chapter 21, p. 179.

TWENTY-FOUR

CONCLUSION

Two-hundred-and-ninety years have elapsed since British forces took over the Rock of Gibraltar. Two-hundred-and-eighty-one years have passed since the Treaty of Utrecht granted Britain jurisdiction over Gibraltar in perpetuity. Ever since that time Spain has sought the restoration of its territorial integrity. Since 1963 the demands by Spain for the return of sovereignty over Gibraltar have been at their most persistent. These demands got nowhere in the 1960s because Spain saw the dispute as an issue of decolonisation, whereas Britain has never seen it in those terms. Relations between Britain and Spain, and between Gibraltar and Spain, have clearly improved since the acrimonious '60s and the besieged '70s. Yet Gibraltar remains as firmly British as it was when the ink had dried in 1713, and the Gibraltarians remain resolutely opposed to the solution which Spain seeks. Apart from marginal gains, the negotiations since 1980 have brought Spain no closer to regaining sovereignty over the Rock than did sixteen years of blockade.

If so little progress has been made, the question must therefore be asked: how serious has Britain been in the negotiations since the signing of the Lisbon Agreement in 1980 about securing a lasting solution to the question of the sovereignty of Gibraltar?

To answer that question we need to look again at the 1960s. Britain's reaction to what was seen as United Nations hostility in 1966 and 1967 over the Gibraltar issue, together with increasing restrictions imposed by Spain at the border, was to call a referendum in Gibraltar on the question of its future sovereignty. The result gave both Britain and the colony democratic support for increased autonomy for the Gibraltarians. The 1969 Constitution, which provided that increased autonomy, was immediately followed by the imposition of the blockade by General Franco. But the Preamble to the Constitution gave Britain a permanent justification in subsequent negotiations to act only in accordance with the democratically expressed wishes of the Gibraltarians. Britain already knew what those wishes were—the result of the referendum was an overwhelming commitment to a future with Britain. It could be argued, therefore, that the British Government knew that it was quite safe in agreeing to attempt 'to solve all of the differences over Gibraltar' (the Lisbon Agreement), including an explicit commitment to discuss sovereignty (the Brussels Declaration), because the Gibraltarians would be allowed the power of veto over the question of sovereignty (and as it has turned out, they have also been allowed the power of veto over other issues, such as the 1987 airport agreement). Spain has tried in vain to argue that the 'wishes' of the Gibraltarians ought to be the same as their 'interests'; this has cut no more ice with the British Government (or with the Gibraltarians) than has the same argument put by Argentina about the inhabitants of the Falklands/Malvinas. The words of the Preamble to the 1969 Constitution have therefore served as the quicksands into which all negotiations have run.

The Constitution did not really have an impact until negotiations began, and there was no question of these beginning as long as General Franco's regime was still in place. Spain would have known that the British Government would not hand over a colony to a dictatorship (which is why, subsequently, such great play was made in Spain of Britain's apparent inconsistency when dealing with Hong Kong). With the restoration of democracy following Franco's death, that impediment—as far as negotiations were concerned—was removed, and with Spain's application to join the EC having been accepted, Britain and Spain were obliged to negotiate practical issues like the reopening of the border.

The Lisbon Agreement, which did not specifically mention sovereignty, but which did reiterate Britain's commitment to respect the wishes of the Gibraltarians, was therefore an imperative which stemmed from Britain's desire to see Spain within the European Community (because of the new markets it offered) and within NATO (because it would strengthen Europe's southern flank), rather than from a desire to find a way to accommodate Spain's historical ambition over Gibraltar.

Spain's membership of NATO swiftly followed, but initially it was not supported by all of the major parties (the PSOE stood in 1982 on a platform of campaigning to take Spain out of NATO again), and

Spain did not integrate—and still has not integrated—into the military structure of NATO. Thus membership of NATO only partly served the Spanish cause over Gibraltar, and the attempted coup of 23 February 1981 confirmed the suspicions of some that democracy in Spain was still only skin deep.

A little more than a year later, Britain was at war with Argentina in the South Atlantic. This brought into relief the whole issue of Britain's relationship with its remaining colonies and reinforced the paramountcy of the wishes of their inhabitants. Spain's dilemma during the Falklands/Malvinas conflict—when historical and cultural ties vied with its new loyalties to Europe, to the Atlantic Alliance and to civilised ways of settling disputes—led to ambivalence over the Spanish position and a reminder to Britain that in the dispute over Gibraltar it was dealing with a blood-brother of the Argentinians. The Falklands/Malvinas episode was an undoubted chronological setback to the negotiations over Gibraltar, but the psychological setback was probably even more significant. For Britain, Spain came out of the episode as an unreliable ally which might itself reject the use of force in dealing with territorial disputes, but which, out of sympathy for the motives of others, failed to condemn their use of force with great conviction.

Despite these setbacks, some progress was made in easing restrictions at the border and the Brussels Declaration was seen by both sides as a major advance. It not only resolved the border issue and led to the end of the blockade, but it also made explicit the fact that 'issues of sovereignty will be discussed'. Britain has since interpreted that statement in the letter rather than in the spirit; there has never been any problem about *discussing* sovereignty, but there has equally never been any indication of Britain's willingness to *negotiate* on it. Spain's disillusionment with the post-Brussels process is therefore scarcely surprising.

While the discussion of sovereignty has been the Spanish Government's overriding concern, it has come at the foot of Britain's list of priorities. Britain has had far more interest in making the technical talks work on practical matters such as economic cooperation, tourism and the environment. It is notable that working groups were set up on all practical issues, but the issue of sovereignty was only up for discussion at the annual meetings (often delayed) of the two Foreign Affairs ministers. While this may have been the only appropriate forum for such an issue, it also ensured that Britain could relegate it to the back burner. The annual encounters between Sir Geoffrey Howe and then Douglas Hurd (John Major did not remain Foreign Secretary for long enough in 1989 to attend one) on the one hand, with Fernando Morán, Francisco Fernández Ordóñez and Javier Solana on the other, have proved extremely unproductive. The British Government's failure to respond to the leaseback or condominium proposals in 1985 was a clear indication that they had no interest in discussing the specifics of anything to do with the transfer of sovereignty.

The only sign of encouragement for Spain is that Britain has consistently rejected calls by Gibraltar since 1988, following the election of Joe Bossano as Chief Minister, for moves towards some kind of independence, whether outright or within an EU context. This rejection stems from a desire not to jeopardise Anglo-Spanish relations, which in the long term are more important to Britain than relations with Gibraltar, and explains why in this respect Britain has to contradict its commitment to respect the democratically expressed wishes of the Gibraltarians.

Britain has always been able to argue, to the annoyance of the Gibraltarians, that the Treaty of Utrecht requires Spain to be given the first option if there is to be any change of sovereignty, and therefore independence for Gibraltar has never been a possibility. However, over the years certain aspects of the Treaty (such as communications with Spain) have been conveniently ignored if they do not suit Britain's or Gibraltar's interest. What Britain has been prepared to do is to encourage the colony to exercise greater financial independence in exchange for allowing Gibraltar the continuing power of veto over arrangements which it sees as threats to its sovereignty, such as the joint use of the airport.

Spain's only area of progress in relation to sovereignty has therefore been in the sphere of defence, with the reduction of a British military presence on the Rock itself (by early 1992 only some 1,800 jobs in Gibraltar were directly dependent upon the British Ministry of Defence) and with greater Spanish involvement through NATO in the control of the Strait. But the extent to which this might give Spain a lever with regard to a transfer of sovereignty has yet to be demonstrated.

What of the future? Some proposed solutions will clearly be more

feasible than others. It is unlikely that the idea put forward by the
Tory MP for Salisbury, Robert Key, on 10 July 1990, will be adopted.
He proposed (reiterating a suggestion that had first been made in
Parliament in May 1968) that the 162,000 people in Britain's
remaining 14 dependencies should elect two MPs to the House of
Commons, one to cover the islands in the Caribbean, the other to
cover the Falklands, St Helena and Gibraltar.

The fact is that most Gibraltarians no longer want that kind of
close relationship with Britain, but are seeking a status which puts
them in charge of their own affairs within a European context. In an
interview given to *The Guardian* on 9 November 1991, Joe Bossano
made his views clear: 'I am committed to Gibraltar being decolonised . . . What I am is the result of 300 years of British influence.
That makes me a British Gibraltarian. Spanish is the last thing I want
to be'. His vision of Gibraltar is as an independent off-shore finance
and service centre, which can offer the advantage of being a
member of the EC and therefore having easier access to it than other
off-shore bases such as the Channel Islands, the Isle of Man or
Bermuda. His explanation for Spain's attitude to his ambitions for
Gibraltar is 'because then Madrid will have to recognise Catalan and
Basque and Galician claims'. In another interview for *El País* on 17
February 1992 he argues that it would be much better if Gibraltarians and Spaniards spoke to each other as one European to another,
and he warns the Spanish Government that if all that is going to
happen is that Foreign Ministers meet every year and repeat what
they said twelve months previously then they will be saying the
same things to each other for the next 280 years.

Interestingly, Joe Bossano has support from opposition leaders for
his position: Peter Montegriffo, founder of the Gibraltar Social
Democrats, says: 'We are shifting from a defence-oriented, artifici-
ally protected economy to an internationally-based economy.
Before it was MoD, now it will be finance, shipping, tourism. We
need to market the Rock. Gibraltar should be like Monaco, or Dublin
or Luxembourg. We should look for a niche within Europe'.

Whether or not Gibraltar can find that niche and with what status
depends to a great extent on whether the European Union continues to move towards a greater pooling of sovereignty and to
stronger regional identities. That clearly remains some way away,
and there are other practical issues which have yet to be resolved.

But there are signs that outside the bilateral vision held by Britain and Spain of Gibraltar's future, others have an optimistic view. Late in 1991 confidence in the future of the Rock encouraged a Norwegian company, Kvaerner, to step in and save the ship-repair industry. Gibrepair, the company which had taken on the dockyard in 1984, had lost more than £26 million since 1986. Kvaerner had tried to negotiate a deal in March 1991 but ran into union demands which resulted in the dismissal of staff and the payment of over £6 million in redundancy money. In 1984 the projected number of staff to be employed by GibRepair was 800. Kvaerner planned to re-employ 160 staff—a sign of the changing role of ship-repairing in the Gibraltar economy. But nevertheless, the Norwegian company saw a future in one of the old Gibraltar industries.

Others have put their faith in new developments, and by early 1992 foreign investment was running at £500 million, twice the Rock's GDP. Government borrowing to finance infrastucture projects rose from £4 million (800 million pesetas) in 1987 to £65 million (13 billion pesetas) in 1991, largely to finance construction developments in partnership with the Danish company Baltica Finans on land reclaimed since 1988 by the Gibraltar Land Reclamation Company. Part of the one square kilometre development has been used to build over 2,000 dwellings. On the remainder the firm Bruun Laursen has built Europort, consisting of a luxury hotel, an office complex of eight seven-storey blocks, a set of 200 apartments and a waste incinerator—all part of Joe Bossano's plans to turn Gibraltar into the Hong Kong of the Mediterranean.

However, for the development to succeed, the airport agreement needs to be implemented, and the continuing delay could well explain why the project has run into difficulties. By the end of 1993 only 10 of the apartments had been sold, a mere 22% of the office space had been let, and the hotel remained unfinished. Baltica, one of the biggest insurance and finance groups in Scandinavia, collapsed in 1992 largely as a consequence of its involvement in the Europort venture, and the current Danish owners, Gefion, are now trying to sell the complex for what they can get. The response to other development areas, such as Queensway Quay, has been equally disappointing. Things may improve by 1995 when all flights within the EU are supposed to be viewed as domestic flights, and as the 1997 transfer of Hong Kong to China approaches it may well be that companies will look to Gibraltar as an alternative location.

In the interim, there seems little prospect that Spain will be able to remove the stone of Gibraltar from its shoe, and it will continue to chafe whenever the Spanish Government has occasion to notice it. For its part, the British Government seems to be in no hurry to assist with its removal.

APPENDIX 1
THE TREATY OF UTRECHT (2–13 July 1713)

Extract from Article X, translated from the Latin

The Catholic King does hereby, for Himself, His heirs and successors, yield to the Crown of Great Britain the full and intire propriety of the Town and Castle of Gibraltar, together with the port, fortifications, and forts thereunto belonging; and He gives up the said propriety, to be held and enjoyed absolutely with all manner of right for ever, without any exception or impediment whatsoever. But that abuses and frauds may be avoided by importing any kind of goods, the Catholic King wills, and takes it to be understood, that the above-named propriety be yielded to Great Britain without any territorial jurisdiction, and without any open communication by land with the country round about. Yet whereas the communication with the sea by the coast of Spain may not at all times be safe or open, and thereby it may happen that the garrison, and other inhabitants of Gibraltar may be brought to great straits; and as it is the intention of the Catholic King, only that fraudulent importations of goods should, as is abovesaid, be hindred by an inland communication, it is therefore provided that in such cases it may be lawful to purchase, for ready money, in the neighbouring territories of Spain, provisions, and other things necessary for the use of the garrison, the inhabitants and the ships which lie in the harbour. But if any goods be found imported by Gibraltar, either by way of barter for purchasing provisions, or under any other pretence, the same shall be confiscated, and complaint being made thereof, those persons who have acted contrary to the faith of this Treaty shall be severely punished. And Her Britannic Majesty, at the request of the Catholic King, does consent and agree, that no leave shall be given under any pretence whatsoever, either to Jews or Moors, to reside or have their said dwellings in the town of Gibraltar; and that no refuge or shelter shall be allowed to any Moorish ships of war in the harbour of the said town, whereby the communication between Spain and Ceuta may be obstructed, or the coasts of Spain be infested by the excursions of the Moors. But whereas Treaties of friendship, and a liberty and intercourse of commerce are between the British and certain territories situate on the coast of Africa, it is always to be understood, that the British subjects cannot refuse the Moors and their ships entry into the port of Gibraltar purely upon the account of merchandising. Her Majesty the Queen of Great Britain does further promise, that the free exercise of their religion shall be indulged to the Roman Catholic inhabitants of the aforesaid town. And in case it shall hereafter seem meet to the Crown of Great Britain to grant, sell, or by any means to alienate therefrom the propriety of the said town of Gibraltar, it is hereby agreed and concluded, that the preference of having the same shall always be given to the Crown of Spain before any others.

APPENDIX 2
THE LISBON AGREEMENT (10 April 1980)

(1) The British and Spanish Governments, desiring to strengthen their bilateral relations and thus to contribute to Western solidarity, intend, in accordance with the relevant United Nations resolutions, to resolve, in a spirit of friendship, the Gibraltar problem.

(2) Both Governments have therefore agreed to start negotiations aimed at overcoming all the differences between them on Gibraltar.

(3) Both Governments have reached agreement on the re-establishment of direct communications in the region. The Spanish Government has decided to suspend the application of the measures at present in force. Both Governments have agreed that future cooperation should be on the basis of reciprocity and full equality of rights. They look forward to the further steps which will be taken on both sides which they believe will open the way to closer understanding between those directly concerned in the area.

(4) To this end both Governments will be prepared to consider any proposals which the other may wish to make, recognising the need to develop practical cooperation on a mutually beneficial basis.

(5) The Spanish Government, in reaffirming its position on the re-establishment of the territorial integrity of Spain, restated its intention that in the outcome of the negotiations the interests of the Gibraltarians should be fully safeguarded. For its part the British Government will fully maintain its commitment to honour the freely and democratically expressed wishes of the people of Gibraltar as set out in the preamble to the [1969] Gibraltar Constitution.

(6) Officials on both sides will meet as soon as possible to prepare the necessary practical steps which will permit the implementation of the proposals agreed to above. It is envisaged that these preparations will be completed not later than 1 June.

APPENDIX 3
THE BRUSSELS DECLARATION (27 November 1984)

1. The Foreign and Commonwealth Secretary, the Right Hon. Sir Geoffrey Howe, and the Spanish Foreign Minister, His Excellency Sr Don Fernando Morán López, held a meeting in Brussels on 27 November during which they agreed on the way in which the Spanish and British Governments will apply by not later than 15 February 1985 the Lisbon Declaration of 10 April 1980 in all its parts. This will involve simultaneously:

(a) The provision of equality and reciprocity of rights for Spaniards in Gibraltar and Gibraltarians in Spain. This will be implemented through the mutual concession of the right which citizens of EC countries enjoy, taking into account the transitional periods and derogations agreed between Spain and the EC. The necessary legislative proposals to achieve this will be introduced in Spain and Gibraltar. As concerns paid employment, and recalling the general principle of Community preference, this carries the implication that during the transitional period each side will be favourably disposed to each other's citizens when granting work permits.

(b) The establishment of the free movement of persons, vehicles and goods between Gibraltar and the neighbouring territory.

(c) The establishment of a negotiating process aimed at overcoming all the differences between them over Gibraltar and at promoting cooperation on a mutually beneficial basis on economic, cultural, touristic, aviation, military and environmental matters. Both sides accept that the issues of sovereignty will be discussed in that process. The British Government will fully maintain its commitment to honour the wishes of the people of Gibraltar as set out in the preamble of the 1969 Constitution.

2. Insofar as the airspace in the region of Gibraltar is concerned, the Spanish Government undertakes to take the early actions necessary to allow safe and effective air communications.

3. There will be meetings of working groups, which will be reviewed periodically in meetings for this purpose between the Spanish and British Foreign Ministers.

APPENDIX 4
THE GOVERNMENT OF GIBRALTAR

The Constitution of 1969 established a House of Assembly, consisting of a Speaker appointed by the Governor, 15 elected members (of whom no more than eight may come from the winning party) and two ex-officio members (the Attorney-General and the Financial and Development Secretary).

Executive authority is exercised by the Governor, who is also the Commander-in-Chief. He is normally required to act in accordance with the advice of the Gibraltar Council, consisting of four ex-officio members (the Deputy Governor, the Deputy Fortress Commander, the Attorney-General and the Financial and Development Secretary), together with five elected members of the House of Assembly appointed by the Governor after consultation with the Chief Minister.

There is a Council of Ministers presided over by the Chief Minister. Britain is responsible for external affairs, defence and internal security; other areas of responsibility are devolved to elected Ministers.

BIBLIOGRAPHY

Bradford, Ernle. *Gibraltar: The History of a Fortress*. London: Rupert Hart-Davis, 1971.

Garratt, G. T. *Gibraltar and the Mediterranean*. London: Jonathan Cape, 1939.

Gibraltar—Recent Differences with Spain. London: HMSO, Misc. No. 12, 1965.

Gibraltar: The Situation of Gibraltar and United Kingdom Relations with Spain. House of Commons, Seventh Report from the Foreign Affairs Committee (Session 1980–81). London: HMSO, 1981.

Gibraltar: The Situation of Gibraltar and United Kingdom Relations with Spain. Observations by the Secretary of State for Foreign and Commonwealth Affairs on the Seventh Report from the Committee in Session 1980–81. House of Commons, First Special Report from the Foreign Affairs Committee (Session 1981–82). London: HMSO, 1982.

Hills, George. *Rock of Contention: A History of Gibraltar*. London: Robert Hale, 1974.

Jackson, Sir William. *The Rock of the Gibraltarians: A History of Gibraltar*. Gibraltar: Gibraltar Books, 1990.

Morán, Fernando. 'Las relaciones hispano-británicas', *Revista de Occidente*, No. 89 (October 1988), pp. 5–20.

Morris, D. S. and R. H. Haigh. *Britain, Spain and Gibraltar 1945–90: The Eternal Triangle*. London: Routledge, 1991.

Palasi, José Uxo. 'Gibraltar: el istmo', *Ejército*, August 1986, pp. 3–9.

Palasi, José Uxo.'Gibraltar: aguas y aeropuerto', *Ejército*, September 1986, pp. 3–9.

Palasi, José Uxo.'Gibraltar: situación actual', *Ejército*, December 1986, pp. 19–25.

INDEX